福建古驿道

POST ROAD IN ANCIENT FUJIAN

楼建龙 著
福建画报社 编

海峡出版发行集团
THE STRAITS PUBLISHING & DIBLISHING GROUP
海峡书局

目录
CONTENTS

006 前言
Preface

第一章 Chapter I

012 山亘水阻 路凿东南
Continuous mountains and dangerous rivers, dig roads in the southeast

018 山行而水处，飘风去难从
Walk in the mountains and live by the water, and it's difficult for blinding wind to leave

026 汉晋往来徙，古道渐成形
The ancient road gradually took shape with the migration in Han and Jin Dynasties

036 五州拓闽境，唐驿通四方
The territory of Fujian was expanded, the post road connected all sides in the Tang Dynasty

044 冠盖投于铺，商旅络于途
Official hats and canopies were sold in shops, and businessmen and travellers came and went in a continuous stream

050 道路织密网，人物汇川流
A dense road network was built, people gathered in an endless stream

第二章 Chapter II

058 随山奠川 岭道翠微
Along with mountains and rivers, the mountain roads are green

066 西北险道，水陆互通
The dangerous northwest road, interconnection of water and land

114 西南隘道，客家通廊
Southwest Pass Road, Hakka Corridor

148 中南鸟道，千山飞渡
Dangerous roads in central and southern area, flying across thousands of mountains

170 东南间道，桥渡相济
The remote road in the Southeast, bridges and ferries coordinate with each other

208 东北岭道，山高路峻
Northeast ridge road, with high mountains and dangerous road

第三章 Chapter III

238 关隘寨亭　驿馆铺塘
Passes and Villages, Posthouses and Shops

242 关隘寨堡，据险以设
Passes and villages were set up depending on the strategical location

268 驿馆铺递，置廪传食
Posthouses and shops were set up for grains

282 路亭接引，送别赋游
The road pavilions becomes a place for reception and writing poems when bidding farewell

302 木石成桥，凌空渡水
The bridge is made of wood and stone, crossing the water and the sky

第四章 Chapter IV

324 **山水福建　闽道人文**
Fujian with mountains and rivers, Human culture of Fujian roads

326 **修路旌善，碑铭纪事**
Building roads for commending goodness, inscriptions for chronicles

340 **题刻垂彰，共襄盛绩**
Inscriptions are engraved for inheritance and recognition, to make great achievements together

358 **拍摄后记**
Postscript

前言
PREFACE

驿道，是古时地方联络中央的专用交通线，即古代的官道。早在殷商时代，为战争服务的驿道就已出现。唐代为宣传政令、收集边情、迎送官员、运输货物，在全国主要道路上设置驿站，驿道因而得名。

福建地势背山面海，境内山岭连绵，河流交错，交通亘阻，较中原地区开发较晚。唐朝以前福建与中原的交流只能依靠跋山涉水，崇山峻岭中的出省古道屈指可数，素有“蜀道难，闽道更难”之说。《福建通志》称：“宋承唐制，三十里有驿，非通途大道则曰馆”。说明福建在唐朝已有驿馆的设置，五代闽王王审知轻徭薄赋，奖励通商，驿道得到进一步发展。宋代，福建贸易兴盛，福州、泉州成为著名的商业城市和对外贸易港口，与此相适应，交通驿道也得到发展。元明清时代，继续沿袭邮驿制度。随着交通路线逐渐增加，官方交通机构的邮驿网点亦随之不断扩充，清代较元代的驿铺总数增长近 14 倍之多。至 1913 年 1 月，北洋政府以中央命令的形式将驿站全部裁撤，驿道主干线相继被修建的铁路和公路取代，千百年来“黄尘腾万丈，驿马如流星”的驿道繁荣景象，成为历史云烟。

福建境内山势起伏，丘陵连绵，河谷、盆地穿插其间，故有“蜀道难，闽道更难”之说。图为闽赣交界的武夷山分水关 阮任艺 陈映辉 摄

In Fujian, the mountains are undulating and the hills are continuous, with valleys and basins interspersed among them. Therefore, there is a saying that "Sichuan Roads are hard, and Fujian Roads are even harder". Photographed by Ruan Renyi and Chen Yinghui

福建驿道分布图

DISTRIBUTION MAP OF FUJIAN POST ROAD

The post road is a special transportation line for local contact with the central government in ancient times, that is, the ancient official road. As early as the Yin and Shang Dynasties, the post road serving the war appeared. In the Tang Dynasty, in order to publicize government decrees, collect border information, welcome officials and transport goods, post stations were set up on major roads across the country, hence the name of post roads.

Fujian faces the sea with the hills for a background, with continuous mountains, crisscrossed rivers and blocked traffic, which was developed later than the Central Plains. Before the Tang Dynasty, the communication between Fujian and the Central Plains could only rely on wading across mountains and rivers, and there were only a handful of ancient roads out of the province between high mountains, which was known as "Sichuan Roads are hard, and Fujian Roads are even harder". "*Chorography of Fujian*" says that"The Song Dynasty inherited the system of the Tang Dynasty, a posthouse is set up every 30 kilometres, which is called a pavilion if it is not a thoroughfare". This shows that Fujian had already set up posthouses in the Tang Dynasty. Wang Shenzhi, the emperor of Min State in the Five Dynasties, reduced corvee and decreased taxes, rewarded barter trade, thus further developed post roads. In the Song Dynasty, Fujian's trade flourished. Fuzhou and Quanzhou became famous commercial cities and foreign trade ports. In line with this, traffic post roads also developed. In the Yuan, Ming and Qing Dynasties, the post system continued to be followed. With the gradual increase of transportation routes, the postal outlets of official transportation organizations have also been continuously expanded. The total number of postal outlets in Qing Dynasty has increased by nearly 14 times compared with that in the Yuan Dynasty. By January 1913, the Beiyang government had abolished all the post stations in the form of a central order, and the main post roads had been replaced by railways and highways built one after another. For thousands of years, the prosperity of post roads with "Yellow dust swirls in the air and post-horses are like meteors" had become a thing of the past.

第一章

Chapter I

山亘水阻　路凿东南

福建

CONTINUOUS MOUNTAINS AND DANGEROUS RIVERS, DIG ROADS IN THE SOUTHEAST

大雁从长空飞过，追寻的是祖先的气息；我们重走古道，体验到的是先民们筚路蓝缕以启山林的艰辛。山水之间的八闽古道，是祖先伟绩的忠实遗留，虽无语蛰伏，或荆榛覆面，但屈曲盘转而光亮平整的古道路石，仍然以直指前方的勇力，唱咏着祖辈拓荒东南的历史与荣光。

历时 3 年的古道调查，让我们有机会重温这些满布福建乡野之间的历史印迹，也让我们有机缘走进福建交通发展的各个历史时期。回顾既往，如果时间回溯 30 年以至于远古时代，生活在福建的人们，无论贵贱，恐怕都不会将出门远游视为一件易事。

哲人有云，走的人多了，也就形成了路。在远古时代，人们用双脚踩出最为原始的道路，但是随着社会的进步与发展的需要，人们对于路况的优劣或是路径的通达又会产生更高的要求。福建古道形成既晚，路况异常险峻、崎岖，即便只在不远的清朝，一县之内的日常巡视，普通官吏也要“动须旬月”；就百姓而言，一辈子都没有机会走出小山村的，也是占了相当多数。但道路对于古代福建的意义，不啻血脉之于身体，对这一僻处东南一隅的区域繁荣，始终起着至关重要的作用；古道的发展与完善，也成为地方社会成长与区域成熟的主要标志。

如今的古道，已经多数湮没于苍苔与青草丛中。曾经的热闹与喧嚣成为过往，古道也成为“线性文化遗产”的代表性家族成员。但如果要评价历史上曾做出过卓越贡献的文化古迹，古道可谓首屈一指、最为劳苦功高的遗产存留！

上　图：仙霞古道位于浙江江山县和福建浦城县。狭义的仙霞古道，仅指仙霞岭上长约 10 公里的山道，但现在通常理解的仙霞古道，则是指江山和浦城之间长约 120 公里的旱路 朱晨辉 严硕 摄

下　图：位于浦城县盘亭乡深坑村枫岭关古道尽头的“仙霞古道”石碑 赖小兵 摄

The upper picture: Xianxia Ancient Road is located in Jiangshan County of Zhejiang Province and Pucheng County of Fujian Province. In a narrow sense, Xianxia Ancient Road only refers to the mountain road about 10 kilometers long on Xianxia Ridge, but now commonly understood Xianxia Ancient Road refers to the overland road about 120 kilometers long between Jiangshan and Pucheng. Photographed by Zhu Chenhui and Yan Shuo

The lower picture: The stone tablet of "Xianxia Ancient Road" at the end of Fengling Pass Ancient Road, Shenkeng Village, Panting Township, Pucheng County. Photographed by Lai Xiaobing

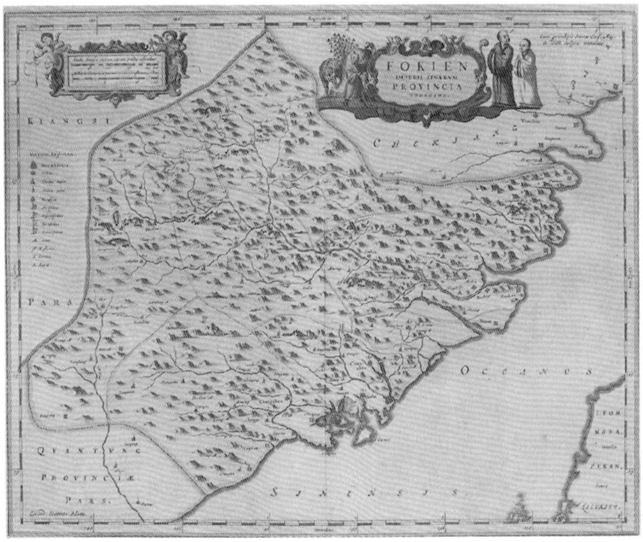

1665 年，荷兰人 Joan Blaeu 完成的福建地图。从此图可以看出当时福建群山环拥、地势险峻的地貌特征

In 1665, a map of Fujian was completed by Joan Blaeu, a Dutch. From this map, we can see the geomorphic characteristics of the surrounding mountains and steep terrain in Fujian at that time.

福建素有“东南山国”之称，西部以武夷山脉为主体的闽西大山带以及中部由鹫峰山–戴云山–博平岭山脉组成的闽中大山带，北接浙江仙霞岭，南连广东九连山，绵亘南北，阻绝东西。在两条平行的大山带之间，是相对低平的长条状山间盆地和谷地。丰沛的溪水在大山之间纵横切割，东向入海。它们所形成的山间盆地、谷地以及低山丘陵、滨海平原等，成为福建先民活动的主要场所。

群山环拥，河流湍急，闭合的地理环境，几乎将福建各处的聚落与城镇完全独立地隔离开来。但朝夕相处于其间的先民们，又凭着坚强的毅力，硬生生地用双手、双脚，在莽莽丛林、尖锐崖壁与汹涌急流中，闯出了条条古道。“道与天齐”，形容的绝不只是这些盘旋接天的古道石阶，更是这种与天地相持的勇力。

福建的古道在各个历史时期反映出来的特征与面貌并不相同，因应着开凿目的以及使用主体的嬗变，大概经历了军旅征伐、移民往来、官巡驿驻、仕商通达、人旅物流等几个阶段的功能演变。古道见证了不同时期“奔赴于途”的各色人等，也成为各个历史时期人文交往与经济增长的历史再现。

福建素有“东南山国”之称，古时与中原的交流，只能靠跋山涉水，出省古道屈指可数。图为武夷山的峰岩幽谷　阮任艺　陈映辉　摄

Fujian is known as the "Southeast Mountainous Country". In ancient times, communication with the Central Plains could only rely on wading across mountains and rivers, and there were only a handful of ancient roads out of the province. The picture shows mountains, rocks and valleys in Wuyi Mountain. Photographed by Ruan Renyi and Chen Yinghui

The ancient post road of Fujian is not only a footprint left by ancestors, but also a history book recording Fujian's historical and cultural changes.

The three-year investigation of the ancient post road has given us the opportunity to relive the historical traces between mountains and rivers of Fujian, and has also given us the opportunity to enter various historical periods of Fujian's transportation development. Looking back on the past, If the time went back 30 years or even ancient times, it would not be easy for people living in Fujian, whether high or low social status, to go out and travel far away.

As the saying of a philosopher goes that, where there are more people walking, a road is formed. In ancient times, people trampled out various primitive roads with their feet. With the progress and development of the society, the ancient post road of Fujian gradually formed.

The road condition of the ancient post road in Fujian was very complicated and dangerous. In the Qing Dynasty, which is closest to us, even if it was only a daily inspection tour within a county, it would take half a month for ordinary officials; As for the common people, most of them even had no chance to get out of small mountain villages in their lifetime. Although the road is dangerously steep, the significance of the road to ancient Fujian is just like blood to the body, which always plays a vital role. The development and perfection of the ancient road has also become the main symbol of local social growth and regional maturity.

Fujian is known as the "Southeast Mountainous Country". The western Fujian mountain belt with Wuyi Mountains as the main body in the west and the central Fujian mountain belt composed of Jiufeng Mountain-Daiyun Mountain-Bopingling Mountains in the middle are connected to Xianxialing Mountain in Zhejiang Province in the north and Jiulian Mountain in Guangdong Province in the south, stretching from north to south and blocking east and west. Between the two parallel mountain belts are relatively low and flat long-strip-shape intermontane basins and valleys. Abundant streams cut vertically and horizontally between the mountains and enter the sea eastward, forming intermontane basins, valleys, low mountains and hills, coastal plains, etc., which became the main places for Fujian ancestors to exercise.

The closed geographical environment, surrounded by mountains and fast-flowing rivers completely isolates settlements and towns everywhere in Fujian. However, with strong perseverance, Fujian ancestors, with both hands and feet, broke through ancient roads in the vast jungle, steep cliffs and surging rapids.

The characteristics and features of Fujian's ancient roads are not the same in each historical period, which probably experienced several stages of functional evolution, such as military conquest, immigration, official tour, official business access, and human travel and circulation of materials. The ancient road witnessed all kinds of people who "rushed to the road" in different periods, and also became the reappearance of cultural exchanges and economic growth in various historical periods.

山行而水处，飘风去难从

古代福建的交通受制于崇山峻岭的地理环境，但智慧的先民创造性地利用了遍布山间的大小溪流。在福建的远古时代，出行方式一是缘溪行，“探路之远近”；二是制作舟板，“浮于天地之间”。但河道与水流弯曲不定，当认知发展到一定程度时，先民们也就自然而然地“裁弯取直”，翻山越岭，辟草成径，由此水陆兼备，实现以最佳或最快方式“到达”的目的。但陡峻的山地与险滩急流，使为了实现“路路通达”目标的福建先民，付出了长达千年的努力。

福建有文字记载的最早族群，称为“闽”或“闽族”。“七闽”是先秦古籍《周礼》对南方向周朝进贡的闽地七个部落的统称，其文明程度大略接近于古代“方国”的水平。当时“七闽”的活动范围包括现在的福建全境、浙江温台、赣西南及广东潮梅等地区。在这片广袤的东南山地，数以千计

武夷山汉城遗址。崇阳溪环绕，依山傍水，风景优美。1999年12月被列入世界文化遗产名录。从航拍图可见城村古汉城遗址周边沃野平畴，沿溪而建，出行便利 阮任艺 陈映辉 摄

Hancheng Ruins of Wuyi Mountain. Surrounded by Chongyang Creek, it is situated at the foot of a hill and beside a stream with beautiful scenery. It was included in the World Cultural Heritage List in December 1999. From the aerial photos, it can be seen that there are flat farmlands and fertile fields around the ruins of Ancient Hancheng in Chengcun, which is built along the stream and is convenient to travel. Photographed by Ruan Renyi and Chen Yinghui

上　图：武夷山汉城遗址是全国保存最完整的汉代古城遗址之一。2200年前，闽越王无诸在此建城立国，成为汉代时东南一带势力最强的国家。城墙内的遗址早已灰飞烟灭，但其根基轮廓仍依稀存在　赵勇 摄

下　图：武夷山城村古汉城遗址出土的文字瓦当，具有很高的书法艺术价值

The upper picture: Hancheng Ruins of Wuyi Mountain is one of the most complete sites of the ancient city in the Han Dynasty. 2200 years ago,Wu Zhu, the emperor of Minyue State built a city and established a state here, then became the most powerful state in the southeast during the Han Dynasty.The ruins in the city wall have long been destroyed, but the foundation outline still exists vaguely. Photographed by Zhao Yong

The lower picture: The inscriptions on eaves tiles unearthed from the ruins of Ancient Hancheng in Chengcun, Wuyi Mountain, have a high artistic value of calligraphy

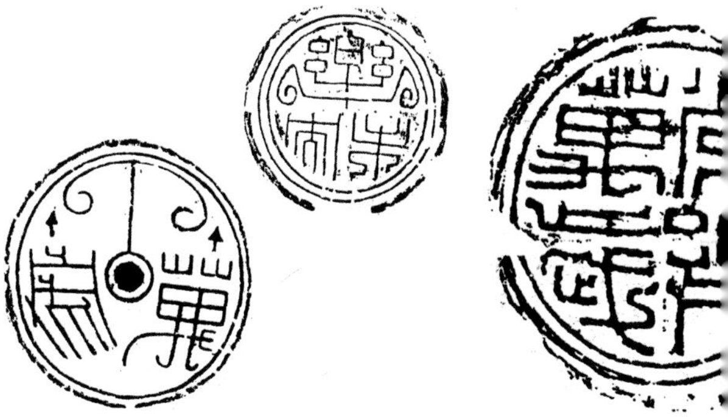

金溪之畔泰宁闽越王无诸校猎雕塑反映了无诸王在金铙山周边建宁、泰宁、明溪等地校猎的史实 崔建楠 摄

The hunting sculpture of Wuzhu, the emperor of Minyue State in Taining, on the bank of Jinxi River, reflects the historical facts that the emperor Wuzhu hunted in Jianning, Taining, Mingxi and other places around Jinnao Mountain. Photographed by Cui Jiannan

的闽族聚居点散布在各条江河的两岸或滨海地区，而大小族群在渔猎与农耕生活之外的交往与攻伐，成为当时推进大规模人群互动、道路发展的主要社会动力。

“山行而水处”，是当年闽族及后来的闽越族人出行的主要模式。公元前 214 年，秦始皇平定南方百越地区，将闽越王无诸及越东海王摇“皆废为君长，以其地为闽中郡”（《史记·东越列传》）。前 207 年，暴政灭秦；闽越族佐汉有功，于汉高帝五年（公元前 202）和汉惠帝三年（公元前 192）分别受封闽越国和东瓯国。公元前 135 年，闽越王郢发兵攻南越边邑，汉武帝因为南越谨守法度，拟派大行王恢、大农韩安国两位将军攻闽越，淮南王刘安上书谏阻说：“……越，方外之地……吴越人相攻击者，不可胜数，天子未尝举兵而入其地也。臣闻越非有城郭邑里也，处溪谷之间，篁竹之中。习于水斗，便于用舟，地深昧而多水险。……以地图察其山川要塞，相去不过寸数，而间独数百千里。阻险林丛，弗能尽著。视之若易，行之甚难。……舆轿而隃领（岭），柁舟而入水，行数百千里，夹以深林丛竹，水道上下击石，林中多蝮蛇猛兽。……限以高山，人迹所绝，车道不通，天地所以隔外内也。”

以上所述，可知当时闽越族人在“习于水斗，便于用舟”的同时，还以“舆轿而隃领”的方式通行于迂回曲折的山间小径，但“车道不通”，与外界基本隔绝。闽越立国仅 92 年，在此之前，闽越族群与中原及江淮、吴越、南越等百越地区间肯定存在着频繁的官方与民间往来；之后，有赖于进出闽境的大规模军队调动，最终在武夷山、仙霞岭的各处谷隘间，形成了通往闽江下闽、浙、赣交界的南浦溪沿岸是当年经济最发达的地区，也是闽浙两省最重要的水路联运线，是商贾仕宦北上中原、南下福州的必经之路，也是物产集散的重要中转。图为当年中原入闽最重要的浦城观前水运码头 赖小兵 摄

The coast of Nanpu River at the junction of Fujian, Zhejiang and Jiangxi was the most economically developed area in those years, which was also the most important waterway intermodal transportation line between Fujian and Zhejiang provinces, and the only way for merchants and officials to go north to the Central Plains and south to Fuzhou, as well as an important transit for the distribution of products. The picture shows the most important Guanqian waterway wharf in Pucheng that the Central Plains entered Fujian in those years. Photographed by Lai Xiaobing

历经艰难，翻山越岭的古人沿着闽江到达福州，形成了通往闽江下游入海口“东冶”（今福州）的陆路通道。图为闽江入海口的梅花水道 阮任艺 陈映辉 摄

After experiencing difficulties, the ancients who tramped over mountains through ravines reached Fuzhou along the Minjiang River, forming a land channel leading to the entrance "Dongye" (now Fuzhou) of the lower reaches of Minjiang River. The picture shows the Meihua waterway at the entrance of Minjiang River. Photographed by Ruan Renyi and Chen Yinghui

WALK IN THE MOUNTAINS AND LIVE BY THE WATER, AND IT'S DIFFICULT FOR BLINDING WIND TO LEAVE

Traffic in ancient Fujian was restricted by high mountains and lofty hills, making it difficult to travel. Intelligent ancestors made use of large and small streams all over the mountains to climb mountains and mountains along the stream current. The interweaving of waterway and landway was the best way to reach their destination. However, the steep mountains and fast-flowing water have also made Fujian ancestors pay thousands of years of exploration.

The earliest ethnic group with written records in Fujian is called "Min" or "Ethnic Min". "Qi Min (Seven Fujian)" is a general designation for the seven tribes of Ancient Fujian that paid tribute to the Zhou Dynasty in the south in the ancient book *Rites of the Zhou Dynasty* in the pre-Qin period. At that time, the scope of activities of "Qi Min (Seven Fujian)" included the whole territory of current Fujian, Wenzhou and Taizhou in Zhejiang, Southwest Jiangxi and Meizhou and Chaozhou in Guangdong,etc. The mass communication among thousands of Ethnic Min settlements became the main social driving force to promote the road development at that time.

The earliest road to Fujian recorded in historical records was the route of the army that Emperor Wu of the Han Dynasty attacked and destroyed Fujian and State Yue. According to comprehensive archaeological findings, the Bronze Age settlement sites in the upper reaches of Minjiang River known in Fujian mainly exist in Chongyang Creek in Wuyishan, Nanpu Creek in Pucheng and Chongren Creek in Guangze, which are the most economically developed tribal settlements in those years. The route for the Han army to enter Fujian should be as follows: first, from Nancheng County of Jiangxi Province to cross Shan Mountain in Guangze County and then down along Futun Creek; Second, to Yanshan County of Jiangxi Province, after crossing Fenshuiguan in Chong'an, down along Chongyang Creek; Third, from Longquan City of Zhejiang, across Zhe Mountain into Pucheng, and then down along Nanpu Creek and Jian Creek. The route of Han soldiers entering Fujian also roughly overlapped with the passage of the Min and Yue people entering and leaving Fujian.

游入海口“东冶”（今福州）的三条主要陆路通道，以及从入海口北往会稽（今绍兴）、南达交趾（今越南北部）的海上交通线。

史籍记载的最早入闽道路，就是当年汉武帝攻灭闽越军队的行军路线。其一，“出梅岭”；其二，“出武林”；其三，“出若邪（绍兴南）、白沙（乐清南）”；其四，“出句章（宁波），浮海从东方往”。以上四处出发点自无异议，但其行进路线特别是前三条的入闽道路却一直存在争议。综合考古发现，福建目前已知的闽江上游青铜时代聚落遗址，主要存在于与浙、赣交界的武夷山崇阳溪、浦城南浦溪、光泽崇仁溪等处。这些在当年属于经济最为发达的部族聚居区，既是闽越国建造“拒汉六城”的地方，也自然成为当时随军辎重有限、需“随地就食”的大部队有序推进的唯一选择。因此，汉军入闽的路线应是：其一，自江西南城越过光泽杉岭，再沿富屯溪而下；其二，至江西铅山，越崇安分水关后，沿崇阳溪而下；其三，由浙江龙泉越过柘岭进入浦城，再沿南浦溪、建溪而下。而汉军的入闽路线，与当年闽越族人进出闽境的通道，也是大致重叠的。

连接浦城与松溪的浦松古道隐匿在翠竹茂林之中 朱晨辉 严硕 摄

Pusong Ancient Road, which connects Pucheng and Songxi, is hidden in the green bamboo forest.
Photographed by Zhu Chenhui and Yan Shuo

汉晋往来徙，古道渐成形

福建是一个移民社会，而福建历史上的移民，又经历了“迁出－迁入－迁出”的往返与反复。从战乱纷争的秦汉交替时期起，直至西晋后期的500年间，见诸史籍的，尽是福建原住民被尽数“掳掠迁出”的画面。汉武帝兵灭闽越国，即以“东越狭多阻，闽越悍，数反复”为由，“诏军吏皆将其民徙处江淮间”（《史记·东越列传》）。原住民被长时期、分阶段地“搜括北上”，是由汉及晋闽境“遂虚”、经济疲弱的主要原因。

社会人群的大规模跨境流动，客观上改变、提升了因地理环境封闭而自然形成的福建各方向“既狭且阻”的交通道路，增进了福建与浙赣、江淮、粤广以及台湾地区的密切交往。因为管理闽越遗民的需要，汉廷在闽地设置了隶属于会稽郡的冶县，并立都尉以镇抚。至东汉，改冶县为侯官都尉，后又分为东南二部都尉，以闽中为南部都尉，临海（温州）为东部都尉。

汉末三国，东吴据有江东，因辖地有限，更加用心经营江浙、平抚闽中，在福建先后设置了建安、建平（建阳）、吴兴（浦城）、东平（松溪）、将乐、昭武（邵武）、绥安（泰宁与建宁两县地）、南平、侯官、东安（南安）等十县，并立建安郡。期间，孙吴军队5次进出福建。

从政区的设置看，当时的闽中与浙江南部的联系最为紧密，因而在原来入闽3处主通道的基础上，由龙泉越柘岭而西入浦城、南下松政（松溪与政和），再沿南浦溪南下建安的陆路，以及经由海路"浮海至东冶"的海上通道的作用大大增强。此外，"建安十县"中东安县的设置，证明当时福州往南海路的通达，而陆上交通路线也已经沿闽江南侧支流上溯，穿越戴云山脉，进抵晋江流域。

西晋太康三年（282），闽中行政建制增为建安、晋安两郡。建安郡治在今建瓯，下辖7县，即建安、吴兴、东平、建阳、将乐、邵武、延平，地属闽江上游建溪、富屯溪流域。晋安郡治在福州，下辖8县，为原丰（闽县）、新罗、宛平（福州与南平间）、同安、侯官、罗江（今罗源）、晋安（今南安）、温麻（今霞浦），多分布在沿海，说明当时沿海航运的发达；而其中新罗县的设置，说明当时的行政管辖已经随着道路的通达而进抵博平岭，远达汀漳腹地。

西晋元康元年（291）至光熙元年（306）间，中原地区发生极其凶残的“八王之乱”，使得晋室南迁，东晋政权偏安南京，但随后又有南朝的“侯景之乱”接踵而至。中州板荡，衣冠入闽，魏晋南朝士人由此掀起南迁入闽的“移民潮”。至南朝（先后含宋、齐、梁、陈四朝）梁天监元年（502），因晋安郡人口增加，又析置南安郡，下辖兴、泉、漳等地。陈朝永定（557~559）年间，升晋安郡为闽州，领晋安、南安、建安三郡，始为刺史治所。

梁朝叛乱四发，晋安豪强陈宝应乘机而起，“自海道寇临安、永嘉及会稽、余姚、诸暨，又载米粟与之贸易，多致玉帛子女，其有能致舟乘者，亦并奔归之，由是大致赀产，士众强盛”（《陈书·陈宝应传》）。南朝天嘉四年（563），陈朝以陈宝应资助江浙豪族叛乱，兵分两路攻闽，其中西路由江西南城“逾东兴岭（杉岭）”，东路“自临海道袭于晋安”，两路夹击，统一闽中。

人口的往来迁徙，促进了福建海、陆交通的不断发展和完善。从目前考古所见的三国两晋南北朝时期古墓葬分布情况看，主要分布于建溪（含崇阳溪、南浦溪、松溪）、富屯溪（含金溪）、闽江、晋江等大水量江河两岸，也是当时古道的所经、所停之处。这一时期的古道已经翻越了闽中戴云山，抵达博平岭，形成以福州为中心、泉州为次中心、建州为枢纽的三足鼎立之势。

左　图：建于清代的寿宁车岭古道平氛关段，地势险要，一士当关可敌万夫　赖小兵 摄

右　图：愁思岭隘道是古代邵武通行于江西、泰宁、建宁、汀州的咽喉要道，是福建出省三道之一，通过此隘道可达江西黎川。因山高路险，崎岖难行，令人望而生愁，故此道名“愁思岭”　吴军 摄

The left picture: Built in the Qing Dynasty, the Pingfenguan section of Cheling Ancient Road in Shouning is dangerous in terrain. If one man guards the pass, ten thousand cannot get through. Photographed by Lai Xiaobing

The right picture: Chousi Ridge Pass Road is the throat main road through Jiangxi, Taining, Jianning and Tingzhou in ancient times, which is one of the three roads out of Fujian Province. Through this pass road, you can reach Lichuan in Jiangxi Province. Because of high mountains and precipitous paths, it is difficult and rough to walk, which makes people sorrowful. Therefore, the road is called "Chousi Ridge". Photographed by Wu Jun

左上图：19 世纪，京城官员通过古道入闽
右上图：19 世纪的官员驿马入闽的场景
下　图：19 世纪上半叶福州城外的驿站小路

The upper left picture: In the 19th century, officials from the capital entered Fujian through the ancient road
The upper right picture: The scene of officials and post-horses entering Fujian in the 19th century
The lower picture: The post path outside Fuzhou City in the first half of the 19th Century

福建的山并不十分高耸，但由于江河的切割，造成的悬崖峭壁随处可见，进出福建的古道正是修建在如此复杂的地形中。图为武夷山脉岚谷乡沟壑纵横的铜钹山 阮任艺 陈映辉 摄

Fujian's mountains are not very high, but because of the cutting of rivers, the cliffs here can be seen everywhere, and the ancient road into and out of Fujian is built in such a complicated terrain. The picture shows Tongbo Mountain with criss-crossing ravines in Langu Township of Wuyi Mountain. Photographed by Ruan Renyi and Chen Yinghui

The Ancient Road Gradually Took Shape with the Migration in Han and Jin Dynasties

Fujian is an immigrant society. Immigrants in Fujian's history have experienced the round-trip and repetition of "emigration—immigration—emigration". From the alternation period of the Qin and Han dynasties filled with wars and disputes to the 500 years in the late Western Jin Dynasty, the history books basically recorded the forced emigration of Fujian aborigines.

The large-scale cross-border flow of social groups has objectively changed and upgraded the closed traffic road in Fujian and enhanced Fujian's close contacts with Zhejiang, Jiangxi, Jianghuai, Guangdong and Taiwan. In order to facilitate the rule and management of the adherents of Ancient Fujian, the imperial court specially set up corresponding administrative positions and administrative regions.

During the Western Jin Dynasty, Jian'ou city was the political, economic and cultural center of Jian'an County; Fuzhou was the political, economic and cultural center of Jin'an County. At that time, coastal shipping had developed considerably, and the administrative jurisdiction also reached Tingzhou, Zhangzhou and other places with the access of roads.

From the first year of Yuankang (291) in the Western Jin Dynasty to the first year of Guangxi (306) , extremely brutal wars took place in the Central Plains region. As a result, scholars in the Wei-Jin-Southern dynasties set off a "wave of immigrants" from the north to Fujian, and Fujian's population increased. Theemigration and migration of population has promoted the continuous development and improvement of Fujian's sea and land transportation. Judging from the current archaeological research, it is mainly distributed on both sides of Jian Creek (including Chongyang Creek, Nanpu Creek and Song Creek), Futun Creek (including Jin Creek), Minjiang and Jinjiang rivers with large water volume, which were also the places where the ancient road passed and stopped at that time. During this period, the ancient road has crossed Daiyun Mountain in central Fujian and reached Boping Mountain, forming a tripartite confrontation with Fuzhou as the center, Quanzhou as the sub-center and Jianzhou as the hub.

从文献记载看，至南朝后期，福建经由北面仙霞岭、西北面杉岭通往浙江南部以及三吴内地的陆路商业网络逐步形成，但当时出省之陆路所经，仍然只是通往浙南、赣东北等方向。大量的移民和经济往来，以及军事行动等，直接促成了道路的增加与路面的改造提升。虽然如此，当时的道路仍然只是泥土路面，陆上交通主要靠人力和马驮；在有水道利用的地方，则可乘坐排筏、小船，闽江水运及以福州为中心的南北海路在当时的交通体系中占有举足轻重的地位。

19 世纪的闽江上游，水运在当时的交通体系中占有举足轻重的地位

In the upper reaches of Minjiang River in the 19th century, water transportation played an important role in the transportation system at that time

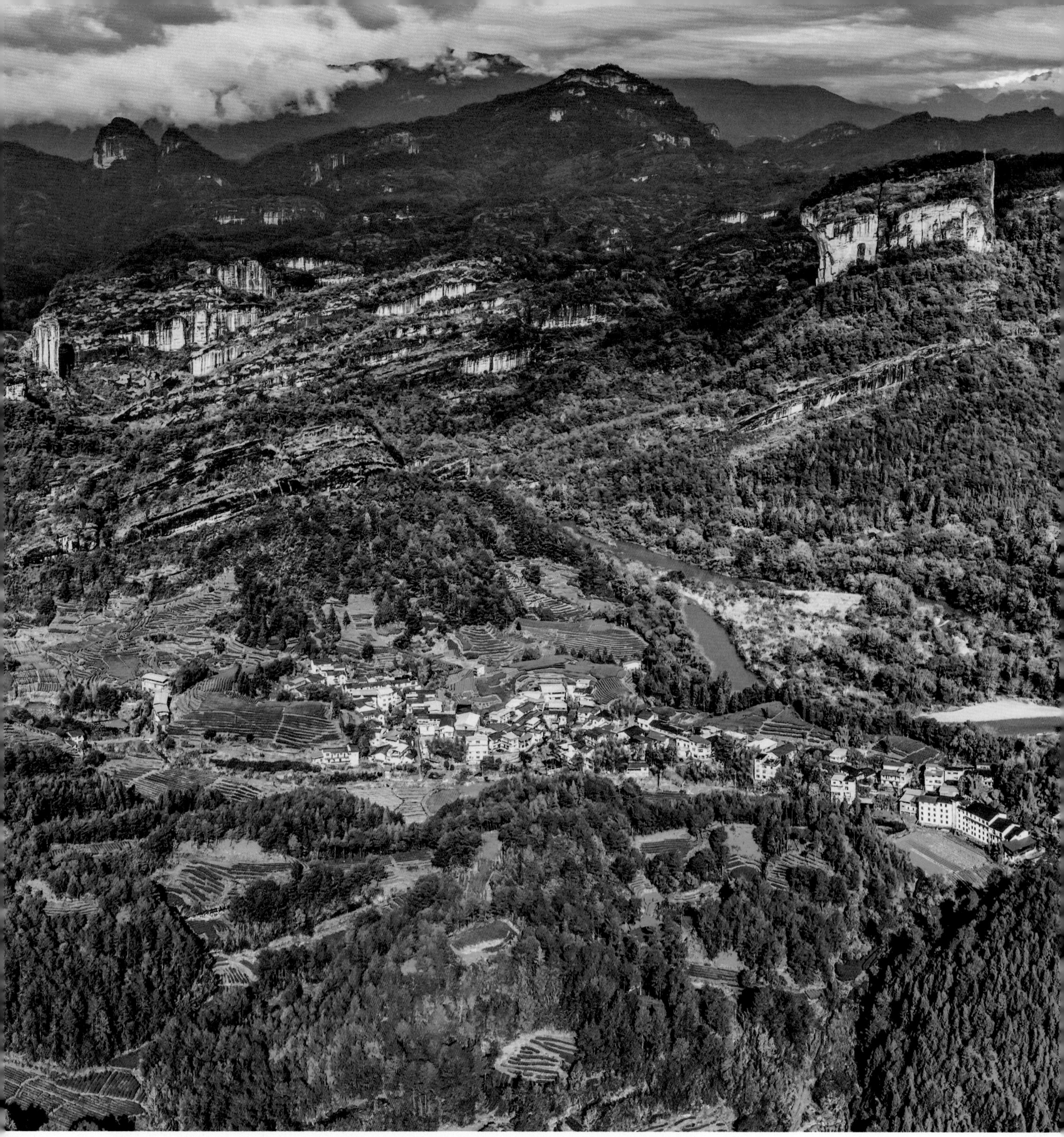

五州拓闽境，唐驿通四方

“闽、浙之盛，自唐而始”（元《文献通考》）。隋末天下大乱，群雄逐鹿，福建原来人迹罕至的各处“僻壤”开始与外界通联。入唐之后，天下大治。福建先是有因“泛筏闽吴间”而“厚赀坐拥、集众辟土”的宁化黄连峒巫罗俊于贞观三年（629）亲赴京师，“纳土中原”；与此同时，又有武夷山彭汉“赴阙，请以新丰乡为温岭镇，设官管领”。唐开元二十八年（740），世居侯官古田山洞之间的刘疆请于朝廷，将他们开垦的土地纳入国家版籍。除以上民间自愿归附的案例外，更多的还是借助于军事的平定，如唐高宗总章二年（669），以泉漳间蛮獠多事，勅岭南行军总管事陈政出以镇之。仪凤二年（667）政殁，子元光代领父众，先巩固云霄故地后，又提兵入潮，“伐山开道”，岭表平定。

唐垂拱二年（686），置漳州；开元二十四年（736），置汀州。至天宝元年（742），福建全境共5州25县，即福州长乐郡（辖闽、侯官、长乐、连江、长溪、古田、梅溪、永泰、尤溪、德化10县）、建州建安郡（辖建安、邵武、浦城、建阳、将乐5县）、泉州清源郡（辖晋江、南安、莆田、仙游4县）、漳州漳浦郡（辖龙溪、龙岩、漳浦3县）、汀州临汀郡（辖长汀、黄连、沙县3县）。至此，福建基本实现了全境通联，以福、建、泉、汀、漳五处州治为中心的驿道网络渐次形成。

福建驿道的大规模系统修建始于唐代，其目的是为了宣传政令、收集边情，并迎送官员、运输货物。驿道是纳入官方管理的大路，沿途设有用

漳浦县佛昙镇轧内村古兵营，据称是唐朝开漳圣王陈元光担任漳州刺史后，建立的四个行台之一 吴瑜琨 摄

The ancient barracks in Yanei Village, Fotan Town, Zhangpu County is said to be one of the four frontier official posts established by Chen Yuanguang, the holy emperor of Kaizhang in the Tang Dynasty, after he became governor of Zhangzhou. Photographed by Wu Yukun

来休息、补充给养的驿站等，与散处城乡的各类古道相比，无论在道路的质量或是日常的维护与管理上，都有着巨大的提升。据《中国通史参考资料》记述："唐凡三十里（约合 14 公里）有驿，驿有长。举天下四方之所达，为驿千六百三十九，阻险无小卒镇戍者，视路要险置官焉。水驿有舟，凡传驿马驴，每岁上其死损肥瘠之数。"福建因为路远行艰，行人相对较少，驿道的规格相对较次，沿途驿站亦少，有的远至 120 里才设一驿。

史载陈元光开漳之时，"奏立行台于四境"。行台其一，为游仙乡松洲堡（今浦南），上游可达苦草镇（今龙岩）；其二，在安仁乡南诏堡（今诏安），下游可至广东潮州之揭阳县；其三，在长乐里佛昙桥，直抵沙澳里太姆山（今龙海港尾）；其四，在新安里芦溪堡，上游直达太平镇（今龙岩永定）。行台所在虽然僻远，但从州治至各行台皆有道路可通，"时时巡守。自此以后，东距泉、建，西逾潮、广，南接岛屿，北抵虔、抚，数千里中，桴鼓不惊，号称平治。"唐朝各地政府对各处驿道实施系统管控，在保障驿传有序、政令畅通的同时，对地方经济的促进与推动作用，也是显而易见的。

据《新唐书地理志》记载：唐代首都长安至福建的干线道路，是由长安至汴州，再由汴州南下，经扬州、杭州、睦州、衢州、江山， 逾仙霞岭入闽，经浦城、建州至福州。在仙霞岭未开通前，由睦州转处州（今丽水）、龙泉，逾柘岭至浦城，或由衢州转常山，经江西玉山、广丰，逾二度关至浦城。这条路称为"福州官路"。

仙霞岭路的开通，缘于唐末的黄巢起义军入闽。仙霞岭自古以险峻著称，人称"飞鸟能度，匹马难施"。据《资治通鉴》："乾符五年（878）三月，巢引兵渡江……八月，攻宣州不克，乃引兵入浙东，开山路七百里，攻剽福建诸州。"入闽后，黄巢兵分两路，一路往东，与唐军大战于政和后，经长溪、宁德往福州；另一路攻克建州，趋古田、过雪峰山抵福州。

The upper left picture: The gateway of Fengling Pass is located at the junction of Fujian and Zhejiang provinces at the foot of Fugai Mountain. The gate is more than 1 meter wide and 3 meters high. Crossing this gateway, you will enter the border of Fujian. Photographed by Wu Jun

The lower left picture: During the reign of Zhenyuan in the Tang Dynasty, the Japanese eminent monk Konghai crossed the sea into Fujian, followed Xianxia Ancient Road, passed through Fengling Pass, went north to the Central Plains, then went to Chang'an to study and learn from the scriptures, and then started the Buddhist mantra system. Now Konghai Pavilion near Fengling Pass was built to commemorate this "Konghai Road". Photographed by Lai Xiaobing

The right picture: Xianxia Ancient Road was the most important commercial passage between Fujian and Zhejiang from Tang Dynasty to modern times, which was the communications hub of Fujian, Zhejiang and Jiangxi provinces and had always been a place for military strategists to contend for. Photographed by Lai Xiaobing

左上图：枫岭关的关口位于浮盖山麓闽浙两省的交界处，关门 1 米多宽、3 米多高，跨过此处关口，便进入福建地界　吴军 摄

左下图：唐贞元年间，日本高僧空海法师渡海入闽，走仙霞古道，经枫岭关，北上中原，赴长安求学取经，后开创了佛教真言系。现在枫岭关旁的空海阁，便是为纪念这一条“空海之路”而修建的　赖小兵 摄

右　图：仙霞古道是唐代至近代闽浙之间最重要的商旅通道，为闽浙赣三省要冲，历来为兵家必争之地　赖小兵 摄

需要说明的是，黄巢于唐末开通仙霞岭山路，据一些地方志的记载，其军锋所指，已经穿越鹫峰山脉到达了闽东沿海，但部队所经的这些道路，多数属于人们称作“鸟道”、“蹊径”的羊肠小路，其危岩仄径，萦纡回曲，步步皆险，所以并未能马上成为官道。福建最早的官道修筑记录，见于《三山志》：“（福州）西路旧无车道抵中国，缘溪乘舟，鼻荡而溯，凡四百六十二里，始接邮道。”至唐元和（807）中，观察使陆庶“铲峰湮谷，停舟续流，跨木引绳，抵延平、富沙（建州），以通京师。”这条驿道自福州西门起，沿闽江西上至延平，路长约182公里；路面宽1.5~2米，用块石或卵石铺砌，虽然路面仍然坎坷，但已是福建最为关键的一段驿道。

汀州设置后，对外的交通路线主要有三条：一是由长汀西北经篁竹岭至江西，巨商小贩悉由此路；二是由长汀西经隘岭至瑞金，前接豫章，后连东粤，为三省通衢；此外，沿汀江南下潮州，可接沿海陆路通道。唐末，由光州刺史王绪率领的光寿移民于唐光启元年（885）率部入闽，先攻破黄连峒，占领汀州后，沿汀江入潮州境，再北上漳州、泉州；在南安附近，王潮取王绪而代之，执掌军权后，继续北上沙县，后接受泉州百姓邀请回攻泉州。以上路线，证明了当时由赣西南、粤东北进出闽西、闽南，以及汀、漳、泉、建、福各州之间主要道路的畅通。

至唐末五代，闽国政权对边境交通也极为重视。如泰宁西北的茶花隘与江西德胜关相近，闽王遣将邓植，屯兵驻守；在福建的东北端，即地处浙江泰顺、苍南与福建福鼎的交界处，也开始设置关隘以据守。据《读史方舆纪要》载：“（福鼎）叠石、分水二关，俱闽王时筑，以备吴越。”由此，最迟至晚唐五代，以福州为中心，通往各方向出境边界要点的福建全境驿道正式形成。

冠盖投于铺，商旅络于途

入宋之后，福建成为独立的省级单位建置，称为“福建路”。宋初，析泉州置兴化军，析建州置邵武军，改剑州为南剑州；至此，福建路共辖6州2军，因而有“八闽”之称。与此同时，增设11县，县数由唐代25个、五代36个，增至宋代的47个县。至元代，福建共分8路48县。

两宋驿道以福州为总枢纽，分为南、北、西3路，全省共有驿四十六、馆十二、铺三十五、亭一、站一。元代，设驿三十、铺二十三、站十。宋元驿道状况如《三山志》所记：“州南出莆田，北抵永嘉，西达

泰宁茶花隘。翻过茶花隘，就越过了武夷山。山的那边是江西，黎川县的德胜关悬在半山 吴军 摄

Taining Chuahua Pass.After crossing Chuahua Pass, thus crossing Wuyi Mountain. On the other side of the mountain is Jiangxi Province. Desheng Pass in Lichuan County hangs in the middle of the mountain. Photographed by Wu Jun

仕

左　图：长汀连接江西的大隘岭古道隘口　崔建楠 摄

右上图：长汀位于汀江上游，主城区分布在汀江两岸，这里是古代汀州府最为繁华的地方　郭晓丹 摄

右下图：北宋时期，福州的西驿道，经闽侯、闽清至延平。进京赶考，金榜题名，回乡省亲，荣归故里，传递文书等都从这条驿道上出入。图为闽侯荆溪镇关西村的“拔仕”榜书、沙溪修路记碑、募修官路碑三段摩崖石刻。其中的沙溪修路记碑记载着这条官路的修建始末　吴军 摄

The left picture: The pass of Da'ai Ridge Ancient Road connecting Changting and Jiangxi. Photographed by Cui Jiannan

The upper right picture: Changting is located in the upper reaches of the Tingjiang River, the main urban area of which is distributed on both sides of the Tingjiang River. This is the most prosperous place in the ancient Tingzhou capital. Photographed by Guo Xiaodan

The lower right picture: During the Northern Song Dynasty, the West Post Road of Fuzhoupassed through Minhou and Minqing to Yanping. Going to the capital to take the examination, succeeding in the government examination, returning to their hometown to visit their relatives, returning to their hometown with honour, and passing on documents all came and went from this post road. The picture shows three cliff stone carvings in Guanxi Village, Jingxi Town, Minhou, namely, the "Ba Shi"list, the Shaxi RoadBuilding Monument and the Monument of Raising and Repairing Official Road. Among them, the Shaxi Road Building Monument records the whole story of the construction of this official road. Photographed by Wu Jun

THE TERRITORY OF FUJIAN WERE EXPANDED, THE POST ROAD CONNECTED ALL SIDES IN THE TANG DYNASTY

At the end of the Sui Dynasty, the world was in chaos, and Fujian's previously inaccessible "backwater" began to communicate with the outside world.

During the Tang Dynasty, Zhangzhou and Tingzhou were set up. Fujian had basically realized the connection of the whole territory, and a network of post roads centered on the five states of Fu, Jian, Quan, Ting and Zhang had gradually taken shape.

The large-scale systematic construction of Fujian post roads, which began in the Tang Dynasty, was aimed at publicizing government decrees, collecting border information, welcoming and sending officials and transporting goods. Post roads were the main roads under official management and post stations are set up along the way to rest and supplement supplies. Compared with all kinds of ancient roads scattered in urban and rural areas, the quality of roads and daily maintenance and management had been greatly improved.

In the Tang Dynasty, local governments implemented systematic control over post roads all over the country, which not only ensured orderly post transmission and smooth government decrees, but also obviously promoted the local economy.

By the late Tang and Five Dynasties at the latest, the post roads throughout Fujian, with Fuzhou as the center and leading to the key points of the exit borders in all directions, were formally formed.

延平。车旌之所宿会，文檄之所往来，求其安便迅驶，而无阻绝沉滞之忧。故更易废置，迄今始定。”但宋代的福建交通仍然极为艰难，正如曾巩在《道山亭记》所称：“其路在闽者，陆出则阨于两山之间，山相属无间断，累数驿乃一得平地，小为县，大为州，然其四顾亦山也。其途或逆坂如缘絙，或重崖如一发，或侧径钩出于不测之溪，上皆石芒峭发，择然后可投步。负戴者虽其土人，犹侧足然后能进，非其土人，罕不蹶也。”

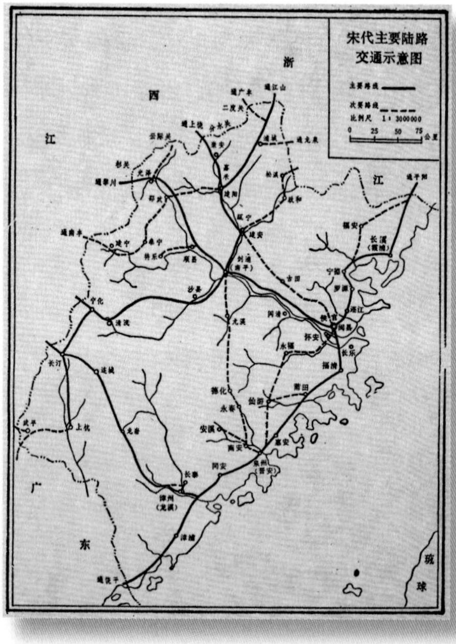

宋代主要陆路交通图（出自《福建公路史》）

Main Land Traffic Map in the Song Dynasty (From *History of Fujian Highway*)

与唐五代相比，宋代福建的水陆交通在通行质量方面，已经有了很大提升。值得记录的事件主要有：1. 天圣年间（1023~1031），南剑州知州刘滋募工整治建溪黯淡滩，“以舒水势”；2. 嘉祐元年（1056），时任福州知州蔡襄令诸邑夹道植松，自大义（属侯官县）至泉、漳，沿途七百余里，以庇道路，堪称福建有史以来首次大规模的道路绿化工程；3. 崇宁二年（1103），新辟福州北门经闽侯雪峰、古田筹岭直达建州的山路，比出福州西门经南平到建州的路程缩短一百余里（约合 46 公里）；4. 嘉祐三年（1058），知县樊纪修砌福州大北岭山磴路一千八百步（约合 3 公里），“夷高直曲，培凹续陷”，便于通行；5. 乾道九年(1173)二月，崇信军节度使史浩改任建州，以石砌仙霞岭路 20 里(约合 9 公里)，共 28 个弯道，3060 级；6. 嘉定六年（1213），李湛知建宁府，铺砌建、剑石路 15000 余丈，方便旅客舍舟就陆，不必冒险过滩等。

以上事件，只是官方的行动组织，而民间的自发行为，更是数不胜数。事实上，当时的道路使用，已经从军旅为主，转而成为商贸货物的主流。所谓“峡深风立豪，石峭湍声泻。古剑成蛰龙，商航来阵马”，就是当年蔡襄在路过南剑州（今延平）时发出的感慨。也正为此，由官绅士民戮力同心、矢志改善交通的努力屡见不鲜，著名者如《读史方舆纪要》所记邵武通往江西南城的道路，“鸟道嵚崎，绵亘六七里，人以为病，戏名愁思。宋上官端义慕

蔡襄

（1012~1067），字君谟，福建仙游（今福建仙游）人，历任西京留守推官、知谏院、知制诰、翰林学士、三司使以及知泉州、福州、开封和杭州府事，以正直端方、敢于直言独立于士林。

蔡襄担任泉州知府时主持修建了城东北洛阳江上的『万安桥』，他以『一太守不费公帑为之』，深受人民的敬重。这条著名的大桥，长360丈，跨海而架，大大方便了往来的旅客。他还亲自作《万安桥记》，每个字直径一尺，刻石矗立在大桥两岸，与大桥相映生辉，一时被传为佳话。

蔡襄曾组织人马，从福州始，沿途植树至泉州、漳州，计长700里。它成为万安桥的配套工程，此即《宋史》本传所说的『植松七百里以庇道路』一事。时人为此作诗赞之：『夹道松，夹道松，问谁栽之我蔡公。行人六月不知暑，千古万古摇清风。』

Cai Xiang (1012-1067), styled himself Junmo, born in Xianyou, Fujian (now Xianyou of Fujian). He has successively served as the garrison enforcement officer in Xijing, the official in charge of imperial censors , the official in charge of secretarial matters, Hanlin academician, Chancellor of the Treasury, and Magistrate of Quanzhou, Fuzhou, Kaifeng and Hangzhou magistrates. He stood among the scholars for his honest and daring to speak bluntly.

When Cai Xiang was the prefect of Quanzhou, he presided over the construction of the "Wan'an Bridge" on the Luoyang River in the northeast of the city. He was deeply respected by the people for "a prefect does not cost public money". This famous bridge, with length of 1.2 km, crosses the sea and stands, greatly facilitating passengers. He also personally wrote "The Story of Wan'an Bridge". Each word is one foot in diameter. The carved stone stands on both sides of the bridge, which reflects the bridge and is widely spread for a while.

Cai Xiang once organized troops to plant trees from Fuzhou to Quanzhou and Zhangzhou, with a length of 700 miles. It became a supporting project for Wan'an Bridge, which is what the biography *The History of The Song Dynasty* said: "Planting pine trees for 700 miles to shelter roads". At that time, people wrote a poem praising it: "Pine trees in the middle lines both sides of the rosd, pine trees in the middle lines both sides of the rosd, if asking who planted them, it's Cai Xiang,Pedestrians do not know the summer heat in June, and the wind will shake through the ages."

蔡襄

（1012~1067），字君谟，福建仙游（今福建仙游）人，历任西京留守推官，知谏院，知制诰，翰林学士，三司使，以及知泉州、福州、开封和杭州府事，以正直端方，敢于直言独立于士林。

蔡襄担任泉州知府时主持修建了城东北洛阳江上的"万安桥"，他以"一太守不费公帑为之"，深受人民的敬重。这条著名的大桥，长390丈，跨海而渠，大大方便了往来的旅客。他还亲自作《万安桥记》，每个字直径一尺，刻石矗立在大桥两岸，与大桥相映生辉，一时被传为佳话。

蔡襄曾组织人马，从福州沿途植树至泉州、漳州，计长700里。它成为万安桥的配套工程，此即《宋史》本传所说的"植松七百里以庇道路"一事。时人为此作诗赞之："夹道松，夹道松，问谁栽之我蔡公。行人六月不知暑，千古万古摇清风。"

Cai Xiang (1012-1067), styled himself Junmo, born in Xianyou, Fujian (now Xianyou of Fujian). He has successively served as the garrison enforcement officer in Xijing, the official in charge of imperial censors , the official in charge of secretarial matters, Hanlin academician, Chancellor of the Treasury, and Magistrate of Quanzhou, Fuzhou, Kaifeng and Hangzhou magistrates. He stood among the scholars for his honest and daring to speak bluntly.

When Cai Xiang was the prefect of Quanzhou, he presided over the construction of the "Wan'an Bridge" on the Luoyang River in the northeast of the city. He was deeply respected by the people for "a prefect does not cost public money". This famous bridge, with length of 1.2 km, crosses the sea and stands, greatly facilitating passengers. He also personally wrote "The Story of Wan'an Bridge". Each word is one foot in diameter. The carved stone stands on both sides of the bridge, which reflects the bridge and is widely spread for a while.

Cai Xiang once organized troops to plant trees from Fuzhou to Quanzhou and Zhangzhou, with a length of 700 miles. It became a supporting project for Wan'an Bridge, which is what the biography *The History of The Song Dynasty* said: "Planting pine trees for 700 miles to shelter roads". At that time, people wrote a poem praising it: "Pine trees in the middle lines both sides of the road, pine trees in the middle lines both sides of the road, if asking who planted them, it's Cai Xiang.Pedestrians do not know the summer heat in June, and the wind will shake through the ages."

众甃路，行者便焉”。此外，如漳州城西北的揭鸿岭，古称葵冈岭，传说唐陈政、陈元光曾走此道并驻兵于此，故又名将军岭。古道沿途崇山峻岭，人烟稀少，但在闽粤沿海大道未畅通前，却是漳州的通京孔道。唐慕容韦《度揭鸿岭》五言诗道：“闽越曾为塞，将军旧置营。我歌胡感慨，西北望神京。”元末，有蔡氏因揭鸿岭路高峻，于西山腰辟一新道，俗称新岭，又名蔡公岭，路通安溪、龙岩、漳平等地。

为了沿海大通道的畅通，以北宋嘉祐四年（1059）泉州洛阳桥的建成为标志，技术含量极高的跨海越江石梁桥在宋元时期大量建造，著名者如漳州江东桥，泉州安平桥、顺济桥，莆田宁海桥、延寿桥，福清龙江桥，马尾迴龙桥等，这些大石桥多为民间集巨资、历时十数年而建成。据统计，宋代全省共建成大小桥梁达646座，这些旷世奇构，与当时普遍设置的渡口一起，共同连接起各处的通衢大道，有的至今仍然发挥着巨大的实际交通功能。

漳州万松关地势险要，既是古代的交通要道，又是历代兵家必争之地 阮任艺 摄

Wansong Pass in Zhangzhou was a dangerous terrain and a major transportation route in ancient times, which was also a place where military strategists of all dynasties must contend. Photographed by Ruan Renyi

OFFICIAL HATS AND CANOPIES WERE SOLD IN SHOPS, AND BUSINESSMEN AND TRAVELLERS CAME AND WENT IN A CONTINUOUS STREAM

After entering the Song Dynasty, Fujian became an independent provincial establishment, called "Fujian Road".

Compared with the Tang and Five Dynasties, Fujian's land and water transportation in the Song Dynasty had greatly improved in terms of traffic quality. The function of post roads had changed from military migration to the transportation of commercial goods.

The smooth flow of the major coastal passage was marked by the completion of the Luoyang Bridge in Quanzhou in 1059. During the Song and Yuan Dynasties, a large number of stone beam bridges across the sea and the river with high technical content appeared. For example, Jiangdong Bridge in Zhangzhou, Anping Bridge in Quanzhou, Shunji Bridge, Ninghai Bridge in Putian, Yanshou Bridge, Longjiang Bridge in Fuqing, Jionglong Bridge in Mawei, etc. These large stone bridges were mostly built by folk with huge amount of funds and took more than ten years to form.

According to statistics, 646 bridges, whether large or small, were built in the province in the Song Dynasty. Some of these bridges still play a huge traffic function even today.

万松关是古时进出漳州的必经隘口，是通往省会、京城的重要古道　楼建龙 摄

Wansong Pass was the only pass to enter and leave Zhangzhou in ancient times, and was an important ancient road leading to the provincial capital and capital city. Photographed by Lou Jianlong

左上图：福州马尾区的闽安古镇宋代古桥迴龙桥南北横跨，为罕见的船形桥墩，花岗石平梁桥 阮任艺 摄

左下图：莆田延寿桥桥构古朴，桥头古榕遮天蔽日，古意悠然 阮任艺 摄

右 图：泉州五里桥是中国现存最长的海港大石桥，号称“天下无桥长此桥” 阮任艺 摄

The upper left picture: Jionglong Bridge in Min'an Ancient Town, Mawei District, Fuzhou is an ancient bridge in the Song Dynasty, which spans from south to north, and is a rare boat-shaped pier and granite flat-topped bridge. Photographed by Ruan Renyi

The lower left picture:Yanshou Bridge in Putian has a simple and unsophisticated structure, and the ancient banyan at the head of the bridge covers the sky and blocks out the sun, which is ancient and leisurely. Photographed by Ruan Renyi

The right picture:Wuli Bridge in Quanzhou is the longest existing harbor stone bridge in China. It is known as "there is no bridge in the world that is longer than this bridge". Photographed by Ruan Renyi

道路织密网，人物汇川流

由明迄清，福建的地方行政建制更趋完善。明代辖八府一州、五十七县，设驿四十九（其中马驿三、水驿三）、铺六百四十五、邮递所十；清代辖九府（后又分置台湾府）二州、五十八县，设驿五十九、铺七百八十四、腰站九。铺递数量呈几何级数的大量增多，意味着路网的密集化，以及政令管理与内外交往的有效通达。

这一时期有关福建交通的记述，条分缕析。大的军事行动以元明交替之际的明军入闽路线为例，洪武元年（1368），朱元璋兵分三路，其陆路分别从衢州攻浦城、由江西越杉关、从铅山破分水关攻崇安，水师则从宁

波由海道直取福州后，上溯至水口驿再分舟师、骑兵两路西进，会攻延平。由此可见，明初入闽的主要通道，仍然遵循着唐、五代形成的驿道路网格局。明中期后，由于倭寇侵扰、矿乱频发，对原本相对“空白”的闽中山区的管控与处置日益加强；明末清初，福建的地方割据以及清后期的太平军入闽等一系列事件，沿海上下以至于山区内陆深受影响，各地的文件往返与汛情急递等得到普遍重视，各地对于交通路网的编织益加严密。与此同时，人口增长、村镇增加以及经济发展的需要，使村镇与城乡之间的往返日益频繁，区域间交往线路随之逐渐增加。

The left picture: Fuding Fenshui Pass, which is located at the junction of Fujian and Zhejiang, was founded in Min State of the Five Dynasties, with a dangerous situation. And it is a place for military strategists to contend for, which is known as the "gateway to northeast Fujian". Photographed by Zhu Chenhui

The right picture: Sketch Map of Main Land Transportation in the Qing Dynasty (From *History of Fujian Highway*)

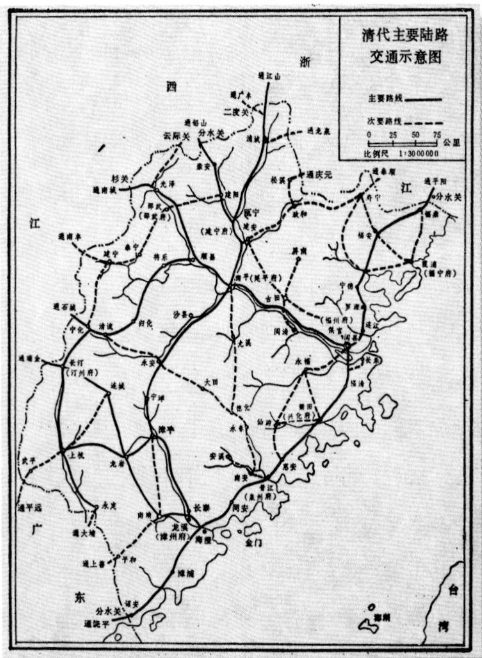

左　图：地处闽、浙交界的福鼎分水关始建于五代闽国，形势险要，为兵家必争之地，号称“闽东北门户”　朱晨辉 摄

右　图：清代主要陆路交通示意图（出自《福建公路史》）

这一时期的驿递要道，往往都有官府拨款或募捐倡修。如清道光三年(1823)，永安知县孙鸿宝捐俸倡修沙县杉口岭至贡川15公里崩塌路段，经3年竣工，费白银千余两。清雍正年间(1723 ~ 1735)，莆田知县汪延英倡议募资修筑沙园至石马段5公里长的驿道；庠生余宗鳌用石头砌筑青龙桥至石马长10公里的驿道等。乾隆二十四年（1759），李拔任福宁知府，"……初至郡，即欲平其险阻，治其茅塞，特以吏事方殷，农功正急，未遑他务。兹当农隙之时，率陂者平之，朽者易之，五里一牌，十里一亭，悬以匾额，涂以丹雘，官道邮亭，岿然相望，一洗从前之陋，盖近日以来未有如此之盛也……今兹之役，自宁德之界首铺，至福鼎之分水关，凡四百五十余里。"（清乾隆《福宁府志》）

明代杰出地理学家和旅行家徐霞客曾五游福建。万历四十四年（1616）第一次入闽，从江西上饶过分水关入福建，主要是赴武夷山游览；泰昌元年（1620），第二次游闽，过枫岭关后，乘船经闽江、南浦溪，抵沿海地区，游兴化府、九鲤湖等；第三次入闽，因为受沿海战乱影响，由仙霞岭经浦城到南平后，因"泉、兴海盗为梗"，遂改经顺昌、将乐、归化（今明溪）抵永安，再由宁洋、漳平等地，到南靖寻访族叔；第四次及第五次赴漳州，过仙霞岭到延平后，逆沙溪水流，经沙县、永安，再水陆兼行到漳州。从徐霞客的五次入闽路线看，其间有着多处重复，这绝非其出行所愿，只能说明闽道艰难，所可选择的途径较少；另外，也说明有限的交通孔道极易受到战乱的牵累，因为沿海大通道受阻，为安全起见，只能经由闽中山区而水陆兼行。时局困顿、旅途艰辛，但精于风光记录的徐霞客，仍然于字里行间，为我们展示了闽中古道的别样风景。

上　图：素有"八闽铜关"之称的南平延寿门楼始建于元代，是古代重要的驿道中转，交通枢纽。图为海外摄影家拍摄的19世纪的延寿楼

下　图：南平延平区延寿楼被誉为八闽铜关的代表性建筑，曾于1609年重修。延寿楼是古代重要的军事指挥机关，文天祥、韩世忠、郑成功、石达开都在此驻扎过　阮任艺 摄

The upper picture: Known as the "Eight Fujian Tongguan", Nanping Yanshou Gate House was built in the Yuan Dynasty and was an important post road transit and transportation hub in ancient times. The picture shows the 19th century Yanshou building. Photographed by an overseas photographer

The lower picture: Yanshou building in Yanping District of Nanping, reputed as the representative building of Eight Fujian Tongguan, was rebuilt in 1609. Yanshou building was an important military command organization in ancient times. Wen Tianxiang, Han Shizhong, Zheng Chenggong and Shi Dakai all stationed here. Photographed by Ruan Renyi

徐霞客

（1587~1641），名弘祖，字振之，号霞客。明代地理学家、旅行家和文学家。徐霞客一生志在四方，足迹遍及今21个省、市、自治区，『达人所之未达，探人所之未知』，所到之处，探幽寻秘，并记有游记，记录观察到的各种现象、人文、地理、动植物等状况。

在游记中，徐霞客对福建山川情有独钟。在他所涉足的十多个省份中，唯独到福建的次数最多、范围最广，历经20多个府、县。他登攀了武夷山、仙霞岭、戴云山三大山系，探察了闽江、九龙江和木兰溪三大水系。福建的武夷山、九鲤湖（仙游）、玉华洞（将乐）、桃花洞（永安）、浮盖山、龙洞（浦城）、石所山（今福清石竹山）等多处，都留下他的足迹。

Xu Xiake (1587-1641), named Hongzu, Styled himself Zhenzhi, with an alternative name of Xiake. He was a geographer, traveler and litterateur in the Ming Dynasty. Xu Xiake has devoted his whole life to all directions and has traveled all over 21 provinces, cities and autonomous regions today. He "has not reached what the people has not reached, and has explored what the people have not known". Wherever he goes, he has explored mysteries and searched for secrets, and has written down his travel notes, recording various phenomena, humanities, geography, animals and plants and other conditions observed.

In his travel notes, Xu Xiake has a special liking for Fujian's mountains and rivers. Of the more than ten provinces he has set foot in, Fujian has been the only one with the largest number of visits and the widest range, going through more than 20 prefectures and counties. He climbed three moutain systems of Wuyi Mountain, Xianxia Mountain and Daiyun Mountain, and explored three water systems of Minjiang River, Jiulong River and Mulan River. Wuyi Mountain, Jiuli Lake (Xianyou), Yuhua Cave (Jiangle), Taohuajian (Yong'an), Fugai Mountain, Longdong (Pucheng), Shisuo Mountain (now Shizhu Mountain in Fuqing) and more than other places in Fujian have left his footprints.

徐霞客

（1587－1641），名弘祖，字振之，号霞客。明代地理学家、旅行家和文学家。徐霞客一生志在四方，足迹遍及今21个省、市、自治区，"达人所之未达，探人所之未知"，所到之处，探幽寻秘，并记有游记，记录观察到的各种现象、人文、地理、动植物等状况。

在游记中，徐霞客对福建山川情有独钟。在他所游历的十多个省份中，唯独到福建的次数最多，范围最广，历经20多个府、县。他登攀了武夷山、仙霞岭、戴云山三大山系，探察了闽江、九龙江和木兰溪三大水系。福建的武夷山、九鲤湖（仙游）、玉华洞（将乐）、桃花涧（永安）、浮盖山、龙洞（浦城）、石所山（今福清石竹山）等多处，都留下他的足迹。

Xu Xiake (1587-1641), named Hongzu, Styled himself Zhenzhi, with an alternative name of Xiake. He was a geographer, traveler and litterateur in the Ming Dynasty. Xu Xiake has devoted his whole life to all directions and has traveled all over 21 provinces, cities and autonomous regions today. He "has not reached what the people has not reached, and has explored what the people have not known". Wherever he goes, he has explored mysteries and searched for secrets, and has written down his travel notes, recording various phenomena, humanities, geography, animals and plants and other conditions observed.

In his travel notes, Xu Xiake has a special liking for Fujian's mountains and rivers. Of the more than ten provinces he has set foot in, Fujian has been the only one with the largest number of visits and the widest range, going through more than 20 prefectures and counties. He climbed three moutain systems of Wuyi Mountain, Xianxia Mountain and Daiyun Mountain, and explored three water systems of Minjiang River, Jiulong River and Mulan River. Wuyi Mountain, Jiuli Lake (Xianyou), Yuhua Cave (Jiangle), Taohuajian (Yong'an), Fugai Mountain, Longdong (Pucheng), Shisuo Mountain (now Shizhu Mountain in Fuqing) and more than other places in Fujian have left his footprints.

延平王

左　图：1998 年，加拿大汉学家鲁克恩在荷兰复制了这幅似地图而非地图、似山水画又非山水画的古画，带到福州。经福州的文博专家曾意丹考证，确认这是一幅清代康熙年间的福州城台景观图，最后由福州画家郑子端，历时半年，根据自己一些新的考证成果，重新绘制了《福州城台景观图》。那些消失了的景观让跨越了 3 个世纪的后人浮想联翩。可见十八世纪中叶的福州因交通驿道而兴盛如斯　郑子端 绘

右上图：19 世纪的福州万寿桥

右下图：福建货物外运大都经行闽江大小支流后，先集中于福州，再由海路输出于江浙。图为 19 世纪繁华的福州台江码头

The left picture: In 1998, Canadian sinologist Rukken copied this ancient painting in Holland, which looks like a map but not a map, looks like a landscape painting but not a landscape painting, and brought it to Fuzhou. After textual research by Zeng Yidan, an expert of culture and museum in Fuzhou, it was confirmed that this was a landscape map of Fuzhou's city and terrace during the Kangxi period of Qing Dynasty. Finally,Zheng Ziduan, the painter in Fuzhou redrew the *Landscape Map of Fuzhou City* for half a year according to some of his new textual research results. Those lost landscapes have inspired future generations spanning three centuries. It can be seen that Fuzhou in the middle of the 18th century flourished as a result of the post roads. Drew by Zheng Ziduan

The upper right picture: Wanshou Bridge of Fuzhou in the 19th Century

The lower right picture: Most of Fujian's goods are transported abroad through tributaries of Minjiang River, then concentrated in Fuzhou and then exported to Jiangsu and Zhejiang provinces by sea. The picture shows the prosperous Taijiang dock in Fuzhou in the 19th century

明清福建商业发达，当时行走于古道之间的主要群体，已经转变成了商旅物流。福建各地尤其是山区土特产的运出，大多经由内河船运，一部分先抵入海口大城市后，再通过海运转销于国内外各地；一部分则肩挑马驮，通过内陆路线与邻省江浙一带互通有无。水陆联运，成为福建货物外走的主要方式。正如王世懋在《闽部疏》中所述："凡福之绸丝，漳之纱绢，泉之蓝，福延之铁，福漳之橘，福兴之荔枝，泉漳之糖，顺昌之纸，无日不走分水岭及浦城小关，下吴越如流水，其航大海而去者，尤不可计。"以出于闽西的福建木材为例，其中一部分陆运进入江西；一部分出于汀江流域者，水运至广东潮州府属；而大部分的福杉，则经行闽江大小支流后，先集中于福州，再由海路输出于江浙。如《明季北略》载，崇桢时浙江巡抚张延登《请申海禁疏》云："福建延建邵汀四府出产杉木，其地木商将木沿溪放至洪塘、南台，装船至宁波等处发卖，外载杉木，内装丝棉，驾海出洋，每赁兴化大海船一只，价至八十余两，其取利不赀。"

事实上，福建各个县、乡之间的路网交通，也是到了明、清两代，凭籍着官宦、学子、商旅、民众等各界人群的共同发力，才逐渐实现了真正意义上的路路贯通。

浦城盘亭乡的小关是闽浙两省商旅物流的重要关隘 吴军 摄

The small pass in Panting Township, Pucheng is an important pass of business and tourism logistics in Fujian and Zhejiang provinces. Photographed by Wu Jun

A DENSE ROAD NETWORK WAS BUILT, PEOPLE GATHERED IN AN ENDLESS STREAM

From the Ming Dynasty to the Qing Dynasty, Fujian's local administrative system was getting perfect. The number of post stations has increased greatly and the road network has become more dense.

During this period, the population growth, the increase of villages and towns and the needs of economic development made the round trip between villages and towns increasingly frequent, and the communication lines between regions also gradually increased.

Fujian's commerce was developed in the Ming and Qing Dynasties, and the ancient roads at that time were mainly used for commercial activities. Local specialties from all parts of Fujian, especially in mountainous areas, were transported by inland river shipping. Some of them first arrived in the big cities at the seaport and then were resold at home and abroad by sea; Some of them were carried by people on their shoulders or carried by horses and then were contacted with neighboring provinces of Jiangsu and Zhejiang through inland ancient roads. Water-and-land combined transportation has become the main way for Fujian goods to be sold.

In fact, the road network transportation between various counties and townships in Fujian, also to the Ming and Qing Dynasties, with the joint action of officials, students, travelling businessmen and common people from all walks of life, gradually realized the real road through.

陆海相连，福建成为海上丝绸之路的重要起点 何清和 摄

Land and sea are connected, and Fujian has become an important starting point of the Maritime Silk Road. Photographed by He Qinghe

第二章

Chapter II

随山奠川 岭道翠微 福建

ALONG WITH MOUNTAINS AND RIVERS, THE MOUNTAIN ROADS ARE GREEN

由“方国”闽族而至“国家”闽越国，再至纳入中央一体政权的地方政府，福建由“僻处一隅”，而逐渐全境融入多元中华文化。漫漫数千年间，逐步繁密且渐渐延展、规范布局的八闽古道，无疑起到了“编织”“缀连”的重要作用。在“车同轨、书同文”的“天下大一统”历史进程中，古道的形式渐趋统一；而道路之成，关键在于使用与维护，随着历代政治管理、文化发展以及经济交流的需要，福建古道的路网分布日益细化，“连结”功能也更趋强化。

由汉迄清，福建古道依势定向，逢山砌蹬，遇水架桥。因为天多阴雨，土路遇雨则泥泞易滑，所以大道的路面无论坦夷，均采取铺石以就的方式。修路的材料，主要以大小石材为骨干，因为溪流资源丰富，石材多数取自溪中的大小卵石，一般取大块的居中、平整面朝上铺砌，稍小的用于外侧砌造路沿，更小的用于路面间填缝平铺；上山的石阶，多采自山石，开凿錾平，平铺使用；遇到山间横亘的大块岩石，或绕行，或直接凿阶而上。修路时，一般利用砂土作为路肩和底部的铺垫，必要时加以一定量的垫或枕木。依赖庞大的人工伟力和简易的工具，先民们将随处可见的土、石、木等有效运用，铺凿出遍及八闽、无限延伸的条条道路。

福建古代道路以险峻著称，穿行于崇山溪谷之间，平坦之处极少。路面宽度常在1~2米间，只有小部分转弯或休息之处，可以超过2米。山路多用块石平铺，高低成阶，同时在依山一侧的路肩处挖出浅沟，以利行洪；水沟宽窄不一，每隔一段距离会以明沟的形式横穿路面，将流水排入另一侧的断坎之下。在临崖道路的断坎外侧，为安全考虑，往往设有栏杆，栏杆立柱下部的长石条多悬空外挑，外沿凿孔，以对接立柱的柱脚；但栏杆立柱或扶手因为多为木质或竹藤，随着时间的流逝，已经很少能够见到完整地保留下来的了。

道路大略分为车（马）道、步道两类。与中原地区不同的是，福建的车（马）道因为纡曲陡峻，并不能通行用马或骡、牛等牲畜拉行的车舆，而是以人力推拉的板车、独轮车等应用较为广泛。马匹等畜力工具只用于

左　图：福建古驿道的路面宽度通常是在 1~2 米之间，图为仙游何岭古道　崔建楠 摄

右上图：武夷山小浆古道上，石阶外端设有榫卯，推测为安装护栏之用　吴军 摄

右下图：古道上挑夫歇脚形成的柱窝　吴军 摄

The left picture: The width of the road surface of Fujian Ancient Post Road is usually between 1 and 2 meters. The picture shows Heling Ancient Road in Xianyou. Photographed by Cui Jiannan

The upper right picture: On Xiaojiang Ancient Road in Wuyi Mountain, mortise and tenon joints are set at the outer end of the stone steps, which are presumed to be used for installing guardrails. Photographed by Wu Jun

The lower right picture: The column socket formed by the porter resting on the ancient road. Photographed by Wu Jun

驮物或骑行，人力肩扛的轿子（舆）主要供官绅人家出行使用，但遇到险峻的部分岭道，都需下马、下轿，缓行通过。相比较而言，车（马）道较为规整，其上下山的台阶石坎不会太高，约10公分左右；步道则路面崎岖高陡，不适合车马通行。因行走之时常需手持棍杖，或负重而行于途中休息时以棍杖驻撑货担，时间久了，拐棍就在路石表面磨出一个又一个的圆窝，称为柱窝，径约6~9公分。

福建古道之险峻，国内堪称"无出其右"，因而使无数入闽官员发出"蜀道无以过"的感叹！明代《邵武府志》载："入闽有三道，建宁为险道，两浙之所窥也。邵武为隘道，江右（江西）之所趋也。广漳航海为间道，奇兵之所乘也。"建宁、邵武分指当时的建宁府、邵武府，建宁路上的"险道"，即指崇安分水关路和浦城仙霞关路；所谓隘道，即指光泽杉关路。历千百年时光而形成的入闽"官马大道"，仍然险、隘如斯，就不难想见其他大小通道的"不堪"了！

左　图：光泽杉关，被誉为"八闽第一关"，是古代闽北重要的军事要塞　吴军 摄

右　图：邵武桂林乡的村前古道　阮任艺 摄

The left picture: Shanguan Pass in Guangze, known as "the first pass in Fujian", is an important military fortress in northern Fujian in ancient times. Photographed by Wu Jun

The right picture: The ancient road in front of the village in Guilin Township, Shaowu. Photographed by Ruan Renyi

福建古道依其通往目的地的不同，可以区分为五类：其一，是通京或通省驿道，或称主驿道、省道，其中通京驿道称作“官马大道”，通省驿道称作“官马支道”。其二，是县际通道，其中多数也是通邮的驿道，可称之为次驿道、大道。以上两类道路因为沿线设有驿站、公馆与铺递，并纳入官方的管理体系，故可统称为“官道”。其三，是县际间的次要道路，连通县城与主要乡镇，多数也与邻县相接，或通往县域内的次要行政与集散中心，也有通往有影响力的寺观或山岳等处的，统称为县道；这类道路有的设有塘汛，以资守备或“会哨及文移往来”。第四类连接各乡镇与较大型村落的，即为乡道。第五类，就是遍布于乡村之间或村域内外的村道，如联络各处的毛细血管，通连于房前屋后、田间地头，其路径时成时改，足迹所至，即成有无。

官道及各类县道的形成，基本都是官方在民间财力的基础上，以“官倡民修”的形式长期延续，但各处道路因为所经过的地形及各地经济能力、使用人群不同，表现方式也各不相同。值得说明的是，各类道路的等级并不是一成不变，随着形势的变化，道路的重要性也会因时而变。主要的变化因素，是出于军事上的防御需求或行政管辖上的隶属变迁。如明代寿宁县隶属于建宁府，其南路过九岭、芹洋、平溪，穿石门隘入政和，为通府正道；东南路经三望洋、车岭、斜滩，至武曲往福安，原为偏道，至清雍正十三年（1735），寿宁改隶福宁府，遂成通府正道，沿路并增设青竹岭、大洋头、三澄、元潭、武曲共 5 处铺递等。

如果我们将“险峻”称之为福建古道的共性，那么由于道路应用目的的不同，以及道路所经之处地理与地方风情的差异，在经历了漫长的时间磨洗后，各地的古道仍然发展出各自鲜明的布局与特性。福建的古道格局大致如蓝鼎元在《福建全省总图说》中的概括，可以区分为北路出仙霞关、西路通赣西南、东北路出闽东、西南路通粤东北，以及东南沿海通道等 5

个方向。结合“入闽三道”等说，参照明清之际的驿铺分布情况，全省古道由此统分为西北险道、西南隘道、中南鸟道、东南间道、东北岭道等五大分区体系。

如果以各处的入省边界为起点，则西北路起于闽浙、闽赣间绵延分布的松政柘岭、浦城仙霞、武夷分水、光泽杉岭等各处古关隘；西南路起点含由闽西转闽西南的建宁、泰宁、宁化、长汀、武平、上杭等闽西客属各县与江西、广东间的各处隘口；中南路起点为与粤东相交接的永定至平和沿线，并北向穿越闽南博平岭、闽中戴云山；东南路起点为诏安及东南沿海各府县；东北路则始于福鼎、寿宁、柘荣等与浙南相接的省界关隘。五大区系以东北 - 西南向的闽中大山带为左右分水，闽江干流及上游富屯溪为南北分界，铺石凿路，水陆相接，织出缀连于山、河、海之间的这片东南路网。

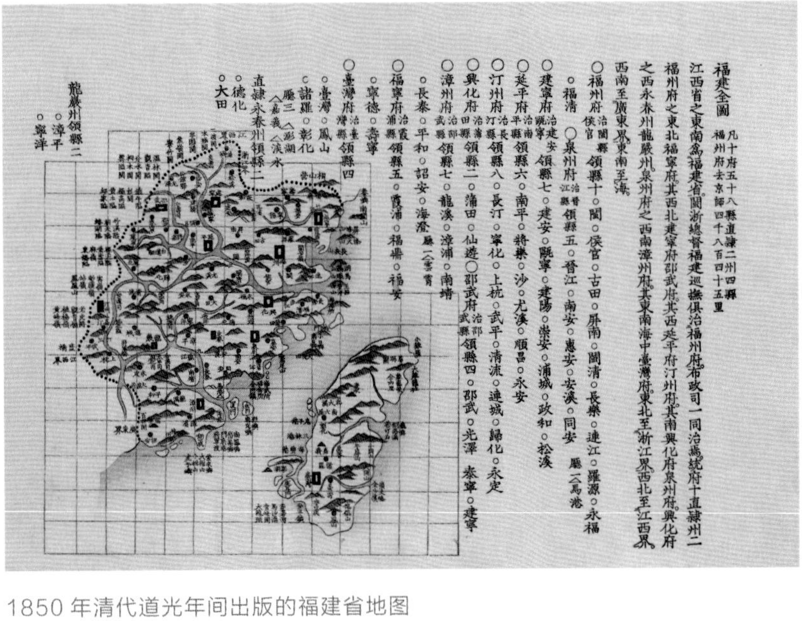

1850 年清代道光年间出版的福建省地图

Map of Fujian Province Published in Daoguang Period of the Qing Dynasty in 1850

各区道路起自于出省各个方向的大关小隘，大致以山水为界，沿山、顺水、趁势，以福州为最后汇集的中心点，但也有部分道路是经由延平这一交换枢纽后，直接转往目的地。古道或收或分，干道与支路有序递进，宛如一只巨掌，以道路作为血脉经络，通连各个府、州、县，形成了以福州为中心的福建古代道路交通体系。

ALONG WITH MOUNTAINS AND RIVERS, THE MOUNTAIN ROADS ARE GREEN

During the development of Minyue Dynasty, Fujian gradually integrated into the diverse Chinese culture. For thousands of years, the ancient roads, which have gradually become dense and laid out, have played an important connecting role. The key to the formation of roads lies in their use and maintenance. With the needs of political management, cultural development and economic exchanges in past dynasties, the road network distribution of Fujian ancient roads has become increasingly detailed and the function of "connection" has become more strengthened.

From the Han Dynasty to the Qing Dynasty, Fujian's ancient roads were built along the mountain, with stairs built on mountain roads and bridges built on waterways. The road surface of main roads is paved with stones. Because of abundant stream resources, most of the stones are taken from pebbles of different sizes in streams. Relying on labor power and the resources and tools endowed by nature, the ancestors dug all roads.

左　图：武夷山古道，依旧还有茶农穿梭其间　吴军 摄

右　图：柘荣县内连接乡村之间的村道　赖小兵 摄

The left picture: There are still tea farmers shuttling through Wuyi Mountain Ancient Road. Photographed by Wu Jun

The right picture: Village roads connecting villages in Zherong County. Photographed by Lai Xiaobing

Fujian ancient roads can be divided into five types according to different destinations: the first is the post road leading to the capital or provinces; the second is the channel between counties. The above two types of roads are collectively referred to as "official roads". The third is the secondary road between counties, which connects the county town with main villages and towns, and most of them are also connected with the neighboring counties, collectively referred to as county roads. The fourth is the connection between towns and larger villages, which is called township road. The fifth is the village road which are scattered between villages or inside and outside the village area, like capillaries connecting everywhere, all the places where people can walk are roads.

After a long period of honing, the ancient roads in all parts of Fujian have developed their own distinct layout and characteristics. According to the distribution of post shops during the Ming and Qing Dynasties, we further divided the ancient road system in the whole province into five regional systems, namely, the northwest dangerous road, the southwest pass road, the south-south bird road, the southeast inter-road and the northeast ridge road.

The roads in each region start from small and big passes in all directions out of the province, which are roughly bounded by mountains and rivers, along the mountains and along the rivers, with Fuzhou as the final gathering center. There are also some roads cerntering on Yanping and directly transferred to their destinations. The ancient road is just like a huge palm, with roads as blood channels and collaterals, connecting various prefectures, states and counties, forming an ancient road traffic system in Fujian with Fuzhou as the center.

西北险道，水陆互通

西北区主要指今天南平市所属各区县，以及沿闽江干流所经的古田、闽清、闽侯等。无论从道路的形成时间，或是路面的便利性以及重要程度，西北路都是福建与外界相连的主要通道，在很长一段时间里，甚至可以称之为“唯一重要”的通道。但这么重要的“官马大道”，却仍然还是被普遍认定为“险道”，而那些“策马驰骋”抑或是“乘风破浪”的想法，对福建先民而言，也只能是“诚不能也，非不为也”的梦想！

福建西北全境皆山，西北险道起于分踞闽浙、闽赣分界的仙霞岭、武夷山脉间的各处隘口，关山万里，岭路崎岖，是以称“险”。而西北路之所以能够成为贯穿福建历史发展始末的最显重要的官马大道，除了这一区域正好处在出省通京的主要方位外，更与其水陆相辅相成的地理特点密切相关。虽然翻山越岭、跋山涉水已是行走之间的常态，西北官路却有闽江上游各大水系相伴，陆路沿山岭蜿蜒而下，只要走出大山，往往不远处就可以到达与大河交汇的口岸，坐船或沿着河岸道路顺势而下，水陆兼程，即可通津千里，直达福州。

但船行有上下、水势有枯汛，闽江水路又险滩密布，所以来回于福建与中原间的不同人群与货物中的多数，还是会选择经行于崎岖蜿蜒的“官马大道”。据《读史方舆纪要》，闽江上游的水运航道艰险无比：“滩石嵯岈，纵横林立，舟行罅隙中，滩高水急，略无安流，流船轻脆，石齿坚利，稍

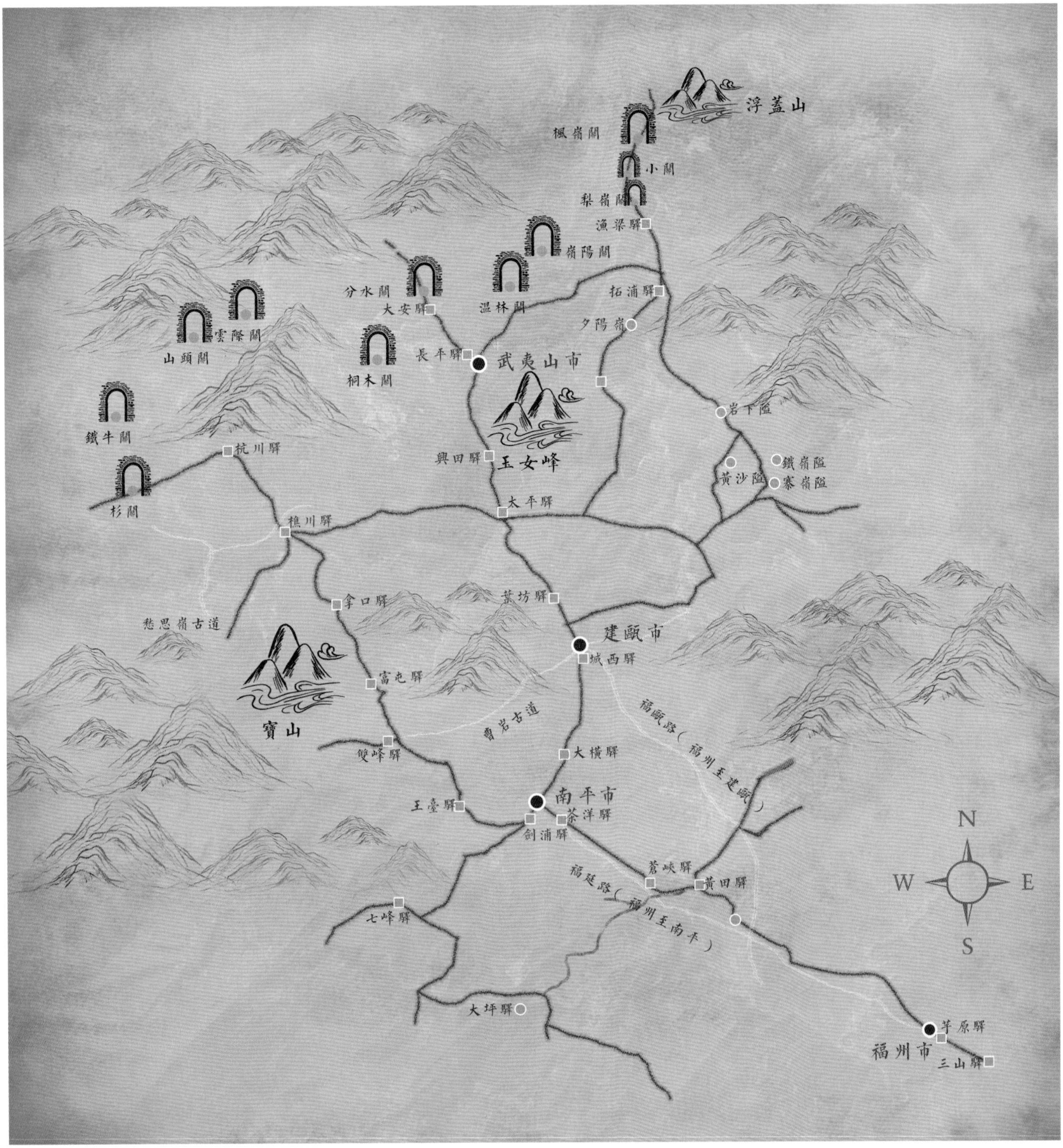

闽西北驿道是福建与外界相连的主要通道，其中浦城仙霞、武夷分水、光泽杉关都是重要的古道关隘

The post road in the northwest of Fujian is the main passage connecting Fujian with the outside world, of which Xianxia in Pucheng, Fenshui in Wuyi and Shanguan in Guangze are all important ancient roads and passes

或不戒，沉溺及之矣。相传始于浦城，迄于水口，诸滩之有名者以三百计，然至险者亦不过数处，曰将军滩在浦城县南十里、和尚滩俗名阿弥陀佛滩在建宁府北六十五里、黯淡滩在延平府北五里、大伤滩在延平府东南十八里、大湾滩在水口北二十里，其最著者也。”而水口往下，水势平稳，方可泛舟无虞！

闽江河道具有显著的山区溪流特点：浅滩更多，水流重疾，礁石更密，季节落差大。即使是土生土长之人，也必须“生而习水者”才“敢以舟楫自任”。对此，北宋陈渊有诗《自浦城放船下建安寄庞几先》称：“扁舟西下趁残阳，目断云边归雁行；短棹莫辞风浪恶，人间平地有羊肠。”闽江上游地区也一直流传有“纸船铁艄公”和“上下三十六滩，滩滩都是鬼门关”的说法；而当逆流经过险滩时，还要多凑人手上岸拉纤，才能让船逆流而上。以林则徐在嘉庆十七年（1812）的出行为例，其十月二十五日从洪山桥登舟，全程坐船，8 日之后，于十一月初二日到达延平府城外泊；初五日至建宁府城，停泊一日后续发，于十四日晚泊浦城观前，“每由此舍舟就陆，此番初亦拟其如是，幸水吉以上连日有雨，溪流复长，故仍令舟人溯流而前。”十六日，到浦城，距离开福州之时，已经过去了 22 天！林则徐在浦城停留多日，因“数日来，浙省无夫到此，官差尚未疏通，催促行户亦属无益，不得不静以待之。”至二十一日，“始有人夫，束装就陆，北风甚大，晚至渔梁宿；二十二日，辰刻行，上午过五显岭，又过大竿岭，入浙界，酉刻至念八都宿。”

由于水路风波险恶，所以不少人从仙霞岭路入闽后，会选择经陆路官道至南平，再坐船往福州。参照清康熙六十一年（1722）首任巡察台湾御史黄叔璥的《南征纪程》，他从农历二月二十一日离京，沿大运河—钱塘江—富春江一路乘船南下，于四月八日经仙霞古道越过浦城梨岭关，先沿建溪陆行至南平，然后登船沿闽江东下，于四月十七日至福州洪山桥上岸入福州城。由此大略推算，经由这条西北官道从浦城至福州的时间，头尾约需十天。

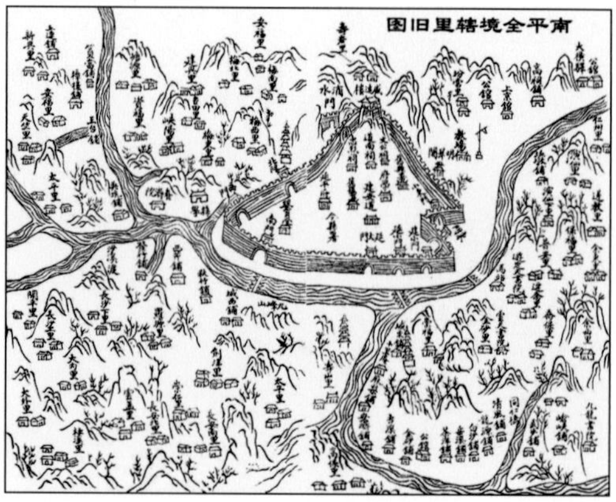

古时南平旧城图，从图中可清楚地看到南平城区在崇山峻岭环抱中

The old city map of Nanping in ancient times clearly shows that Nanping's urban area is surrounded by high mountains

The upper picture: Lilingguan Ancient Road, located in Wuxian Mountain, Jiumu Town, Pucheng County. Photographed by Lai Xiaobing

The lower picture: Andan beach is the most dangerous place in Jianxi River. The boat capsized with a little carelessness, and boats often avoided it in ancients times. After passing through Andan beach, Yanping was just in front of it. Photographed by Ruan Renyi

上　图：位于浦城县九牧镇五显岭的梨岭关古道　赖小兵 摄

下　图：黯淡滩是建溪最险之处，稍有不慎舟船倾覆，古代行舟多避之，过了黯淡滩，延平就在面前了　阮任艺 摄

西北官道的省界起点，由东往西可以区分为松政柘岭、浦城仙霞、崇安分水、光泽杉岭四区，正好分别对应着松溪、南浦溪、崇阳溪、富屯溪等闽江上游的四大支流。古道在跨越关隘之后，顺山势沿溪岸前行，松政之路汇于松溪，再顺流而下至建阳；仙霞各路汇于浦城，沿南浦溪而下，聚于建瓯；崇安各路沿崇阳溪汇于建阳，杉岭各路沿富屯溪东下邵武，与上述各路俱聚于南平。这些支流水势丰沛，几十万年间冲积而成的大河两岸，形成有着优越生产、生活条件且聚散便利的村镇聚落，古道沿河而行，形成蒲扇状的路网，人流汇聚，货物转贮，由此在道路的交汇处，形成了邵武、建阳、建瓯、南平等各处区域中心城市。

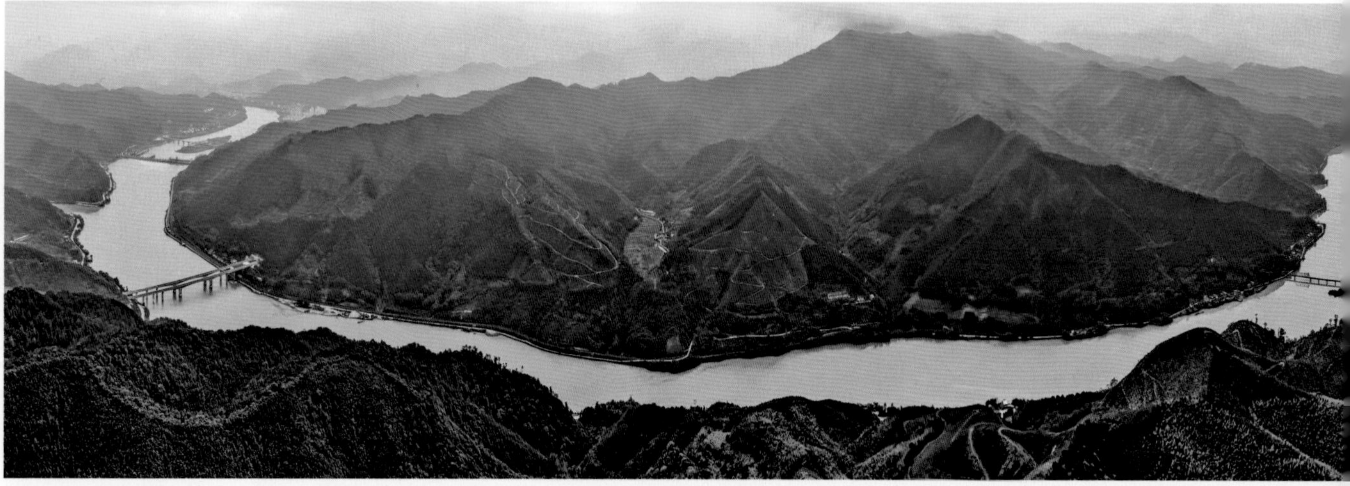

闽江上游富屯溪与沙溪交汇处 阮任艺 陈映辉 摄

The intersection of Futun River and Shaxi River in the upper reaches of Minjiang River. Photographed by Ruan Renyi and Chen Yinghui

The Dangerous Northwest Road Interconnection of Water and Land

The northwest of Fujian mainly refers to today's Nanping City, as well as Gutian, Minqing, Minhou and other places along the Minjiang River. No matter the formation time of the road, or the convenience and importance of the road surface, Northwest Road is the main passage connecting Fujian with the outside world. For a long time, it can even be called the "only important" passage.

The whole territory of northwest Fujian is full of mountains. The northwest road starts from the passes of Xianxialing and Wuyi Mountain at the boundary between Fujian and Zhejiang, Fujian and Jiangxi. The reason why this northwest road can become the most important official road is not only that this area is located in the main direction leading to Beijing, but also related to its geographical characteristics of water and land complementing each other.

Along the northwest road, walking out of the mountain to the southeast can reach the port where the river meets. Then people could take boats or walk along the river. Due to the danger of waterways, many people choose to reach Nanping by land and then Fuzhou by boat after entering Fujian from Xianxialing Mountain and Fengshui Guan. According to records, it takes about ten days for this northwest road to travel from Pucheng to Fuzhou.

The starting point of the Northwest Road in Fujian can be divided into four regions from east to west: Songxi County and Zhenghe County, Pucheng County, Wuyishan County and Guangze County. They correspond to the four tributaries of the upper reaches of the Minjiang River, including Song Creek, Nanpu Creek, Chongyang Creek and Futun Creek. With the plentiful water potential of these tributaries, on both sides of the river formed by hundreds of thousands of years of alluvial, villages and towns have been formed; Along the river, the cattail-leaf-fan-shaped ancient road has been formed; At the junction of roads, Shaowu, Jianyang, Jian'ou, Nanping and other central cities have been formed.

上　图：1870 年的延平区全景图。闽江绕城而过，沿江的建筑鳞次栉比，城市格局已具雏形　约翰·汤姆逊 摄

下　图：闽江沿岸河道交错，水流丰沛，古道沿江而行，商旅如流，形成了流域各处的中心城市。图为延平区沿江景色　阮任艺 陈映辉 摄

The upper picture:Panorama of Yanping District in 1870. Minjiang River passes around the city, buildings along the river are lined up and the city pattern has taken shape. Photographed by John Thomson

The lower picture:The rivers along the Minjiang River are crisscrossed and the water flow is abundant. The ancient road runs along the river with many businessmen and travellers, forming the central city in all parts of the river basin. The picture shows the scenery along the river in Yanping District. Photographed by Ruan Renyi and Chen Yinghui

柘岭松溪

远古福建与浙江同属百越，从浦城、松溪等地出土的大量新石器、青铜时代遗物看，与浙江南部丽水地区的同期文物具有极大的相似性，可为两地先民早期往来频繁的实证。从地理位置看，浦城、松溪、政和三地与浙南地域毗邻，省界之间山多孔道，水源相通，具备极好的通达条件。按《读史方舆纪要》，“泉山，在（浦城）县东北六十里，一名泉嵩，顶有泉二派，一入建溪，一入处州。或曰：《汉书》朱买臣言，东越王居保泉山，盖谓此山云。……柘岭，县东北百二十里，接浙江丽水县界。高千余仞，绝顶周回百余步。旧《记》：柘岭峻极，势彻苍穹，狭道陡绝，不通牛马。是也。有江村溪出焉，亦谓之柘水。谢灵运云：柘水出柘岭，以地多柘树而名。”

柘岭古道应为闽浙之间往来年代最早的通道，也是唐末仙霞岭未开之前最重要的省界古道之一。在柘岭南侧，现仍保存着一座石砌关隘——寨岭隘，为福建浦城与浙江江山、遂昌间的界关。清光绪《浦城县志》：“寨

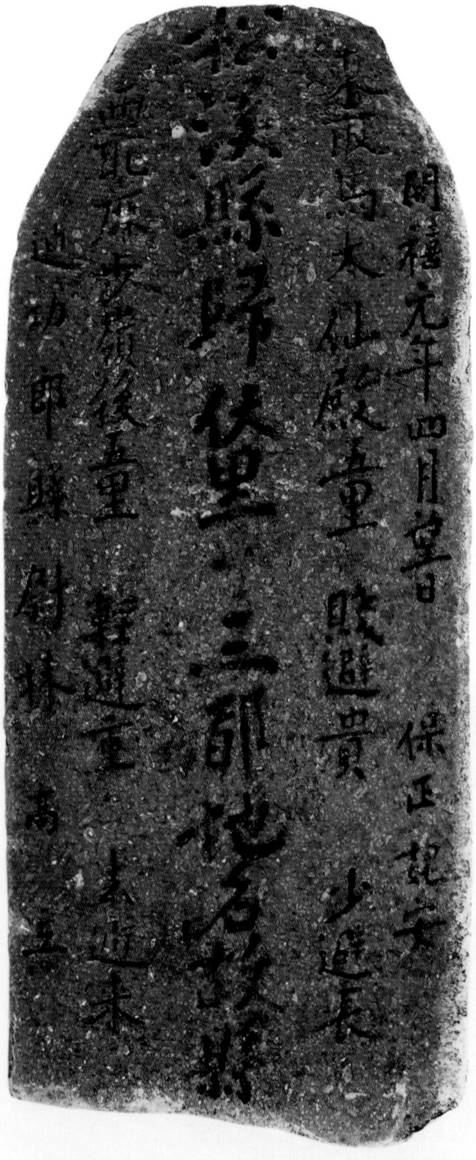

松溪保存着一块我国现存最早、最完整的南宋交通法规碑。碑文为：“贱避贵，少避长，轻避重，去避来” 严硕 摄

Songxi has preserved the earliest and most complete monument of traffic regulations in the Southern Song Dynasty in China. The inscription is: "The lowliness avoid the nobleness, the youthful avoid the elderly, the lightness avoid the heaviness, the going avoid the coming". Photographed by Yan Shuo

THE ROAD CONNECTING SONGXI AND ZHENGHE COUNTY

Zheling Ancient Road is the earliest passage between Fujian and Zhejiang Provinces. On the south side of Zheling, there is still a stone pass—Zheling Pass, which is the boundary between Pucheng in Fujian and Jiangshan and Suichang in Zhejiang. Zheling is also the birthplace of Nanpu River and Songxi River. Songxi River in Songxi County connects Qixing River in Zhenghe County and then flows into Jianxi River in Jian'ou County.

福清山古道山高险峻，风光秀美，早在隋朝以前，就是中原地区联系福建的主要通道 朱晨辉 摄

The ancient road of Fuqing Mountain is high and steep, with beautiful scenery. As early as before the Sui Dynasty, it was the main passage connecting the Central Plains with Fujian. Photographed by Zhu Chenhui

The upper left picture: Yinbin Gate in Songxi County, built in the Ming Dynasty, has been renovated many times and now basically retains the architectural style of the Guangxu period of the Qing Dynasty. It is an important place for Songxi to welcome and send off in ancient times. Photographed by Lai Xiaobing

The lower left picture: The tea garden on Chaping Ancient Post Road in Songxi County was once a busy tea road. Photographed by Lai Xiaobing

The right picture: Huangkeng Pass in Songxi is an important watershed between southern Zhejiang and northern Fujian. Photographed by Lai Xiaobing

左上图：松溪寅宾门，始建于明代，经多次修缮，现基本保留清光绪年间的建筑风格，是松溪古时迎来送往重要之地　赖小兵 摄

左下图：松溪县茶平古道上的茶园，这里曾是繁忙的茶道　赖小兵 摄

右　图：松溪黄坑关，是浙南与闽北的重要分水关　赖小兵 摄

谢灵运

（385～433），原名公义，字灵运，世称谢客。南北朝时期诗人、佛学家、旅行家。

山水诗的鼻祖谢灵运一生酷爱山水，自称『江北倦历览，江南旷周旋』，还特制登山之用的『谢公屐』，他的山水诗多创造于『肆意遨游，寻山陟岭』。

为追求奇险之景，谢灵运把出游的地方选择在危险绝壁的山岚处，出游刻意求奇，『寻山陟岭，必造幽峻，岩嶂千重，莫不备尽』。当年，他经柘岭古道入闽，并留下了『柘水出柘岭，以地多柘树而名』的记录。

这种对奇景的爱好情趣，也表现在他的山水诗中，如他登上天姥山是『高高入云霓』；他登上『群峰首』，感觉『邈若升云烟』；这些游历的风景皆是直插云霄、高耸屹立的奇险之景，可见他所追求的探险式的美趣。

Xie Lingyun (385-433), originally named Gongyi, styled himself Lingyun, traditionally called Xieke, was a poet, buddhist and traveler in the Southern and Northern Dynasties.

Xie Lingyun, the originator of landscape poems, loved mountains and rivers all his life. He claimed to be "tired of looking at the north of the Yangtze River and wandering in the south of the Yangtze River", and also specially made "xie gong ji" for mountaineering. Most of his landscape poems were created in "roaming freely and looking for mountains to climb".

In order to pursue the strange and dangerous scenery, Xie Lingyun not only chose the place to travel in the dangerous cliff, but also deliberately sought strange things when travelling.When looking for mountains to climb, he always went to the deepest and most steep places. Even if there are thousands of rocks and risks, there is no place he couldn't travel. In that year, he entered Fujian via Zheling Ancient Road and left a record that "Zheshui came out of Zheling and was famous for its many trees".

This interest in wonders is also reflected in his landscape poems. For example, the Tianmu Mountain he climbed was "high into the sky"; He climbed to the "highest of the peaks" and felt "as remote as rising up the sky ". These landscapes he travelled are all exotic and dangerous scenes that soar into the sky and stand tall, which can be seen that what he pursues in his traveling landscapes is adventurous beauty.

Xie Lingyun (385-433), originally named Gongyi, styled himself Lingyun, traditionally called Xieke, was a poet, buddhist and traveler in the Southern and Northern Dynasties.

Xie Lingyun, the originator of landscape poems, loved mountains and rivers all his life. He claimed to be "tired of looking at the north of the Yangtze River and wandering in the south of the Yangtze River", and also specially made "xie gong ji" for mountaineering. Most of his landscape poems were created in "roaming freely and looking for mountains to climb".

In order to pursue the strange and dangerous scenery, Xie Lingyun not only chose the place to travel in the dangerous cliff, but also deliberately sought strange things when travelling. When looking for mountains to climb, he always went to the deepest and most steep places. Even if there are thousands of rocks and risks, there is no place he couldn't travel. In that year, he entered Fujian via Zheling Ancient Road and left a record that "Zheshui came out of Zheling and was famous for its many trees".

This interest in wonders is also reflected in his landscape poems. For example, the Tianmu Mountain he climbed was "high into the sky"; He climbed to the "highest of the peaks" and felt "as remote as rising up the sky ". These landscapes he travelled are all exotic and dangerous scenes that soar into the sky and stand tall, which can be seen that what he pursues in his traveling landscapes is adventurous beauty.

谢灵运

（385~433），原名公义，字灵运，世称谢客。南北朝时期山水诗人、佛学家、旅行家。

山水诗的鼻祖谢灵运一生酷爱山水，自称「江北倦历览，江南旷周旋」，还特制登山之用的「谢公屐」，他的山水诗多创造于「肆意遨游，寻山陟岭」。

为追求奇险之景，谢灵运甚至出游的地方选择在危险绝壁的山岚处，出游刻意求奇，「寻山陟岭，必造幽峻，岩嶂千重，莫不备尽」。当年，他经柘岭古道入闽，并留下了「柘木出柘岭，以地多柘树而名」的记录。

这种好奇景的爱好情趣，也表现在他的山水诗中。如他登上天姥山是「高高入云霓」；他登上「群峰首」，感觉「邈若升云烟」；这些游历的风景皆是直指云霄、高耸屹立的奇险之景，可见他所追求的探险式的美趣。

松溪县茶平乡古驿道，传说朱熹曾在此游学讲道　赖小兵 摄

Chaping Ancient Post Road in Songxi County is said to have been where Zhu Xi studied and preached. Photographed by Lai Xiaobing

左　图：政和稠岭茶盐古道。昔日，政和的食盐从闽东福安穆阳运进，完全靠挑夫运送，穆阳到政和，要翻越鹫峰山脉，上牛岭、麻岭，下稠岭。古道曾多次重修，难得的是整条古道大部分是用条石铺成，条石长约 1.4 米、宽约 40 厘米、厚约 12 厘米，在福建古道中极为罕见　吴军 摄

右　图：松溪大布古渡口，这里曾是松溪重要的集市　崔建楠 摄

The left picture: Ancient tea and Salt Road in Chouling Mountain of Zhenghe. In the past, Zhenghe's salt was transported from Muyang of Fu'an in eastern Fujian, and was transported entirely by porters. From Muyang to Zhenghe, it was necessary to cross Jiufeng Mountains, Shangniu Mountain, Maling Mountain and Xiachou Mountain. The ancient road has been rebuilt many times, what is rare is that the whole ancient road is mostly paved with stone, which is about 1.4 meters long, 40 centimeters wide and 12 centimeters thick. It is extremely rare in Fujian ancient roads. Photographed by Wu Jun

The right picture: Ancient Dabu ferry of Songxi used to be an important market in Songxi. Photographed by Cui Jiannan

岭隘，在忠信里，南据县治八十里，东至遂昌县二百三十里，北至江山县二百里。”寨岭隘又名海溪关，位于浦城县忠信镇海溪村北侧约 7500 米处的岭南半山腰上，地势极为险要。关墙用岩石垒砌，关门高 2.4 米、宽 2.1 米、深 2.5 米。关墙总长 23 米，宽 3 米，高 3 米。石砌古道上下尚存 7.2 公里，每级石阶长 1.7 米、宽 0.5 米，沿途房基、商铺遗址尚存。关门内侧往浙江方向接近山脊垭口处的古道边，立有一方摩崖题刻，高 1.8 米、宽 0.8 米，刻于明嘉靖十年（1531），内容为“鉴于古道年久失修，今集资维修……”，以及捐资者姓名、金额等。

柘岭同为西南面南浦溪、南面松溪的发源地。松溪县以溪名，古称东平，因有松溪干流纵贯全境，“百里松荫碧长溪”，故于宋开宝八年（975）改名松溪县。政和于宋政和五年（1115）析置立县，因年号而称政和县。松溪南流接政和七星溪，溪岸宽阔，水流平缓，至建瓯并入建溪。

上　图：锦穆古道，南平政和县至浙江省庆元县古道。图为岭腰乡锦屏村大林洞段，通往浙江省庆元县举水乡的古道　吴军 摄

下　图：西津码头。政和县石圳村三面为七星溪所环绕，千百年前，它不仅曾是政和重要的水陆中转码头所在地，也是政和通往省、府的必经之地。发达的水陆交通催生了商贸服务业，清朝末期，石圳村富庶繁华，华屋连甍。沿路的古门额、封火墙头和古民宅等，都在昭示着这个村落曾经的繁华热闹　吴军 摄

The upper picture: Jinmu Ancient Road, the ancient road from Zhenghe County in Nanping to Qingyuan County in Zhejiang Province. The picture shows Dalin Cave Section of Jinping Village, Lingyao Township, an ancient road leading to Jushui Village, Qingyuan County, Zhejiang Province. Photographed by Wu Jun

The lower picture: Xijin wharf. Three sides of Shizhen village in Zhenghe county is surrounded by Qixing Creek. Thousands of years ago, it was not only the location of Zhenghe's important land and water transfer dock, but also the only way for Zhenghe to the province and capital. The developed land and water transportation hastened the birth of the commercial service industry. At the end of the Qing Dynasty, Shizhen village was rich and prosperous, and gorgeous houses linked together. The ancient horizontal inscribed boards over a door, the head of the fire wall and ancient houses along the road all show the past prosperity and excitement of this village. Photographed by Wu Jun

松政两县地处仙霞岭南端和洞宫山余脉交汇处，为浙西南入闽要道，历代兵家均在此设防。松溪沿岸铺递并行，境内古驿道东达浙江庆元、龙泉两县，北至浦城，西南至建阳，南至建瓯；往东南，可达寿宁，以及屏南、宁德等地。松政与浙江关系密切，往来较多。如宋代在岩下建置的梓亭寨，兼管龙泉、遂昌、政和等县防务，设立之初隶属松溪，至元代改隶龙泉县，至明代则改隶庆元县。

元朝在松溪、政和两县境内置“两寨九隘”，两寨即东关寨、二十四都寨，九隘分别是铁岭隘、寨岭隘、岩下隘、黄沙隘、山庄隘、黄土隘、荷岭隘、翁源隘、红门隘等。隘口多以石砌，门洞为券顶长巷过道式，兼具有路亭的休息功能。

左上图：政和至寿宁澄源乡黄岭村的黄岭古道上的梦龙亭，传说因明朝中晚期的著名文学家冯梦龙途经此地而得名 吴军 摄

左下图：政和澄源乡古道边的定风寺，建于唐朝，是古代旅行者祈福保佑平安之处 吴军 摄

右 图：政穆古道—青丝岭 吴军 摄

The upper left picture: Huangling Ancient Road, located from Zhenghe to Shouning official road in Huangling village, Chengyuan township. Photographed by Wu Jun

The lower left picture: Dingfeng Temple on the edge of the ancient road in Chengyuan Township of Zhenghe was built in the Tang Dynasty and is a place for ancient travelers to pray for peace. Photographed by Wu Jun

The right picture: Zhengmu Ancient Road-Qingsi Mountain. Photographed by Wu Jun

仙霞南浦

XIANXIA ANCIENT ROAD IN PUCHENG COUNTY

浦城位于福建最北端，“山延两脉，水注三江”，境内溪流因仙霞岭而分水，分别流注福建闽江、江西信江和浙江钱塘江，主要河流南浦溪可直通闽江，径达福州。

浦城早在秦汉之时就有翻越东北面柘岭通往浙江龙泉、丽水的大路，唐末黄巢沿山开道仙霞岭，从宋代起，仙霞岭路成为福建的主要进京官路。《读史方舆纪要》云：“浦城北当仙霞，虞浙江突入，西联分水，虑江右之交驰，东界处州，防矿贼之窃发，是诚全闽之头目，保护不可或怠者也。”因为关防紧要，所以历代朝廷都在浦城的各处险要之地叠石为门，境内沿着与浙、赣的省界一线设立的关隘多达二十余处，屯兵数百，以资防御。

仙霞岭横亘于闽浙赣三省之间，又名古泉山、古岭山。从浙江江山绵延至福建浦城，其中以山势相对高峻之处分作六岭，即浙江境内的仙霞岭、窑岭、茶岭、小竿岭，以及浦城境内的大竿岭（又名枫岭）和梨岭（又名五显岭），六岭统称仙霞岭。隋炀帝开通京杭大运河后，中原入闽路线多经运河达钱塘江，再溯江而上至江山清湖渡，改行陆路，翻越仙霞岭到浦城城关，其间230里路，即仙霞古道。

仙霞古道贯通六岭，前后共设五关。第四关枫岭

Pucheng County is located in the northernmost part of Fujian, where streams are separated by high Xianxia Ridge and flow into Minjiang River in Fujian, Xinjiang River in Jiangxi and Qiantang River in Zhejiang.

Since the Song Dynasty, Xianxia Ancient Road in Pucheng Countyhas been the official road leading to Beijing from Fujian. There are six mountains on the Xianxia Ancient Road, with a total of five passes. Among them, Fengling Pass, the fourth pass, is the border between Fujian and Zhejiang. The existing length of the ancient road is more than 2 kilometers, which is one of the most well-preserved ancient roads in Pucheng. The fifth pass is Liling Pass, which is also the only one of the five passes located in Fujian.

左上图：浦城南浦溪源头 那兴海 摄
中上图：盘亭乡刘田村古驿道 严硕 摄
右上图：枫岭关为闽浙界关，现属浙江管辖，古驿道穿村而过，长约两公里，是浦城保存最为完整的古道之一 赖小兵 摄
下 图：仙霞古道上的盘亭乡古道 严硕 朱晨辉 摄

The upper left picture:Source of Nanpu Creek in Pucheng. Photographed by Na Xinghai

The upper middle picture: The ancient post road in Liutian village, Panting Township. Photographed by Yan Shuo

The upper right picture:Fengling Pass is the border between Fujian and Zhejiang and is now under the jurisdiction of Zhejiang. The ancient post road passes through the village and is about two kilometers long, which is one of the most well-preserved ancient roads in Pucheng. Photographed by Lai Xiaobing

The lower picture: The ancient road in Panting Township on Xianxia Ancient Road. Photographed by Yan Shuo and Zhu Chenhui

关为闽浙界关，现属浙江管辖，关墙以下的深坑古道即属浦城盘亭乡的深坑村。深坑因而成为东北连浙江、西北界江西的边界小山村，山村虽小，但鸡鸣三省，素有“深坑深万丈，盘亭在天上”的说法。古驿道穿村而过，现存总长约2公里，是浦城保存最为完整的古道之一。

梨岭关为第五关，也是仙霞五关中唯一位于福建境内的关。梨岭又称五显岭，北距浙、赣不足10公里，岭上的石砌古关四周高墙危堑，林木稠密，道路崎岖。《读史方舆纪要》载：“五显岭高峰连云，前横大壑，傍岩飞阁又类仙霞。其危崖仄径，真是令人一夫当关，千人自废。”据《浦城县志》，明洪武元年（1386），知县张鹏举于岭畔树华表，匾书“梨关”。正德七年（1512），重立关门。清嘉庆十五年（1810），重建关楼，南面书“全闽锁钥”，北面书“越闽砥柱”，梨岭关的重要性可见一斑。

据2014年9月的考古勘探资料，关墙正面朝北，呈自南向北防御态势。关墙正中及南北均存古驿道，南高北低，其中北段出露较长，南段出露较少。测量东西总长度31.8米（包括东西关墙和关门）。关口平面近方形，北端（前）底部宽2.6米，两侧墙均仅存基石；南端（后）底部约宽2.9米。西侧墙与驿道之间设排水沟，沟宽0.25米，沟底不规则，深约0.25米。门道从底向上稍外侈，上大下小，用较大块毛石砌造。东侧关墙连接岩壁，长度为10.9米，除保存较好下部外，还残存跑马道和跑马道面至垛口下部的部分墙体（矮墙）。西关墙长度为19米，高度从0.5~6.2米不等；此段关墙继续向西延伸，呈逐步提高的趋势。驿道在关口外向北延伸出露长49.5米，向南出露7米。路面宽度大多3.5米左右，进深0.7米，每级高差有0.15米、0.12米、0.1米不等。台阶前缘以较大石砌造，内侧用小片和卵石铺设。

除仙霞岭路外，浦城还有通往浙江龙泉、江西广丰以及各县的古道，沿路关隘矗立，保存较好的，还有毕岭关、海溪关、太平关和葛山隘等处。

境内主驿道分为北道、正南道、偏南道，3条道路每约10里分别设铺，共27铺。北道经仙阳逾渔梁岭，过九牧逾梨岭关，经庙湾、深坑至枫岭关出境，通浙江江山二十八都；正南道经下沙逾西阳岭，过临江逾大湖岭，过石陂越塔岭隘，经蒋溪口至濠岭出境，通建阳水吉；偏南道经水北越翁村岭，至翁源隘出境，通松溪留源。

The upper picture: Liling Pass is densely forested and has rugged roads. Photographed by Lai Xiaobing

The lower left picture: Liling Pass is the only pass of five passes of Xianxia within Fujian. The picture shows the drinking tank for the post horses to rest in front of Liling Pass. Photographed by Wu Jun

The lower right picture: Pucheng is the birthplace of ancient Minyue culture, with exquisite kiln technology. The kiln site at the back of the bowl kiln is mostly celadon, with bowls as the main part and a small number of bottles and jars. Due to its border with Zhejiang, it is greatly influenced by Longquan kiln. The picture shows the ancient road leading to the kiln site. Photographed by Lai Xiaobing

上　图：梨岭关林木稠密，道路崎岖　赖小兵 摄

左下图：梨岭关是仙霞五关中唯一位于福建境内的关隘。图为梨岭关前驿马休息的喝水槽　吴军 摄

右下图：浦城是古闽越文化的发源地，制窑技术精湛，碗窑背窑址多为青瓷。以碗为主，兼有少量瓶罐等，由于与浙江接壤，受龙泉窑影响较大，图为通往窑址的古道　赖小兵 摄

The upper picture: The Ancient Road of Xiyang Mountain in Shuidong village, Linjiang town, Pucheng. Photographed by Yan Shuo

The lower left picture: Geshan Pass of Fuling Mountain in Pucheng is the boundary between Fujian and Zhejiang provinces. Photographed by Wu Jun

The lower middle picture: The ancient road leading to Songxi behind Beiyanjing in Xudun village, Linjiang town, Pucheng still retains the bluestone road of the original post road. Photographed by Lai Xiaobing

The lower right picture: The Ancient Bridge leading to Songxi behind Beiyanjing in Xudun village, Linjiang town, Pucheng. Photographed by Wu Jun

上　图：浦城临江镇水东村夕阳岭古道　严硕 摄

左下图：浦城富岭葛山隘 是闽浙两省的分界关　吴军 摄

中下图：浦城临江镇徐墩村北岩井后通往松溪的古道还保留着原有驿道的青石路　赖小兵 摄

右下图：浦城临江镇徐墩村北岩井后通往松溪的古桥　吴军 摄

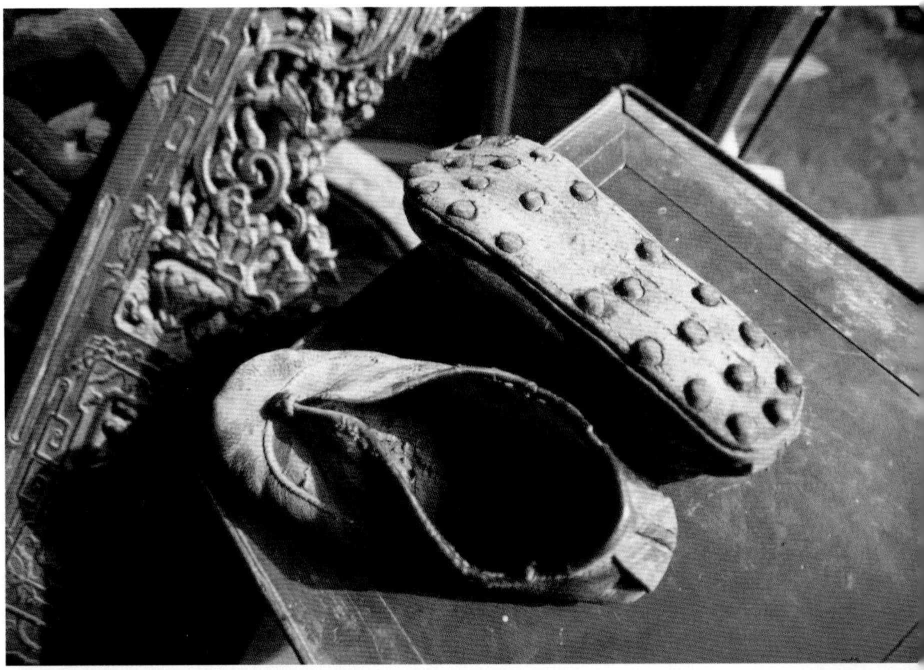

上　图：仙霞古道上古人跋涉驿道所用之鞋　阮任艺 摄

下　图：古驿道的发展也带来文化融合，赣剧是江西地方剧种之一，随着交通的便利也带来了异地的文化，浦城赣剧就是在此之下盛行的，如今在百姓中依然喜闻乐见　赖小兵 摄

The upper picture: Shoes used by ancient people to trek through post roads on Xianxia Ancient Road. Photographed by Ruan Renyi

The lower picture: The development of ancient post roads also brought about cultural integration. Jiangxi opera is one of Jiangxi's local operas. With the convenience of transportation, it also brought culture from other places. Jiangxi opera of Pucheng is popular under this circumstance and is still popular among the people today. Photographed by Lai Xiaobing

左　图：通往浙江江山的廿八都古道　阮任艺 摄
右　图：仙霞古道关雄峡险，如今大部分已被宽敞的公路覆盖，仅余仙霞关到枫岭关山岭之间尚有保存完整的古驿道　阮任艺 摄

The left picture: The 28-Capital Ancient Road leading to Jiangshan of Zhejiang Province. Photographed by Ruan Renyi

The right picture: Xianxia Ancient Road is with impregnable passes and dangerous valleys. Now most of it has been covered by spacious roads. Only between Yu Xianxia Pass and Fengling Pass, there are still well-preserved ancient post roads. Photographed by Ruan Renyi

武夷分水

今之武夷山古称崇安，即崇山峻岭之间的开阔安稳之地。其地处闽、赣两省交界，境内东、西、北部群山环抱，峰峦叠嶂，逐次向中、南部的崇阳溪谷降低。沿闽赣省界山脊之马鞍形坳谷处，历代筑关，控临山溪，扼险以守。据《读史方舆纪要》：“崇安有八关之阻。八关者，曰分水，曰温林，路出江西铅山及上饶县；曰岑阳，路出江西上饶及永丰县；曰桐木，曰焦岭，曰谷口，曰寮竹，曰观音，皆接铅山及上饶县界。”其中，“分水、温林、岑阳三关，商旅出入，恒为孔道。桐木、蕉岭、谷口、寮竹、观音五关，虽接连江右，而羊肠鸟道，人迹罕至，惟桐木关尚通行旅。”分水关古称大关，当闽赣之交通要冲，又称“八闽第一关”。

分水关位于崇安县境西北七十里之分水岭上。分水岭为入闽第一山，有二水发源岭下，一入江西铅山，一入福建为崇仁溪之源。分水关建于其上，历称江闽之襟要，五代至宋皆置寨于此。嘉定间，郡守史弥坚增修，后废。开庆元年（1259）修复，并置大安驿，

CHONG'AN ANCIENT ROAD IN WUYI MOUNTAIN

Today's Wuyi Mountain was called Chong'an in ancient times, which means an open and stable place between mountains. It is located at the junction of Fujian and Jiangxi provinces, surrounded by mountains in the east, west and north. Among them, the watershed is the first mountain from Jiangxi to Fujian, so the Fenshuiguan is called "the first pass of Eight Fujian ".

上　图：立关北望，两侧高山耸峙入云，“V”形的大峡谷犹如一道天堑，直向江西铅山县伸展。这是地质活动造成的桐木关断裂带，极其雄奇壮观　朱晨辉 严硕 摄

左下图：隐藏在峡谷深处古道边的这个小山村，叫桐木村。早在宋代，这里就已经种植茶树。图为与江西接壤的桐木关口　赖小兵 摄

右下图：黄连坑地形狭长，中间是一条明清时期就修筑的官马大道，它全由鹅卵石和大石板铺就，宽敞坚实，成为村庄的中轴线。两侧的吊脚楼板壁房，就是商铺和客栈　吴军 摄

The upper picture: Standing in the north of the pass, the mountains on both sides stand up into the clouds, and the "V" shaped Grand Canyon is like a natural moat stretching straight to Jiangxi's Qianshan County. This is the tongmuguan fault zone caused by geological activities, which is extremely spectacular. Photographed by Zhu Chenhui and Yan Shuo

The lower left picture: Hidden in the deep valley by the ancient road, this small mountain village is called Tongmu village. As early as the Song Dynasty, tea trees were already planted here. The picture shows the Tongmu Pass bordering Jiangxi Province. Photographed by Lai Xiaobing

The lower right picture:Huanglian Pit has a long and narrow terrain. The middle is an official road built in the Ming and Qing Dynasties, which is paved with pebbles and large stone slabs. It is spacious and solid, and becomes the central axis of the village. On both sides of pile dwellings and wooden partition houses,which are shops and inns. Photographed by Wu Jun

左上图：清末民初，随着福州开埠，外国传教士顺闽江北上，沿着古驿道进入福建腹地，最远到达武夷山分水关。桐木天主教堂建于清道光三年 赖小兵 摄

右上图：武夷山桐木村的烘茶作坊茶风景 崔建楠 摄

左下图：崇阳溪源头洋庄乡大安村的清澈溪流，无名拱桥是古代出省古道必经之路 吴军 摄

右下图：站在分水关上看古道，虽纤若游丝，却编织了闽赣繁荣的文明历史。古道上河口、苏州馆等古村镇遗存的格局和风貌，当年的辉煌从中可见一斑 吴军 摄

The upper left picture: At the end of the Qing Dynasty and the beginning of the Republic of China, with the opening of Fuzhou as a port, foreign missionaries went north along the Minjiang River, entered the hinterland of Fujian along the ancient post road, and reached Fenshui Pass in Wuyi Mountain as far as possible. Tongmu Catholic Church was built in the 3rd year of the Daoguang period in the Qing Dynasty. Photographed by Lai Xiaobing

The upper right picture: Tea scenery of Tea Baking Workshop in Tongmu Village, Wuyi Mountain. Photographed by Cui Jiannan

The lower left picture: The clear stream in Da'an Village, Yangzhuang Township, the source of Chongyang Creek and the nameless arch bridge is the only way out of the province in ancient times. Photographed by Wu Jun

The lower right picture: Standing on the Fenshui Pass and looking at the ancient road, although it is as delicate as a hairspring, it weaves the prosperous civilization history of Fujian and Jiangxi. The pattern and style of the remains of ancient villages and towns such as Hekou and Suzhou Pavilion on the ancient road can be seen from the glory of that year. Photographed by Wu Jun

元废。明洪武初，复置关，设巡司戍守，亦曰大关。关口平面呈“S”形，东西走向。关口及关门在1937年建101省道时损毁，现仅存两侧关墙，残长500余米。关墙用毛石干砌，顺山坡而建。西关墙保存相对完整，墙底部到顶部高3米至4米不等，内侧有一跑马道，厚6米；外侧垛墙高0.9~1.1米，厚0.6米。

岑阳即岭阳关，东隔铜钹山入浦城，北出则为上饶县封禁山，周边广谷深林，常为盗薮。关外内皆险，林深径窄，悬崖陡峭，措足殊艰。关寨呈西北向东南方向，现仅存关门、残墙和石基。关门平顶，用长方形石块砌筑，宽2.8米、进深2.5米、高2.7米。关口平面呈“一”字形，垛墙高0.5~1米。墙垛残宽0.45米、高0.65米。走马道宽2~4米。隘口左右门为框条石干砌，上槛石压顶，关墙为夯土城墙。土墙外侧高在2~5米之间。两侧关墙沿左右山脊至山顶，南侧残存城墙约300米，北侧残存城墙450米。

温林关又称温岭关，与寮竹关、观音关向称“三关”，皆外控上饶，分道通关，喉束衢、信，旧设巡司，地旷民聚，坡岭易登。关寨所在山体为南北走向，现存关门、残墙和石基。关门已塌陷，但门柱、关墙、

左　图：岭阳关关口位于武夷山市北部洋庄乡坑口村与江西交界的深山之中　吴军 摄

中　图：地势险要的温林关古道　吴军 摄

右　图：福建武夷山，小浆古道上，古时候用于安插护栏的坑槽（榫卯），是古道高工艺建造的证据　吴军 摄

The left picture: The gate of Lingyang Pass is located in the remote mountains at the junction of Kengkou Village, Yangzhuang Township, northern Wuyishan City and Jiangxi Province. Photographed by Wu Jun

The middle picture: Wenlin Pass Ancient Road with dangerous terrain. Photographed by Wu Jun

The right picture: In Wuyi Mountain of Fujian Province, the pits (mortise and tenon joints) used to install guardrails on the Xiaojiang ancient road in ancient times are evidence of the high-tech construction of the ancient road. Photographed by Wu Jun

墙垛、驿道等保存良好。隘口筑于北侧山脚，左右关墙用 1.2 × 0.27 × 0.3 米至 1.5 × 0.24 × 0.37 米不等长方形条石砌筑。关门平顶，高 2.7 米，下宽 1.8 米、进深 3.7 米，上槛用大形条石压顶。倒伏草中的门楣上书“温林关”字样，字幅 22 × 25 厘米，阴刻。两侧关墙用荒石干砌，外侧城墙垂直高峭处 4.5 米，最低处 2.7 米，沿左右山脊至山顶，南侧残存城墙约 300 米。北侧残存城墙 450 米。墙垛高 0.65 米，残宽 0.5 至 0.8 米，走马道宽 3.7 至 5 米。

界关以内的道路以崇安城关为中心，北道有 3 路，分别经分水关、岭阳关、寮竹关通往江西铅山、广丰，也可从焦岭关、温林关等越境到江西；南道有 2 路，一沿崇阳溪南下，一从赤石沿梅溪而上，越梅岭至五夫再沿潭溪而下至建阳，再抵建瓯；东道有 2 路，通浦城；西道亦 2 路，接建阳、光泽。

其中北上通往分水关的官道最为重要。现存大安岭段古驿道，自小浆村永丰桥自然村北侧至大安岭顶，全长 540 米。驿道大体呈东南 – 西北走向，斜长 542 米，宽 2.5~3.3 米，踏步宽 0.5~0.7 米。驿道用长方形条石、大小不一河卵石铺设而成，在驿道陡峭处间隔 1~1.2 米左右就铺设长条形石阶。石阶西端有榫卯，榫卯用于安装护栏，以利安全。

武夷山自然风景区内，大王峰星村古道上的送茶人 黄景业 摄

The tea deliverer on XingcunAncient road of Dawang Mount in Wuyi Mountain Natural Scenic Area. Photographed by Huang Jingye

上　图：武夷山五夫古镇兴贤书院，朱熹曾在此讲学传道
邱汝泉 摄

下　图：下梅古时是商贾云集之地，山西晋商在这里施展才华，武夷山的岩茶、红茶便从这里起运，北至山西、内蒙、俄罗斯，南至福州、厦门、印度。因此，下梅村又称"晋商万里茶路起点" 丁李青 摄

The upper picture: Zhu Xi gave lectures and preached at Xingxian Academy in Wufu Ancient Town of Wuyi Mountain. Photographed by Qiu Ruquan

The lower picture: Xiamei was a place where merchants gathered in ancient times. Shanxi merchants displayed their talents here. The transportation of rock tea and black tea of Wuyi Mountain started from here, reaching Shanxi, Inner Mongolia and Russia in the north and Fuzhou, Xiamen and India in the south. Therefore, Xiamei Village is also called "the starting point of Shanxi Merchants' Tea Road of thousands of miles". Photographed by Ding Liqing

杉岭富屯

光泽长期隶属于邵武军、州、府，有“邵光一家”之说。两者地处福建西北之闽赣边陲，西溪、北溪于光泽县城回龙潭汇合后称作富屯溪，经邵武后直下延平，达福州，是古代主要的运输通道。富屯溪河床坡度大，仅光泽至南平就有500余滩，回程上溯，全靠人力拖拉，故有“一滩高一丈，光泽在天上”之说。富屯溪滩多流急，舟船航行艰险，也有“一溪十八滩，滩滩鬼门关”之叹。

光泽、邵武历代为兵家必争之地，光泽古称“战城”，邵武则因城池雄峻，有“铁城”之称。光泽境内通往江西的古道众多，省界之间关隘林立，统称“九关十三隘”。从北向南，分别为鸭母关、马铃关、云际关、火烧关、山头关、分水关、铁牛关、杉关、王际坳关等九座山关，以及金家隘、蛇岭隘、台尖隘、孔坑隘、白虎隘、牛田隘、风扫隘、羊头隘、岩岭隘、杨公隘、义角隘、毛家隘、仙人隘等13座山隘。邵武地处光泽水陆下行之要津，境内又有金坑、桂林与江西交界，

如今古码头虽然失去了昔日的枢纽作用，但依然是村民生活中的一部分 吴军 摄

Although the ancient dock has lost its former pivot role, it is still a part of the villagers' life. Photographed by Wu Jun

THE NORTHWEST ROAD THROUGH GUANGZE AND SHAOWU

Guangze County was called "Zhancheng" in ancient times, which was the main transportation channel in ancient times and also an important military location in history. Shanling between Guangze and Jiangxi is aplace Easy to defend but hard to attack because of the deep and dangerous canyon.

Shaowu County was called "Tiecheng" in ancient times and was connected with the lower reaches of Guangze County Basin. Shaowu County is also a strategic place, guarding Fujian's northwest border because Guilin Township under its jurisdiction borders Jiangxi.

Today, people still regard these provincial passes as the end point of entering and leaving Fujian on land, while Fuzhou, the provincial capital, becomes the starting point of these "Official Avenue". This northwest road is the area with the most complete post station facilities in the province, connecting the central cities in northwest Fujian and the surrounding towns to build a perfect transportation system.

左　图：光泽铁牛关层峦叠嶂，峭壁挺立，山高谷深，地形十分险要，历来为兵家攻掠福建的必争之地　吴军 摄

右　图：山头关古称老关，位于离光泽县城110多里的寨里镇山头村，是与江西交界的千年古关隘。过去赣东人入闽走古道都从村口经过　吴军 摄

The left picture: Tieniu Pass in Guangze, with mountainous peaks, upright cliffs, high mountains and deep valleys, and very dangerous terrain, Tieniu Pass in Guangze has always been a crucial place for strategists to attack Fujian. Photographed by Wu Jun

The right picture: Shantou Pass, known as Laoguan in ancient times, is located in Shantou Village, Zhaili Town, more than 110 miles away from Guangze County, which is a thousand-year-old pass bordering Jiangxi. In the past, people from eastern Jiangxi passed through the village entrance when they entered Fujian and took the ancient road. Photographed by Wu Jun

左上图：光泽杉关已经改建为 332 省道，这条通往江西黎川的出省大道建在古道的基础之上
阮任艺 摄

左下图：光泽县寨里镇山头村古道上的迎仙桥。相传古时山头村常发水灾，古人建此桥以防御洪水 吴军 摄

右　图：新中国成立后，光泽城关（含儒州至司前）到山头关，至江西贵溪公路开通，山头关这条古道逐渐落败下来，无人行走，只留下关名唤起人们昔日的记忆 吴军 摄

The upper left picture: Shanguang Pass in Guangze has been converted into 332 Provincial Highway, which is built on the basis of the ancient road leading to Lichuan in Jiangxi Province. Photographed by Ruan Renyi

The lower left picture: Yingxian bridge on the Ancient Road of Shantou village, Zhaili town, Guangze county. Legend has it that floods often occurred in Shantou Village in ancient times and the ancients built this bridge to prevent floods. Photographed by Wu Jun

The right picture: After the founding of New China, from Chengguan Pass in Guangze (including Ruzhou to Siqian) to Shantou Pass, until Guixi Highway in Jiangxi Province was opened. Shantou Pass, the ancient road, gradually lost. No one walked, leaving only the name of the pass to arouse people's memories of the past. Photographed by Wu Jun

亦为战守之地，又有“铁城”之称。关隘遥相呼应，如屏障雄立，守护着福建的西北边境。

光泽与江西之间的杉岭，因峡谷深险，涧溪分流，山道崎岖，“九关十三隘”都设在地势险要、易守难攻之处，其中最有名者，当属杉关。按《读史方舆纪要》的说法：“仙霞之途，纡回峻阻，其取之也较难。杉关之道，径直显露，其取之也较易。闽之有仙霞、杉关，犹秦之有潼关、临晋，蜀之有剑阁、瞿塘也。一或失守，闽不可保矣。”

左　图：光泽县鸾凤乡油溪村承安桥建于明万历年间，距今已有400多年。每年“七夕”之夜的走桥活动吸引了十里八乡的村民　赖小兵 摄

右　图：光泽三角戏是一种起源于江西的传统戏曲艺术。约明清间传入福建邵武，如今盛行于闽北一带，节目内容贴近百姓，演的是家长里短的百姓故事，表演生动、语言诙谐有趣　赖小兵 摄

The left picture: Chengan bridge in Youxi village, Luanfeng township, Guangze county was built in the Wanli period of the Ming Dynasty, more than 400 years ago. Every year, the bridge walking activity on the night of "Chinese Valentine's Day" attracts villagers from all over the country. Photographed by Lai Xiaobing

The right picture: Triangle play of Guangze is a traditional opera art originated from Jiangxi. It was introduced to Shaowu in Fujian during the Ming and Qing Dynasties and is now popular in northern Fujian. Its content is close to the common people and plays the stories of small household affairs of the common people. The performance is vivid and the language is humorous and interesting. Photographed by Lai Xiaobing

邵武黄土关古称黄土寨、黄土隘，南宋时成为福建与江西的界关，故改称王虎关，元代始设“黄土寨巡司”，明朝为增强军事防御效果，以石砌关墙。明正统十三年（1148）沙县农民起义军邓茂七率军占领邵武后，攻克杉关、黄土关。清道光十五年（1835），邵武县令曹衔达重新修筑；咸丰三年（1853），邵武府知府周揆源扩建黄土关，筑关楼 2 层，两翼设雉堞，并著《黄土关诗》：“绝顶千寻凤鹤静，悬崖百丈鸟猿愁，竹排箭笱青围帐，云作旌旗翠拥楼”，是壁垒森严、雄关如铁的具体写照。

黄土关地势险要，关墙坚固，崖峭削壁，深涧环护，居高临下，进可攻，退易守，是八闽重要军事要塞之一。穿关而过的古道东连和平、邵武，西接黎川，成为古时沟通赣闽贸易的动脉。明清鼎盛时期，古道上的和平、金坑、黎川等城镇成为商埠重镇，商风鼎盛，集市兴旺，商铺林立，往来客商众多，豪门巨富迭出，一派兴盛气象。

愁思隘位于和平镇通往金坑乡、江西省的愁岭山古道上，古道险峻，苔深路滑，让出行之人油然而生愁思之苦。隘门筑在古道之接近山脚处，条石当路砌门，坐西朝东，门东面门楣上条石阴刻楷书“永安门”，门两侧山墙南北长 7.5 米，厚 1.4 米。

入隘门上行，在通往翠云庵的山道旁，镌有宋、清两方摩崖石刻。宋代石刻刻在稍加修整的光面天然岩壁上，离路面约 1.2 米高。分为两部分，一幅为“弥陀会记”，整幅高 3.5 米，宽 1.6 米，楷书阴刻“本会於大宋绍熙四年□丑冬出既劝化四方……里人张子充□草为之众化救治炼药修行……庆元五年五月……”等约 500 字；另一幅书“佛”及其他模糊字迹约 400 余字，整体高 1.9 米，宽 1.8 米，底部刻划莲瓣纹。清代石刻刻于一整块光面岩石上，为左右相连的两幅，内容为当地村民捐款修愁岭古道之事，落款为“大清嘉庆二十年刻”。

当年愁思岭隘道商贸往来十分密集，直到上世纪 70 年代，邵武和平镇往金坑镇的公路建通以后，愁思岭才慢慢失去了它的咽喉作用　吴军 摄

The business and trade exchanges on Chousi Ridge Pass Road were very intensive at that time, until the 1970s that the road from Heping Town in Shaowu to Jinkeng Town was built, Chousi Ridge slowly lost its throat function. Photographed by Wu Jun

上　图：黄土关古道从邵武经朱山、大埠岗、和平、金坑黄土岭隘口出关，直下五里到甘竹，一路平走过熊村，到达黎川　吴军 摄

左下图：今日的黄土关，关门依然雄踞在闽赣二省交界的黄土岭上，前来探访的人们可以体会到“一步跨两省”的神奇　吴军 摄

右下图：邵武和平古镇愁思岭古道上的指路碑　阮任艺 摄

The upper picture: Huangtu Pass Ancient Road passes through Zhushan, Dabugang, Heping and Huangtuling Pass in Jinkeng from Shaowu for out of the pass, straight down five miles to Ganzhu, passes through Xiong Village, and thus reaches Lichuan. Photographed by Wu Jun

The lower left picture: Today's Huangtu Pass is still located on the Huangtu Ridge at the junction of Fujian and Jiangxi provinces. Visitors can realize the magic of "crossing two provinces in one step". Photographed by Wu Jun

The lower right picture: The guiding stele on the ancient road of the Ancient Heping Town in Shaowu. Photographed by Ruan Renyi

上　图：和平古镇地处闽赣交通节点上，是古代邵武通往泰宁、将乐、宁化、长汀的咽喉要道，同时也通往江西黎川、南城、南丰等县　吴节俤 摄

下　图：傩舞是中原文化驱疫逐鬼的一种仪式，传入邵武之后，演变成为祈福驱疫的民间活动。邵武傩舞是中原文化、楚文化、古越文化的融合，也是各种文化在闽北地区积淀的遗存　赖小兵 摄

The upper picture: The Ancient Heping Town is located on the transportation node of Fujian and Jiangxi, which is the throat main road from Shaowu to Taining, Jiangle, Ninghua and Changting in ancient times, and also leads to Lichuan, Nancheng and Nanfeng counties in Jiangxi Province. Photographed by Wu Jiedi

The lower picture: Nuo dance is a ritual to drive out epidemic diseases and ghosts in the Central Plains culture. After it was introduced into Shaowu, it evolved into a folk activity to pray for blessings and drive out epidemic diseases. Nuo dance of Shaowu is the fusion of Central Plains culture, Chu culture and ancient Yue culture, and is also the remains of various cultures accumulated in northern Fujian. Photographed by Lai Xiaobing

黄峭

（872~953），字峭山，又名岳，字仁静，号青岗，后裔尊称为峭公或峭山公，远祖自河南光州固始入闽，自幼沉宏，有智略，官至工部侍郎，娶上官氏、吴氏、郑氏三郡君，共生二十一子。

黄峭弃官归隐时创建和平书院，是闽北历史上创办最早的书院。和平书院自创办后历时1000余年，新中国成立后还作为『和平小学』校址，不但开了宗族办学的先河，更是造福桑梓，为和平历史上教育发达、文风炽盛作出重大贡献。

Huang Qiao (872-953), styled himself Qiaoshan, also named Yue, styled himself Renjing, with an alternative name of Qinggang. Descendants honored him as Qiaogong or Qiaoshangong. His distant ancestors entered Fujian from Gushi, Guangzhou, Henan Province. Since childhood, he was grand and wise. He was appointed vice minister of public works. He married Shangguan, Wu and Zheng, and had 21 sons of symbiosis.

Huang Qiao founded Peace Academy when he abandoned his official position and retired, which was the earliest academy in the history of northern Fujian. The Peace Academy lasted more than 1,000 years since its establishment. After liberation, it was still the site of the "Peace Primary School". It not only set a precedent for clans to run schools, but also benefited the native place and made great contributions to the development of education and the flourishing style of writing in the history of peace.

黄峭

（872~953），字峭山，又名岳，字仁静，号青岗，后裔尊称为峭公或峭山公，远祖自河南光州固始入闽，自幼沉雄，有智略，官至工部侍郎，娶上官氏、吴氏、郑氏三妻，共生二十一子。

黄峭弃官归隐时创建和平书院，是闽北历史上创办最早的书院。和平书院自创办后历时1000余年，解放后还作为“和平小学”校址，不但开了宗族办学的先河，更是造福桑梓，为和平历史上教育发达、文风炽盛作出重大贡献。

Huang Qiao (872-953), styled himself Qiaoshan, also named Yue, styled himself Renjing, with an alternative name of Qinggang. Descendants honored him as Qiaogong or Qiaoshangong. His distant ancestors entered Fujian from Gushi, Guangzhou, Henan Province. Since childhood, he was grand and wise. He was appointed vice minister of public works. He married Shangguan, Wu and Zheng, and had 21 sons of symbiosis.

Huang Qiao founded Peace Academy when he abandoned his official position and retired, which was the earliest academy in the history of northern Fujian. The Peace Academy lasted more than 1,000 years since its establishment. After liberation, it was still the site of the "Peace Primary School". It not only set a precedent for clans to run schools, but also benefited the native place and made great contributions to the development of education and the flourishing style of writing in the history of peace.

左　图：和平古镇聚奎塔，塔名为明代大将袁崇焕所题　阮任艺 摄
右　图：和平书院为五代后唐工部侍郎黄峭所建，是闽北历史上最早的书院　朱晨辉 摄

The left picture: The name of Jukui Tower in ancient heping town was inscribed by Yuan Chonghuan, a general of the Ming Dynasty. Photographed by Ruan Renyi

The right picture: Heping Academy was built by Huang Qiao,vice minister of public works of the Five Dynasties and the Later Tang Dynasty, which is the earliest academy in the history of northern Fujian. Photographed by Zhu Chenhui

福延福瓯

从福建本省的角度出发，文献与今人通常会将省界上的关隘作为陆出福建的终点，而福州则成为这些“官马大道”的起点。如《福建通志》的路程记录，自闽县三山驿起，经侯官县芋源驿、古田县水口驿、延平府南平县岭峡驿、建宁府建安县太平驿、瓯宁县城西驿、建阳县建溪驿、浦城县人和驿，至浙江衢州府江山县交界，全程一千零八十五里（约合 625 公里）。如从剑浦驿分路，由顺昌县双峰驿、邵武县拿口驿、光泽县杭川驿，至江西南城县交界，全程九百八十五里；如从建溪驿分路，经崇安县兴田驿，至江西铅山县交界，全程八百三十五里。

自唐代开通经由古田直通建瓯的道路后，从福州通往西北的早期官道即沿闽江北岸通往延平的路被称为“福延路”，与其北面的这条“福瓯路”相对应。福瓯路自福州至建瓯，全长 480 里，比经由福延路至建瓯可缩短里程 182 里。唐乾符五年（878），黄巢农民起义军入闽后，其中一路即由此路进入古田，东下直取福州，福瓯路也由此成为历史上著名的用兵之路。宋崇宁二年（1103），福瓯路设 6 驿 14 铺。该路自福州北门起，越小北岭，经闽侯大湖、雪峰，由闽清县渡塘入古田境，再经常洋、大桥、沽洋，至东门头搭船过渡到对岸的溪山书院，出北门经凤埔、官亭、旧镇，出筹岭隘入建瓯境。虽为官道，但福延路与福瓯路的路宽也仅仅在 1.5~2 米间，路面用块石或卵石铺砌，沿途山岭逶迤，路面坎坷不平。

福建西北路是省内驿站、铺递设施最为完备的地区，驿站与众多铺递一起，连接起区域内各个中心城市以及周边的次中心城镇，构建起完善的交通体系。驿站位于官马大道上，由北往南，主要有浦城北面的小关驿（在庙湾），下 120 里至柘浦驿（位于城关，设有水驿），下 70 里至人和驿（在石陂）。从崇安分水关往下，依次有大安驿（原为分水关驿）、长平水马驿、兴田水马驿。两路汇于建阳，由北而南，则有太平驿、叶坊驿、城西驿抵建瓯。从建瓯而下，经大横驿，至南平的剑浦驿。从光泽杉关驿，往下是位于城区的杭川驿，再至邵武的樵川驿、拿口驿；再接顺昌的富屯驿、双峰驿；经王台驿，汇于南平。由南平往东，经茶洋驿、苍峡驿，进入古田县境，又经黄田驿、水口驿，至闽侯的白沙驿、芋原驿。闽侯西北面，经由大湖，均接入福州城区的三山驿。

上　图：建瓯鼓楼城门，昔日南来北往的旅人皆从此门通过　赖小兵 摄

左下图：位于建瓯房道镇曹岩村崇山峻岭中的千年古道，是古代建瓯通往顺昌县之路　吴军 摄

右下图：建瓯曹岩村龙门古道尚存 10 多公里长，至今东面仍然可以通往建瓯七里街，西面延伸至顺昌县交界处　吴军 摄

The upper picture: In the past, travelers from south to north all passed through the gate of the Gulou Tower in Jian'ou. Photographed by Lai Xiaobing

The lower left picture: The millennium ancient road, located in the mountains of Caoyan Village, Fangdao Town, Jian'ou, is the road from Jian'ou to Shunchang County in ancient times. Photographed by Wu Jun

The lower right picture: The Longmen Ancient Road in Caoyan Village of Jian'ou is still more than 10 kilometers long. Up to now, it can still lead to Qili Street in Jian'ou in the east and extend to the junction of Shunchang County in the west. Photographed by Wu Jun

左上图：建瓯东峰镇的一块矮脚乌龙茶园，成了百年乌龙的原产地，深刻影响了闽台两岸的茶历史 崔建楠 摄

右上图：北苑凤凰山上的茶神庙，当地茶农茶工采制春茶前夕，都要到庙里烧香礼拜，祈佑茶事 Frank Folwell 摄

左下图：北苑御茶园“凿字岩”摩崖石刻，岩高约 3 米，长约 4 米，刻于北宋时期，记载了北苑贡茶的地理位置、自然环境、御焙年代、上贡名品、官焙作坊、茶园范围等内容，落款为“北宋庆历戊子仲春朔柯适记” 吴军 摄

右下图：水路与古道互联，便捷的交通条件为建瓯桂林村乌龙茶种植提供了良好的发展条件。至今桂林村仍保存着 15 亩百年矮脚乌龙茶园 吴军 摄

The upper left picture: A short-footed oolong tea garden in Dongfeng Town of Jian'ou has become the origin of a century-old oolong. It has profoundly influenced the tea history on both sides of Fujian and Taiwan. Photographed by Cui Jiannan

The upper right picture: At the Tea Temple on Phoenix Mountain in Beiyuan, local tea farmers and tea workers all go to the temple to burn incense and pray for tea before picking spring tea. Photographed by Frank Folwell

The lower left picture: The cliff inscriptions of "Chisel Rock" in Beiyuan Imperial Tea Garden, with a height of about 3 meters and a length of about 4 meters, was carved in the Northern Song Dynasty, which recorded the geographical location, natural environment, royal baking age, tributes, official baking workshops, and the scope of tea gardens of Beiyuan Imperial Tea Garden. The inscription was "Ke Shiji in February 1 of the 8th year of the Qingli regin of the Ming Dynasty ". Photographed by Wu Jun

The lower right picture: Waterways are interconnected with ancient roads, and convenient traffic conditions provide good development conditions for oolong tea cultivation in Guilin Village of Jian'ou. Up to now, Guilin Village still has 15 mu of 100-year-old short-footed Oolong Tea Garden. Photographed by Wu Jun

FU'OU OF FUYAN

From the perspective of Fujian Province, these provincial passes are the last stop out of Fujian, and Fuzhou has become the starting point of these "Official Avenue". Since the opening of the road through Gutian to Jian'ou in the Tang Dynasty, the early official road from Fuzhou to the northwest is called "Fuyan Road", which corresponds to the "Fu'ou Road" to the north. Fu'ou Road runs 240 kilometers from Fuzhou to Jian'ou. In the Tang Dynasty, after the Huang Chao peasant rebel army entered Fujian, one of them entered Gutian through this road and took Fuzhou directly from the east. Fu'ou Road also became a famous military road in history. During the Song Dynasty, there were 6 post stations and 14 shops on Fu'ou Road. The road starts from the north gate of Fuzhou, crosses the small north ridge, passes through Minhou Great Lake and Xuefeng, passes through the pond in Minqing County to enter Gutian territory, then passes through the ocean, bridge and Guyang, passes to the east gate head by boat, transits to Xishan Academy on the other side, passes through Fengpu, Guanting and Jiuzhen, and passes through the raising ridge pass to enter Jian'ou territory. The road width of Fuyan Road and Fu'ou Road is only 1.5 ~ 2 meters. The road surface is paved with stones or pebbles, which makes the road surface bumpy and difficult to level.

Northwest Road in Fujian is the area with the most complete post stations and delivery facilities in the province. The post stations, together with many delivery stations, connect the whole area and build a perfect transportation system.

Minhou Great Lake Pass, also known as Village Pass. Located at the junction of Minhou and Gutian, it is an important relic for studying ancient military buildings.

左上图：建阳出土的宋盏底部，刻有“供御”两字，说明了此盏专为皇家烧制。两宋时，因为“斗茶”的流行，建盏也风靡一时　阮任艺 摄

右上图：20 世纪 80 年代，建窑建盏技艺复原，建盏工艺重现人间。图为仿宋茶盏　叶峰 摄

下　图：建瓯坤口村莲花坪，烧盏工人正在窑场作业　吴军 摄

The upper left picture: The bottom of the Song cup unearthed in Jianyang is engraved with the word "provide for royal", which indicates that this cup is specially fired for royal families. During the Song Dynasty, because of the popularity of "tea fighting", Teacup was also popular for a while. Photographed by Ruan Renyi

The upper right picture: In the 1980s, the skill of teacups was restored, and the skill of teacups reappeared in the world. The picture shows the imitation of teacups in the Song Dynasty. Photographed by Ye Feng

The lower picture: In Lianhuaping, Kunkou Village, Jian'ou, cup-burning workers are working in the kiln yard. Photographed by Wu Jun

上　图：保存完好的麻沙雕刻版　赖小兵 摄

左下图：建阳书坊乡饶坝村拿坑自然村是当年邵武和建阳之间的交通要道，短短的一段溪流上有十三座石拱桥。当年有许多建本图书便是经由这条驿道外运至全国各地，不仅促进了文化传播，也对闽学的发展起到了积极的推动作用　阮任艺 摄

中下图：书坊乡的书坊门，昔日建本印刷的一条街，来自全国各地的书商，都需要经过这道窄窄的小门　赖小兵 摄

右下图：南宋时，建阳雕版是全国三大刻书中心之一，刻印书籍的数量居全国之冠，有“图书之府”的美誉　赖小兵 摄

The upper picture: Well-preserved Masa engraving plate. Photographed by Lai Xiaobing

The lower left picture: Nakeng Nature Village, Raoba Village, Shufang Township, Jianyang was the main traffic route between Shaowu and Jianyang in that year. There were 13 stone arch bridges on a short stream. In that year, many books were transported to all parts of the country through this post road, which not only promoted the spread of culture, but also played a positive role in promoting the development of Fujian studies. Photographed by Ruan Renyi

The lower middle picture: The shufang gate of Shufang township in the street where books of Jianyang version were printed in the past, booksellers from all over the country need to pass through the narrow gate. Photographed by Lai Xiaobing

The lower right picture: In the Southern Song Dynasty, Jianyang engraving was one of the three major book engraving centers in the country. The number of engraved books was the highest in the country and it was reputed as the "Home of books". Photographed by Lai Xiaobing

The left picture: The crown prince bridge on the Tea-Horse Ancient Road in Huangkeng town, Changjian village,Jianyang, is the largest span of the nine stone arch bridges in the Ming Dynasty. The ancient road leads to Tongmu pass in Wuyi Mountain. Photographed by Wu Jun

The upper right picture: Flat farmlands and fertile fields of Houshe village, Chongluo township, Jianyang District. Photographed by Lin Wenqiang

The lower right picture: Tengling Stone Pavilion in Jukeng village, Zhangdun town, Jianyang district, the ancient road leads to Tengkeng in Waitun Village and connects with Dongping Town in Zhenghe. Photographed by Wu Jun

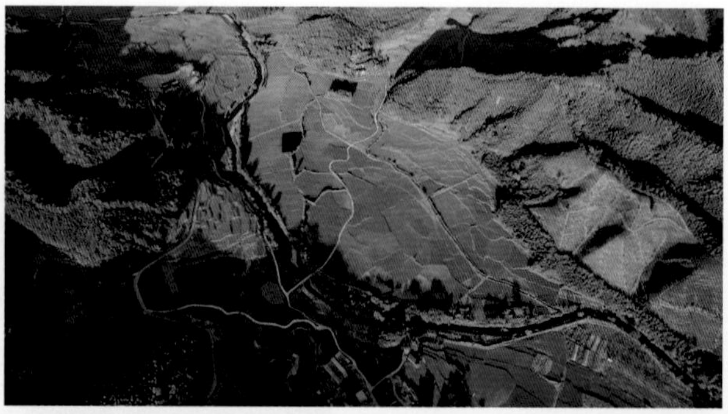

左　图：在建阳黄坑镇长见村茶马古道上的太子桥，是九座明代石拱桥中跨度最大的一座，古道通往武夷山桐木关　吴军 摄

右上图：建阳区崇雒乡后畲村的沃野平畴　林文强 摄

右下图：建阳区漳墩镇橘坑村的滕岭石亭，古道通往外屯村藤坑，与政和东平镇交接　吴军 摄

闽侯大湖关，又称寨上关。关隘处宋代设有“五县寨巡检司”，位于闽侯与古田之交界处。1941年5月，为纪念在大湖阻击日军战斗中以身殉国的第二十五集团军第一纵队装备团副团长郭志雄，更名为“志雄关”。关隘墙体用块石垒砌，关门嵌“志雄关”匾额。大湖五县寨巡检司，宋元丰四年（1081）置，为闽、侯、怀安、闽清、古田五县的屯兵之所。现存“大湖五县寨巡检司碑”为平首花岗岩，高1.3、宽0.5米，碑面竖刻“五县寨巡检司薛典立，右至过隘门，外大坪基路界，按察司委官，经勘旧寨衙门基址，左至溪边又小井止，对面山下路界。丙子年十月吉日记”等碑文，字径0.05米，是研究古代军事建置的重要遗物。

左　图：闽侯大湖志雄关石碑　楼建龙 摄
右　图：“志雄关”原名“寨上关”，以抗日英雄郭志雄的名字命名　吴军 摄

The left picture: The stone tablet of Zhxiong Pass in Dahu township, Minhou county. Photographed by Lou Jianlong

The right picture: "Zhixiong Pass", formerly known as "Zhaishang Pass", was named after Guo Zhixiong, an anti-Japanese hero. Photographed by Wu Jun

西南隘道，客家通廊

福建特别是闽中、闽西各区，山势陡峻，水流湍急，内外交通殊为不便。正如明代王世懋在《闽部疏》中所述："上四郡，大都山郡，路皆逐溪行。溪中无石子，而皆巉岩大石，险恶百态，故其地有怒舟而无怒马。舟多三板薄装。延津而下，才有官舟。纾行矛戟间，有触立碎。而长年狎习，终不令败。每当急滩一泻，目不及瞬，亦一快事也。闽西诸郡，大都两山壁立，中行一水。亡问巨川细流，中皆悍滩怒石，撞击澎湃。其旁隙地壅为圳亩，千塍百圩，仅如盘盂。久行登顿，山麓忽开。瞥见旷土漫川，柳塘桃坞，便似游子还乡。"

西南区隘道的范围，主要包括今天闽中戴云、博平岭山脉以西的三明、龙岩所属区县。从地理形势区分，主要有北面金溪流域的泰宁、建宁、将乐，中部沙溪（其中由清流至永安段

汀属八县客家开基始祖分布图 赖小兵 摄

Distribution Map of Hakka Ancestorsfor laying the foundation in Eight Counties of Tingzhou. Photographed by Lai Xiaobing

《闽部疏》

王世懋（1536~1588），苏州太仓（今属江苏）人，字敬美，号麟洲、损斋、墙东生、少美。历南京礼部主事、江西参议、陕西提学副使、福建布政司左参政、南京太常寺少卿等。万历十五年（1587）以病归。好文学，习农艺。著有《学圃杂疏》《艺圃撷余》《墙东类稿》《闽疏》《王奉常集》等。

王世懋撰《闽部疏》一书，多记闽地风物，对于后人研究福建的历史地理有很大帮助。

Geographical Journal of Central Fujian

Wang Shimao (1536-1588), a native of Taicang in Suzhou (now in Jiangsu), styled himself Jingmei, with alternative names of Linzhou, Sunzai, Qiangdongsheng, Shaomei. He had served as the head of the ministry of Rites in Nanjing, a counsel in Jiangxi, deputy secretary for education in Shaanxi, chief Secretary for Education in Fujian, and deputy director of Taichang Temple in Nanjing. In the 15th year of Wanli's reign (1587), he returned for illness. He likes literature and is familiar with farming. His works include *Records of learning to grow vegetables, Collection of the garden for growing flowers, Similar draft of Qiangdong, Records of Ancient Fujian, CollectionWang Fengchang, etc.*

Wang Shimao wrote the book "*Geographical Journal of Central Fujian*", which kept a lot of records of Fujian's local customs, which is very helpful for future generations to study Fujian's historical geography.

王世懋（1536~1588），苏州太仓（今属江苏）人，字敬美，号麟洲、损斋、墙东生，少美。历南京礼部主事，江西参议，陕西提学副使，福建布政司左参政，南京太常寺少卿等。万历十五年（1587）以病归。好文学，习农艺。著有《学圃杂疏》《艺圃撷余》《墙东类稿》《闽疏》《王奉常集》等。

王世懋撰《闽部疏》一书，多记闽地风物，对于后人研究福建的历史地理有很大帮助。

《闽部疏》

Geographical Journal of Central Fujian

Wang Shimao (1536-1588), a native of Taicang in Suzhou (now in Jiangsu), styled himself Jingmei, with alternative names of Linzhou, Sunzai, Qiangdongsheng, Shaomei. He had served as the head of the ministry of Rites in Nanjing, a counsel in Jiangxi, deputy secretary for education in Shaanxi, chief Secretary for Education in Fujian, and deputy director of Taichang Temple in Nanjing. In the 15th year of Wanli's reign (1587), he returned for illness. He likes literature and is familiar with farming. His works include *Records of learning to grow vegetables*, *Collection of the garden for growing flowers*, *Similar draft of Qiangdong*, *Records of Ancient Fujian*, *CollectionWang Fengchang*, etc.

Wang Shimao wrote the book "*Geographical Journal of Central Fujian*", which kept a lot of records of Fujian's local customs, which is very helpful for future generations to study Fujian's historical geography.

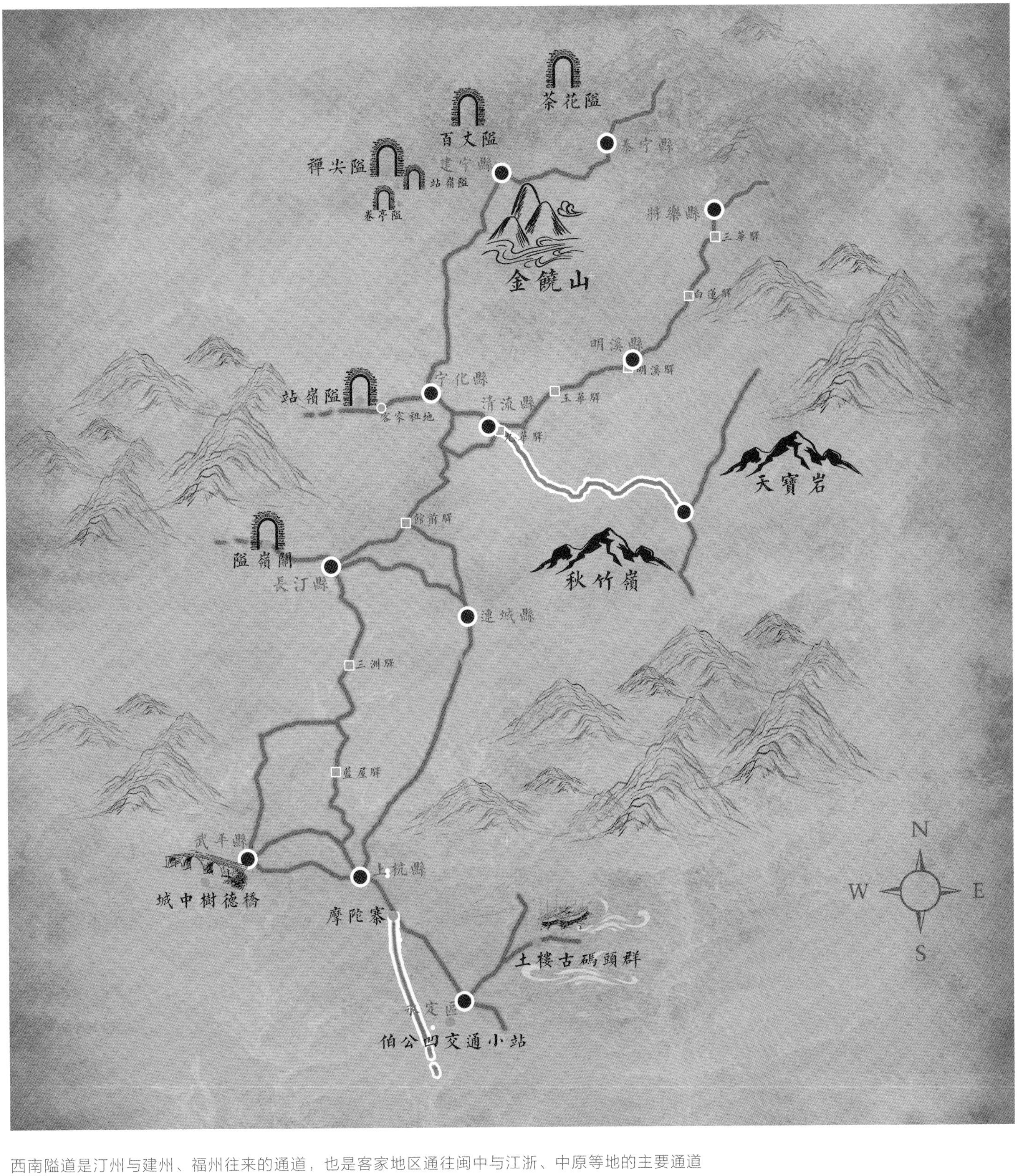

西南隘道是汀州与建州、福州往来的通道，也是客家地区通往闽中与江浙、中原等地的主要通道

Southwest pass road is the passage between Tingzhou and Jianzhou and Fuzhou, and also the main passage from Hakka area to Fujian, Jiangsu and Zhejiang, Central Plains and other places.

称作九龙溪）流域的宁化、清流、明溪、三明（指三元与梅列区）、永安、沙县，以及南部汀江流域的长汀、武平、连城、上杭、永定（主要指西部的汀江谷地）等县。这一区域多属客家，其中宁化为客家祖地，而长汀则为客家首府所在地。

据《重修长汀县志》记载：开元二十四年（736）置汀州，领长汀、黄连、龙岩三县。长汀西北经篁竹岭至江西瑞金一百三十里（约合 59 公里），巨商小贩悉由此路。长汀西经隘岭至瑞金一百四十里（约合 64 公里），前接豫章，后连东粤，为三省通衢。又据《重修宁化县志》：天宝元年（742），改黄连县为宁化县。县西的站岭隘与江西石城相界连。光启元年（885）王绪等由江西入闽，攻陷汀州，击破黄连峒等记载，说明闽西长汀、宁化与赣南瑞金、石城之间的交通，到了唐代已趋频繁。

西南路隘道西侧一线基本都位于闽西与赣东南的边界线上，西南侧的武平、上杭及永定则与广东相接。由于通往的目的地是赣东南或粤东北，其重要性要逊于西北区的道路。西路隘道沿武夷山脉东坡的平缓谷地设置，西界江西，北起泰宁，南迄永定，主要河流有闽江上游的金溪、沙溪以及汀江这一福建唯一出省可通航河流，基本涵括了省内客家的分布区域。

这一区域以客家首府长汀为地区中心，各地路网由驿、铺连接，依序形成西面的泰宁－建宁－宁化－长汀通道，通道北连邵武，南接武平，东南接连城、上杭、永定，东北经清流、明溪后，交汇于将乐，再至顺昌汇入西北的官马大道。从道路自身的条件看，虽然也有一部分翻山越岭的岭道，但大部分还是沿着河谷的平地；同时，由于主要通连汀州与建州、福州，也是客家地区通往闽中与江浙、中原等地的主要通道，人流与物流均相对繁盛。

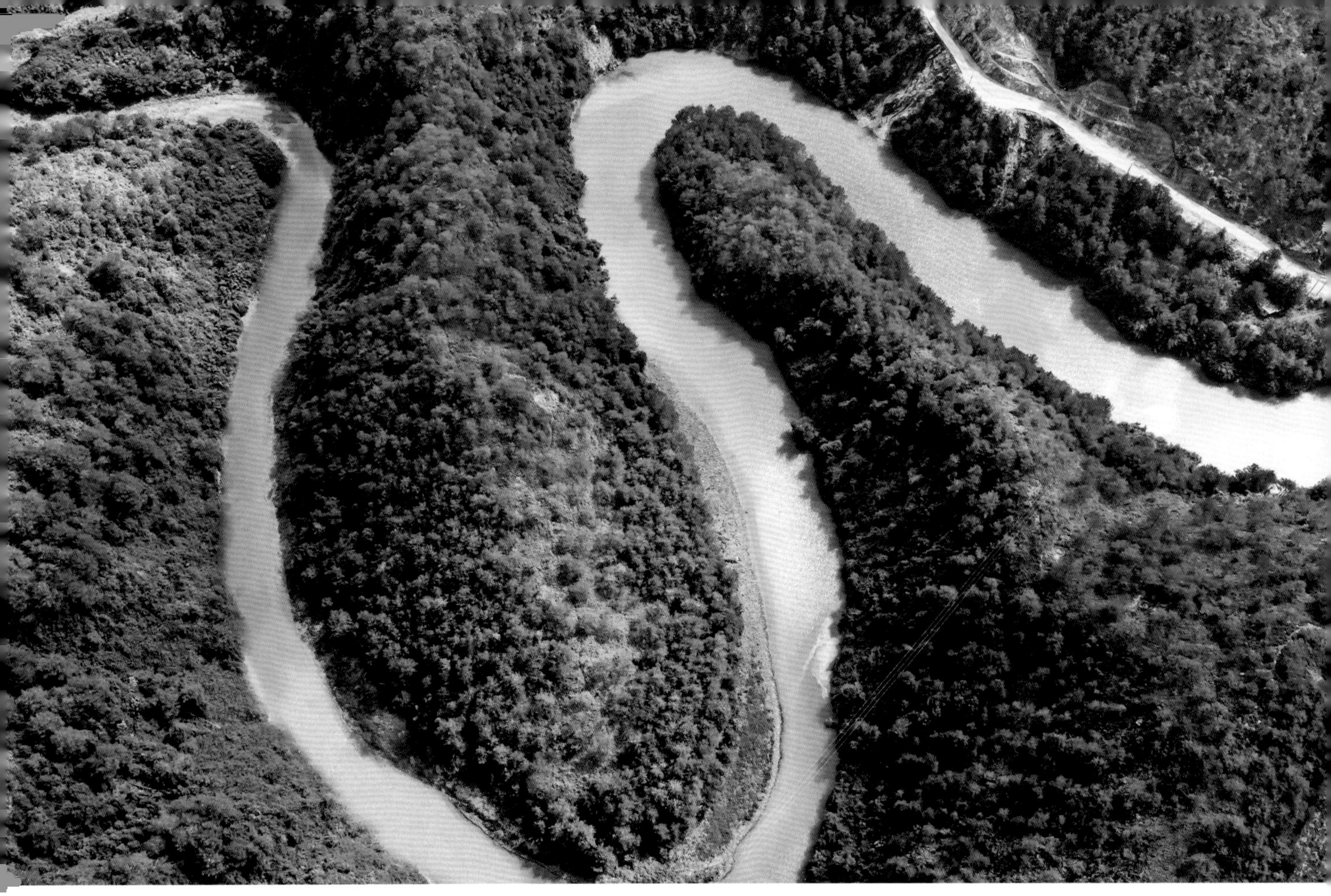

上　图：汀江进入上杭境内，两岸多河谷山间盆地，被誉为汀江的“黄金水道”。图为羊牯乡回龙村的弯道　朱晨辉 严硕 摄

左下图：19 世纪，大批客家人沿着汀江南迁广东，并由此走向海外。图为当年汀州城码头的风貌　长汀县博物馆提供

右下图：宁化站岭隘古驿道是客家人的迁徙之路

The upper picture :The Tingjiang River enters Shanghang and has many river valleys and mountain basins on both sides, which is known as the "golden waterway" of the Tingjiang River. The picture shows the bend of Huilong Village in Yanggu Township. Photographed by Zhu Chenhui and Yan Shuo

The lower left picture: In the 19th century, a large number of Hakkas moved south to Guangdong along the Tingjiang River and went overseas. This was the style of the dock in Tingzhou City in those days. Provided by Changting County Museum

The lower right picture:The Ancient Post Road at Zhanling Pass in Ninghua County is the migration road of Hakkas

左　图：上杭庐丰畲族乡摩陀寨，曾是一座设防的古城堡，汀江环抱，山林耸立，绿树葱茏　邱开勇 摄

右　图：金溪上游的疍民　阮任艺 摄

The left picture: Motuo Village, She Nationality Township, Lufeng, Shanghang County, was once a fortified ancient castle surrounded by the Tingjiang River, with towering mountains and lush green trees. Photographed by Qiu Kaiyong

The right picture: Tan people in the upper reaches of Jinxi river. Photographed by Ruan Renyi

由于西南区内的金溪上游、九龙溪、汀江等大都险滩密布，通航条件较为恶劣。由北面的金溪而联络成片的建宁、泰宁、将乐三县，属于广义上的福建客家分布区。因为金溪上流险滩较多，所以部分建宁、泰宁的道路会选择经由邵武通往建州再分赴福州或中原。而九龙溪历史上一直都是连接汀州与福州、建州的重要水路，也是汀粮东运、福盐西解的主要通道。

九龙溪尤其是清流到永安的九龙滩段凶险异常，事故频发，由此磨炼出福建历史上操船技术最为娴熟的船工，称“清流帮”。“闽船之篙师，多清流县人”，航行在闽江上游各支流的小型船只，都被称为“清流船”。

据《读史方舆纪要》：“九龙滩县东南百里。上六龙属本县，下三龙属永安县。九龙上下二十余里，每龙两崖石峡逼窄如关隘，仅可丈余，而石龙横截水中，高可数丈，乘舟下龙，如在高山坠于平地，舟子欲下，必倚铁石矶，人尽遵陆，空舟而行，雇土著篙师栏头，庶可无恙。以县境止有六龙，亦曰六龙滩。元季陈友定尝开凿之，以通汀州粮运。明成化十八年，县令张霖募工凿去恶石，滩势稍杀，然险峻犹为七闽最。”“遇龙处，水之高低常数丈，舟从高坠下，钻入浪中，跃起，即有巨石当头，相去才尺许，

土人以篙轻拄即转前滩，水既悬奔，又转折于乱石之间。两山夹峙，险隘阴翳，一瞬迟误，便为齑粉，天下之险无逾于此矣。”

汀江上邻赣南，下出粤东与韩江相通。航道多险阻，古时只能分段通航。宋时，长汀运福盐，官给纲本，至福州买盐，运至本州。后因上杭、潮州接壤，易走私贩，郡守李华申请更运粤省潮盐。到南宋嘉定六年（1213），汀州知事赵崇模奏准，将汀江流域原食福、漳盐的长汀、上杭、连城、武平 4 县，改食潮州盐。同时，大力整治永定峰市至上杭段的河道滩险，使潮盐可以从广东韩江上溯入汀江直至上杭。端平三年（1236），长汀县知县宋慈在汀江上游炸石，除七滩，使潮盐可以从上杭回龙滩过驳运至长汀。汀属各县盛产的烟叶、土纸及煤炭等，也源源不断地由汀江船运进入粤省转往各地。

汀江航道有漈滩、龙滩两处，最为险峻，舟师视为畏途，一失趋避，靡不颠覆，莫可援救。明代汀州郡守陈华山，捐资招匠，冬水浅涸，群起攻凿，摧其坚刚，以杀湍悍，于是两滩之险稍平。他滩亦稍整治，并于岸旁开辟纤道，舟行称便。明嘉靖三十年(1551)，汀州知府陈洪范又招石匠，炸上杭县漈、龙两滩，使汀州上下贯通，船只可从长汀直达峰市。

与凶险的水路交通相比，西南陆路通往福州的道路条件相对较好，驿站铺递体系较为完备。事实上，清流、明溪的县城原本就是这条通道上的主要驿站，由驿站而分别在宋代、明代升格为县，充分说明了驿路在这些区域的重要性。

九龙溪清流到永安的九龙滩段两岸险峻 阮任艺 摄

Jiulongxi Waterway passenger ships commute between Qingliu Chengguan and Songkou Wharf once a day. Photographed by Ruan Renyi

宋慈

（1186~1249），字惠父，建阳（今属福建南平地区）人，中国古代杰出的法医学家，被称为『法医学之父』，他所写的《洗冤集录》是世界上第一本法医专著。

南宋端平三年（1236），时任长汀知县的宋慈亲自沿着汀江一路勘探，开辟出长汀至回龙段航道。至此，回龙成为长汀、上杭两地的航运接驳点，来往船只装卸频繁，客商络绎不绝，二十世纪五十年代以前一直是重要的商贸集散地。

后人感念宋慈的拓开航道，便于江边建『宋慈亭』。此亭面向江流，背倚大块乌石，乌石上镌有『龙潭』二字。亭子周围，有几棵老树笼罩着，环境甚为清幽。

Song Ci (1186-1249), a native of Jianyang (now Nanping, Fujian), was an outstanding forensic scientist in ancient China and was called the "Father of Forensic Medicine". His "Record of Redressing Mishandled Cases" is the first forensic monograph in the world.

In the third year of the reign of EmperorDuanping in the Southern Song Dynasty (1236), Song Ci, then a magistrate of Changting County, personally explored along the Tingjiang River and opened up a channel from Changting to Huilong. So far, Huilong has become a shipping connection point between Changting and Shanghang, with frequent loading and unloading of ships and an endless stream of merchants. It was an important commercial distribution center until the 1950s.

In order to empathize with Song Ci's opening the channel, later generations built a pavilion along the river, which is called "Song Ci Pavilion".The pavilion faces the river and leans against a large piece of black stone inscribed with the character"Longtan". Around the pavilion, there are several old trees hanging over it, and the environment is very quiet.

宋慈

宋慈（1186~1249），字惠父，建阳（今福建南平地区）人，中国古代杰出的法医学家，被称为“法医学之父”。他所写的《洗冤集录》是世界上第一本法医学专著。

南宋端平三年（1236），时任长汀知县的宋慈亲自沿着汀江一路勘探，开辟出长汀至回龙段航道。至此，回龙成为长汀、上杭两地的航运接驳点，来往船只装卸频繁，客商络绎不绝，二十世纪五十年代以前一直是重要的商贸集散地。

后人感念宋慈的拓开航道，便于江边建“宋慈亭”。此亭面向江流，背倚大块乌石，乌石上镌有“龙潭”二字。亭子周围，有几株老树笼罩着，环境甚为清幽。

Song Ci (1186-1249), a native of Jianyang (now Nanping, Fujian), was an outstanding forensic scientist in ancient China and was called the "Father of Forensic Medicine". His "Record of Redressing Mishandled Cases" is the first forensic monograph in the world.

In the third year of the reign of EmperorDuanping in the Southern Song Dynasty (1236), Song Ci, then a magistrate of Changting County, personally explored along the Tingjiang River and opened up a channel from Changting to Huilong. So far, Huilong has become a shipping connection point between Changting and Shanghang, with frequent loading and unloading of ships and an endless stream of merchants. It was an important commercial distribution center until the 1950s.

In order to empathize with Song Ci's opening the channel, later generations built a pavilion along the river, which is called "Song Ci Pavilion".The pavilion faces the river and leans against a large piece of black stone inscribed with the character"Longtan". Around the pavilion, there are several old trees hanging over it, and the environment is very quiet.

上　图：汀江险滩重重，早年返航时都需要船工艰难的拖船上岸　袁松树 摄

下　图：汀江航道多险阻，只能分段通航，图为 20 世纪 50 年代汀江上游羊牯乡放排的场景　袁松树 摄

The upper picture: The Tingjiang River is full of dangerous beaches. In the early years, when returning home, boatmen had to tug boats ashore with difficulty. Photographed by Yuan Songshu

The lower picture: The Tingjiang waterway is so dangerous that it can only be navigated in sections. The picture shows the rafting scene of Yanggu Township in the upper reaches of the Tingjiang River in the 1950s. Photographed by Yuan Songshu

铺递完备的“汀州大道”以长汀为中心，东南可通漳州、龙岩，东北经清流、明溪、将乐后至延平，北面沿武夷山东侧谷地的道路，由宁化、建宁、泰宁而达于邵武，接入福建西北区的交通路网。其中，东北线是西南区道路的主线，驿站系统从顺昌双峰驿析分，沿金溪上溯，西行至将乐的三华驿后，再由北往南经白莲驿、明溪驿、清流皇华驿，至宁化的石牛驿，再至长汀的馆前驿、临汀驿、三洲驿，达上杭的蓝屋驿、平西驿（因改路，后移永定）。乾隆十九年（1754）裁驿，多数驿站改称为馆。

西南路隘道的主要特点是设隘以守、筑寨以固。关、隘、寨，都是古代在险要地方或边界设立的守卫处所。与西北通道上普遍设置的大关小隘相比，西南路通道在省或县界之间的险要处一般只设隘，大关基本不见，但寨的数量却显著增加。由于隘的规模较小，驻兵亦少，从一个侧面也说明了西路通道在交通上的重要性相对于西北路的“官马大道”要低，关隘及相关驿铺的设置主要是为了满足军事或管理上的通达诉求，而交通沿线的地方社会安全在更多时候主要采取“筑寨（堡）以自卫”的方式来解决。

SOUTHWEST PASS ROAD, HAKKA CORRIDOR

The main characteristic of the pass roads in the southwest of Fujian is to set up passes to guard and to build military camps to consolidate. Passes, barriers and stockades are all ancient guard places set up in dangerous places or borders. Due to the small scale of the pass and the small number of troops stationed, it also shows from the side that the importance of traffic here is lower than that of the "Official Avenue" on the northwest road. The setting of the pass and post stations is mainly to meet the convenience of military or management, and the social security of the places along the traffic is mainly solved by "building stockades for self-defense".

The scope of ancient roads and passes in southwest Fujian mainly includes the districts and counties to which Sanming City and Longyan City belong today. According to the geographical situation, it is mainly divided into three parts: Jinxi River Basin (Taining County, Jianning County and Jiangle County), Shaxi River Basin (Ninghua County, Qingliu County, Mingxi County, Sanming City, Yong'an County and ShaCounty), and Tingjiang River Basin (Changting County, Wuping County, Liancheng County, Shanghang County, Yongding County and other places).

左上图：连城新罗村白石岭古驿道，1929 年 5 月红四军从井冈山转移到长汀，曾途经此地
崔建楠 摄

左中图：连城文川桥建于宋代，是古代县城南门前的重要建筑，通向南线驿道的津梁，至今仍为百姓往来的主要通道
崔建楠 摄

左下图：白石岭古道上留下的红军标语
崔建楠 摄

右 图：永定抚市镇古码头土楼群
阮任艺 摄

The upper left picture: Baishiling Ancient Post Road in Xinluo Village, Liancheng City. In May 1929, the fourth red army passed through here when moving from Jinggang Mountains to Changting. Photographed by Cui Jiannan

The middle left picture: Wenchuan Bridge of Liancheng built in the Song Dynasty is an important building in front of the south gate of the ancient county seat. Jin Liang, which leads to the post road on the south line, is still the main passage for people to travel. Photographed by Cui Jiannan

The lower left picture: Red Army Slogans Left on Baishiling Ancient Road. Photographed by Cui Jiannan

The right picture:Ancient Wharf Earth Buildings in Fushi Town, Yongding. Photographed by Ruan Renyi

金溪建泰将

建宁、泰宁地处闽西北偏远山区，与江西交界，为由赣入闽的主要通道。境内主河道古称大溪，源出宁化，亦为闽江之源。大溪在建宁境内称濉江，与泰宁之杉溪于梅口交汇。因水险滩多，素有“金溪十八滩，滩滩鬼门关”的说法，其中最有名的当属梅口的火夹滩，乱石巉岩，石崖壁立，奔湍激浪，其声若雷，舟楫至此，最为艰阻。大溪因今之泰宁金湖而被称为金溪，在流入将乐万全境后，水势平缓，平沙旷堤，雨涨则弥，霜凋则平，可舟航直下至延平。

金溪上游与江西接壤，扼汀、邵往来之冲，地理位置极为重要。境内南北向驿道即官马大道为邵武至长汀之间的重要组成部分，路宽 1.5 ~ 2 米，砂石路面。主要大道通往江西的南丰、广昌、石城、瑞金、黎川以及省内的明溪等地。

据清乾隆年《邵武府志》所记，建宁与四周邻县交界处有隘口及营寨等 33 处，其中隘 18 处、寨 15 处。设于险要之地的隘口主要有朝天隘（即百丈隘）、蟠湖隘、邱坊隘、紫云隘、岭头隘、茱萸隘、界头隘、邱家山隘、小坳隘、沙罗隘、九傀儡隘、卷岭隘、竹溪隘、里岭隘、禅尖隘、松根隘、

建宁闽江源国家级自然保护区内的高峰古道 陈伟凯 摄

Gaofeng Ancient Road in Minjiang Source National Nature Reserve of Jianning. Photographed by Chen Weikai

The upper left picture:Overlooking Jiangxi from Baizhang pass. Photographed by Wu Jun

The upper right picture: Gangu Pavilion, Wengjiakeng, Guiyang Village, Huangbu Township, Jianning County, is located on the ancient road leading to Chanjian. There are four villages along the ancient road, each of which has a road pavilion. Photographed by Wu Jun

The lower picture: The steep Gaofeng Ancient Road of Jinnao Mountain circled past. Photographed by Wu Jun

左上图：从百丈隘远眺江西
吴军 摄

右上图：建宁县黄埠乡桂阳村翁家坑甘谷亭，座落在通往禅尖古道上。该古道沿途4个村子，每个村子都有一个路亭
吴军 摄

下 图：险峻的金铙山高峰古道盘旋而过
吴军 摄

上　图：客坊乡里源村茱萸隘全景图　吴军 摄

左下图：茱萸隘隘口现还保存一座石砌风雨亭，古道穿亭而过。风雨亭建于清代康熙年间，两面石门上阴刻“木湖亭”，因年代久远，字迹已难以看清　吴军 摄

右下图：茱萸隘古隘旁有闽赣两省界碑，一不小心就出了省　吴军 摄

The upper picture: Panorama of Zhuyu Pass in Liyuan Village, Kefang Village. Photographed by Wu Jun

The lower left picture: A stone-built fengyu pavilion is still preserved at the pass of Zhuyu Pass. The ancient road passes through the pavilion. The fengyu pavilion was built during the reign of Emperor Kangxi of the Qing Dynasty. The two sides of the stone gate were inscribed with "Muhu Pavilion". Due to its age, the handwriting is difficult to read clearly. Photographed by Wu Jun

The lower right picture: There are boundary monuments between Fujian and Jiangxi provinces beside the ancient Zhuyu pass, which left the province carelessly. Photographed by Wu Jun

左　图：古道上千亩梯田依山就势盘旋于群山沟壑之间　吴军 摄
右　图：建宁县有古关隘近百个，具名的就有40多个，皆为闽、赣两省南来北往的陆路交通要道。图为赴卷亭隘的古驿道　吴军 摄

The left picture: On the ancient road, thousands of acres of terraced fields circled between the mountains and ravines. Photographed by Wu Jun

The right picture: Jianning County has nearly 100 ancient passes, of which more than 40 are named. They are all major land transportation routes from south to north in Fujian and Jiangxi provinces. The picture shows the ancient post road to Juanting Pass. Photographed by Wu Jun

下坊径隘、界牌隘，此外，不同时期用于驻兵的营寨主要有军口寨、西安寨、永平寨、将屯寨、巢隔寨、罗汉寨、东土寨、乌龟寨、太平寨、楚王寨、香炉寨、仙山寨、仁寨、青龙寨、龚家寨等。隘寨数量之多，足以说明这一区域的通道之多且便于往来，为有效管控，于是处处据险设隘，或是沿着重要节点修筑寨堡。

朝天隘位于溪口镇杉溪村上杉溪自然村百丈隘的古驿道上，海拔 624 米。建于清代，坐南朝北，石木结构，是由两座形制相同的石拱中间加覆廊屋而成的关隘，占地面积 33.75 平方米。古驿道由南向北穿过驿站，是古代江西入闽的主要通道之一。民国版《建宁县志·卷一》记载："百丈隘，旧名朝天隘，此通南丰、康都之达道，行旅络驿往来繁杂。昔传越王无诸畋猎至朝天岭尝筑台云。台久荒没，山极陡峻，鸟道盘回，行者苦之。明弘治间，县令李雍构庵其上，以憩行旅。清初置隘建关于扼界处，并设望烽墩。"

泰宁古代的陆路交通只有供步行的古驿道和大小山路，东北往邵武要上"高坡岭"，东去将乐要翻"苦岭"，西走建宁要越"挽舟岭"，西北到江西黎川要登"巫寮隘"。营寨则有虎头寨、钟石寨、南石寨、黄石寨等，分布于梅口、杉城、朱口等重要防御之地。梅口寨在县西梅口保。宋绍定五年（1232），统领刘纯分忠武军于此，以镇罗源箐竹之寇，后废。又朱口寨，在县东三十里。宋绍定中设，元改为巡司，寻废。又石门隘，在县西五十里。又县北四十里，有澹子隘。五十里有茶花隘，以茶花岭名。

上　图：以水上丹霞地貌名闻世界的泰宁大金湖景观独特、风景秀丽 郑惠平 摄
下　图：金溪泰宁池潭镇江段 阮任艺 陈映辉 摄

The upper picture: Dajin Lake in Taining, famous for its Danxia landform on the water, has a unique and beautiful landscape. Photographed by Zheng Huiping

The lower picture: Zhenjiang section of Jinxi River in Chitan village, Taining county. Photographed by Ruan Renyi and ChenYinghui

茶花隘位于新桥乡大源村以北约 4 公里处，路面石铺，宽约 1~1.5 米，沿山势蜿蜒而上；关隘建在两山间之极狭处，居中建隘，内有单孔石拱休息亭。休息亭名曰“爱亭”，面宽 3.8 米，进深 3.88 米，高 2.72 米，石壁厚 0.33 米。券顶，琢制长方条石砌，西侧后壁用条石垒砌。亭始建于清乾隆二十七年（1762）。关隘两侧面，沿山脊建有寨墙，并分段建有圆形的寨堡等。寨堡用卵石垒砌，平面圆形，外部直径约 7.4 米。

由茶花隘往南，大源村所处的长条形盆地内，石铺古驿道保存得极为完整。大块的卵石路面曲折延伸，一路伴杉溪之水南下，穿越古村，将村内外重要古建筑贯穿成有机的一个整体。古道连接泰建黎三县，是古代重要的商贸交通要道。

左　图：通京桥，取意通往京城考取功名，桥的对面山上建有一座魁星楼，学子们进京赶考时都要祭拜孔圣人和魁星，希望高中功名　吴军 摄

中　图：泰宁新桥镇文昌阁，横跨古道，北额“章阁”，南题“文亭”，嵌有“文章”二字　吴军 摄

右　图：泰宁大源村南溪圣殿和文昌阁　崔建楠 摄

The left picture: Tongjing Bridge leads to the capital to obtain fame. There is a Kuixing Building on the mountain opposite the bridge. When students went to the capital to sit an examination, they had to pay tribute to Confucius and Kuixing, hoping for the success in imperial exam. Photographed by Wu Jun

The middle picture: Wenchang Pavilion in Xinqiao Town, Taining, spans the ancient road, with a horizontal tablet of "Zhang Ge" in the north and an inscrirtion of "Wen Ting" in the south, embedded with two characters "Wen Zhang". Photographed by Wu Jun

The right picture: Nanxi Temple and Wenchang Pavilion in Dayuan Village, Taining. Photographed by Cui Jiannan

Ancient Roads in Jinxi River Basin

Due to the poor navigation conditions in the upper reaches of Jinxi River, some roads in Jianning County and Taining County would choose to pass through Shaowu County to Jianzhou and then go to Fuzhou or the Central Plains.

Jianning County and Taining County are located in remote mountainous areas in northwest Fujian, bordering Jiangxi, and are the main passages from Jiangxi to Fujian. The source of the main river in the territory is located in Ninghua County, which is the source of Minjiang River, Fujian's mother river. The ancient post road in the territory is an important part from Shaowu County to Changting County. According to records, there are 33 passes and camps at the junction of Jianning County and its neighboring counties, which shows that this area is closely connected. In order to manage effectively, passes must be set up everywhere, or fortresses must be built along important nodes.

九龙宁清归

宁化、清流、归化（今明溪）属汀州八县中的北路，九龙溪穿行其南，是闽西、赣南地区通往福州的重要途经。“宁化清流归化，路隘林深苔滑”，是当年毛泽东行军途中，对以上三县古道的精辟概括。

宁化古称黄连峒，早在隋唐年间便可由县西境直通赣江，顺流“泛筏于吴”；境内沙溪上游又称翠江，河道狭窄，滩多水浅，行驶艰难。驿道则西出江西石城，东通清流、明溪，南达长汀，北往建宁，四面通达。县境山峻水急，峰峦万叠，至县治则四围平坦，形如大釜，旁挹嶂岫，下瞰溪湖，称为形胜。

宁化共建有隘18处，西通江西石城的主要有凤凰山、堑头、站岭、黄柏岭、狐栖岭等，现存最好的当属站岭隘。

站岭隘位于石壁镇西北与江西石城交界的站岭隘口，建有片云亭，与江西境内介福亭相接，两亭相连，中部共用一墙，以墙界分闽赣两省。

片云亭坐西北朝东南方向 145°，平面呈横向长方形，通面阔 4.57 米，通进深 11.91 米，面积 54 平方米。中轴线上由东南向西北依次建有：亭前通道、亭门、围墙、分界墙等。抬梁式结构、硬山顶。用凿面条石砌外墙及隔墙，梁架直接安于墙上，亭名书于门额上方，墙内嵌石碑一方。上注明亭始建于康熙五十七年（1718）。

站岭隘片云亭，位于石壁镇西北与江西石城交界的站岭隘隘口福建一侧，海拔约 569 米，与江西境内介福亭界分闽赣两省。两亭相连，中部共用一墙，此墙即为两省分界线。站岭隘历史上是闽赣两省往来的重要通道，它见证了一个中国移民史上最重要的事件，即客家先民由武夷山东南麓西出江西，到达闽西客家祖地的全过程，是客家移民路上的一座标志性建筑　吴军 摄

Pianyun pavilion of Zhanling Pass is located on the Fujian side of Zhanling Pass at the junction of northwest Shibi Town and Shicheng in Jiangxi Province with about 569 meters away from the sea, and is divided into Fujian and Jiangxi provinces with Jiefu Pavilion in Jiangxi Province.The two pavilions are connected, and the middle part shares a wall, which is the dividing line between the two provinces. Zhanling Pass is an important passage between Fujian and Jiangxi provinces in history, which witnessed the most important event in the history of Chinese immigrants, that is, the whole process of Hakka ancestors leaving Jiangxi from the southeast foot of Wuyi Mountain to reach the ancestral land of Hakka in western Fujian, which is a landmark building on the road of Hakka immigrants. Photographed by Wu Jun

清流古称黄连，宋元符元年（1098）置县，因清溪环绕，碧水萦回，故名清流。置县时设二驿：皇华驿和九龙驿。明洪武间，皇华驿改为玉华驿，明成化十年（1474）改为玉华公馆，成化二十七年复设驿，驿道40公里，由县城至嵩溪至林畲至五通凹与明溪县交界；九龙驿于明崇祯二年（1629）裁撤，后由铁石矶巡检司兼领。

九龙滩中的上六龙属清流县，下三龙属永安县。据《清流县志》：“每一龙，两岸石峡通窄，仅容舟入口，石梗水中，浪高数丈，舟行如在高山坠平地。行人泛丹者，辄停铁石矶，设牲醴至龙头祭龙王庙，雇土著篙师编竹箬箱裹船头，以拒怒浪。相水势，舞梢入峡，舟疾如飞，虽瞿塘、滟澦之险莫之能过。相传宋、元以前，舟楫不通，往来皆艰隔岭。元末，陈有定凿石去障，水运汀粮，舟始得通。成化十八年，知县凌宲虑滩险舟多复溺，遂因冬季水涸，恶石皆出，发银六十两募石工相险凿之，滩势少平。”

左　图：站岭隘口江西境内的介福亭　吴军 摄
右　图：宁化站岭隘片云亭记事石碑　楼建龙 摄
The left picture: Jiefu Pavilion in Jiangxi Province at Zhanling Pass. Photographed by Wu Jun
The right picture:Chronicle Stone Tablet in Pianyun pavilion, Zhanling Pass, Ninghua. Photographed by Lou Jianlong

Ancient Road in Jiulong River Basin

Ninghua, Qingliu and Guihua (now Mingxi) belong to the north road of the eight counties in Tingzhou. Jiulong River passes through their south and is the important road from Tingzhou to Fuzhou. "Ninghua, Qingliu and Guihua,with narrow roads, deepforestsand slippery moss", which is Mao Zedong's overview of the ancient roads in these three countieson the way to the March.

Jiulongxi River has always been an important waterway connecting Tingzhou with Fuzhou and Jianzhou in history, which is also the main channel for transporting the grain of Tingzhou to the east and unloading the salt of Fuzhou to the west. Jiulongxi River, especially the Jiulong Beach section from Qingliu County to Yong'an County, is extremely dangerous with frequent accidents. As a result, the most skilled boatmen in Fujian's history has been honed, known as the "Qingliu Gang". Small ships sailing in the tributaries of the upper reaches of Minjiang River are all known as "Qingliu Boats".

Compared with the dangerous waterway transportation, the land conditions here are relatively good and the laying of post stations is relatively complete. In fact, the county centers of Qingliu County and Mingxi County evolved from the main post stations on this passage in history. They were upgraded to counties in Song Dynasty and Ming Dynasty respectively, which fully illustrates the importance of ancient roads and post stations here.

宁化客家祖地是客家人的精神家园和朝圣中心，每年都有数以万计的海内外客属后裔来此寻根祭祖。图为客家公祠俯瞰图 阮任艺 摄

Ninghua Hakka Ancestral Land is the spiritual home and pilgrimage center of Hakka people. Every year, tens of thousands of Hakka descendants from home and abroad come here to search for their roots and worship their ancestors. The picture shows a bird's eye view of Hakka public shrines. Photographed by Ruan Renyi

汀州古大道

长汀位于武夷山南麓，处闽、粤、赣三省边陲要冲，素有“福建西大门”之誉。自唐开元二十四年置汀州，长汀一直为州、郡、路、府治所在地，也是闽西客家首府，“阛阓繁阜，不减江浙中州”。

汀江水运历史悠久，由长汀可通航上抗、永定、潮州、汕头，自古享有舟楫之利。自宋端平三年(1236)知县宋慈开辟汀江航运后，水路交通繁忙，往返船只达“上三千、下八百”之数。

陆路交通方面，从宋至清代，县境内建有临汀、馆前、三洲3个驿站，驿道共有5条。历史上，全境共有3关12隘14寨，其中寨的数量与关隘的数量大致相当。

左　图：汀江航道险峻凶险，船工视为畏途　袁松树 摄

中　图：汀州大道遗迹，依稀可见昔日的车马繁荣　崔建楠 摄

右　图：位于闽赣分界处的长汀县古城镇井头村大隘岭古驿栈旧址　阮任艺 摄

The left picture: The Tingjiang waterway is steep and dangerous, and the boatmen regard it as a dangerous way. Photographed by Yuan Songshu

The middle picture: The ruins of Tingzhou Avenue vaguely show the prosperity of chariots and horses in the past. Photographed by Cui Jiannan

The right picture: Located at the boundary between Fujian and Jiangxi, the former site of Da'ailing Ancient Posthouse in Jingtou Village, Gucheng Town, Changting County. Photographed by Ruan Renyi

上　图：上杭回龙镇天后宫与隔江相望的古码头。这里曾是汀江繁忙的水上航运点　吴军 摄

下　图：建于清道光年间的长汀馆前镇沈坊村沈家大院，是一座独特的三堂两横“九厅十八井”府第式住宅，据说这座民居是当地一位商人请京城的工匠到沈坊村建造的　阮任艺 摄

The upper picture: The Tianhou Palace in Huilong Town, Shanghang, faces the ancient dock across the river. This used to be a busy water shipping point on the Tingjiang River. Photographed by Wu Jun

The lower picture: The compound of Shen family in Shenfang Village, Guanqian Town, Changting County built during the reign of Daoguang of the Qing Dynasty, is a unique mansion-style residence with three halls and two horizontal lines and "nine halls and eighteen wells". It is said that this residence was built by a local businessman who invited craftsmen from the capital to Shenfang Village. Photographed by Ruan Renyi

The upper picture:Jichuan Gate of Changting was founded in the third year of the reign of Zhiping of the Song Dynasty, which was once the most important traffic artery in Tingzhou and witnessed the prosperity of Tingzhou capital for a thousand years. According to folk legend, Tingzhou capital has "ten gates and nine locks", of which Jichuan Gate is the only one that is not locked at night. Photographed by Guo Xiaodan

The lower left picture :The stone path of the ancient street in Zhongshan Town, Wuping. Photographed by Cui Jiannan

The lower right picture: Changting Ancient City Gate is the ancient road hub and border crossroads in Fujian, Guangdong and Jiangxi provinces. The thick and long-standing ancient city gate is still intact today. Photographed by Lai Xiaobing

上　图：长汀济川门始建于宋治平三年，曾为汀州最重要的交通要道，见证了汀州府的千年繁华。民间相传，汀州府“十座城门九把锁”，其中济川门是唯一一座夜间不锁的城门　郭晓丹 摄

左下图：武平中山镇的古街石板路　崔建楠 摄

右下图：长汀古城门是闽粤赣三省的古道枢纽和边陲要冲，厚重悠久的古城门至今依然保持完好　赖小兵 摄

左上图：连城四堡书坊间的巷道，当年曾穿梭着书商和印刷工人忙碌的身影 阮任艺 摄

右上图：连城四堡的书坊建筑，多为四合院形式的木结构建筑，既便于聚族而居，又适合家庭手工作坊，图为雾阁村的子仁屋 阮任艺 摄

下　图：连城四堡镇玉砂桥建于清代，是连城现存较完整的四座古廊桥之一 郭晓丹 摄

The upper left picture: In those days, booksellers and printing workers were busy in the roadways of Sibao Bookstore in Liancheng. Photographed by Ruan Renyi

The upper right picture: The bookshop buildings in Sibao of Liancheng are mostly wooden structures in the form of quadrangles, which are not only convenient for people to live together, but also suitable for family handicraft workshops. The picture shows Ziren House in Wuge Village. Photographed by Ruan Renyi

The lower picture: Yusha Bridge in Sibao Town of Liancheng was built in the Qing Dynasty and is one of the four ancient covered bridges in Liancheng. Photographed by Guo Xiaodan

The upper picture: Lianshi paper originated from Jiangxi and Fujia, known as "a thousand years of longevity paper". During the prosperous period, relying on convenient transportation, it was exported to Japan and Southeast Asian countries. Photographed by Lai Xiaobing

The lower left picture: Sibao town of Liancheng is one of the four famous engraving and printing bases in Ming and Qing Dynasties in China. The picture shows engraving woodblocks. Photographed by Lai Xiaobing

The lower right picture:The large number of existing printing houses, engraving plates, printing tools and ancient books are precious cultural relics that are very old and well preserved in China and are rare in the world. Photographed by Lai Xiaobing

上　图：连史纸原产江西、福建。素有“寿纸千年”之称。繁盛时期，依托便利的交通，曾远销日本及东南亚国家　赖小兵 摄

左下图：连城四堡是中国明清两代著名的四大雕版印刷基地之一。图为刻制雕版　赖小兵 摄

右下图：现存的大量印坊、雕版、印刷工具和古书籍，是中国目前年代久远、保存完善、举世罕见的珍贵文物　赖小兵 摄

上　图：位于闽粤交界处的上杭砂睦村旹奎塔，这里古木参天，是省际的古道要隘　阮任艺 摄
左下图：武平至广东平远的古驿道，被称为“盐米古道”。图为松溪上的松溪桥　阮任艺 摄
右下图：武平武东镇川坊村汀洲大道上的“交通碑”　阮任艺 摄

The upper picture: Located at the junction of Fujian and Guangdong, Songkui tower in Shamu Village of Shanghang, with towering ancient trees, is an important pass of ancient roads between provinces. Photographed by Ruan Renyi

The lower left picture: The ancient post road from Wuping to Pingyuan in Guangdong is called "Salt-rice Ancient Road". The picture shows Songxi Bridge on Songxi River. Photographed by Ruan Renyi

The lower right picture:"Traffic Monument" on Tingzhou Avenue, Chuanfang Village, Wudong Town, Wuping. Photographed by Ruan Renyi

客家首府汀州，是连接福建西南部与赣南交通的中心，省界上的隘有：隘岭隘，通江西瑞金；镇平寨隘、七岭半岭隘，通江西石城；牛姆山下隘、分水凹隘、龟龙隘，通江西会昌。另外，有黄峰岭隘，路通武平，崇祯间寇犯隘，官军失利，知府笪继良、知县曾巽捐建敌楼、兵房，掘深堑以防奔突；靖远隘，路通上杭，天启间，推官寇从化增筑墩铺，建靖远庵；人息隘，山顶有铺，崇祯间，知县曾巽立，路通清流、宁化；虎忙隘，路通连城。此外，又有古城寨，在县西古贵六十里，置有巡检司；白花寨，在县东南宣河一百二十里半溪石山下，其上平，四围险塞，可容千余人，乡民避患于此等等。

左　图：武平下坝曾经是闽粤古道上一个繁忙的码头，这里也曾经是闽粤赣边界的重要集镇　崔建楠 摄

右上图：武平永平镇梁野山中连接古道的石桥　崔建楠 摄

右中图：地处闽粤赣三省结合部的武平东留乡，一条古道将三省相连。图为东留乡通往武平县城的古道　崔建楠 摄

右下图：上杭下都古道是闽粤古驿（商）道，与下都交界的梅县松源，自古以来就是著名的闽粤赣边繁华的商品交易、物资集散、人员流动的边贸集市，如今古道已少有人烟　崔建楠 摄

The left picture: Xiaba of Wuping used to be a busy dock on the ancient road between Fujian and Guangdong, and it was also an important market town on the border between Fujian, Guangdong and Jiangxi. Photographed by Cui Jiannan

The upper right picture: Stone bridge connecting the ancient road in Liangye Mountain, Yongping Town, Wuping. Photographed by Cui Jiannan

The middle right picture: Located at the junction of Fujian, Guangdong and Jiangxi provinces, Dongliu Township of Wuping is connected by an ancient road. The picture shows the ancient road from Dongliu Township to Wuping County. Photographed by Cui Jiannan

The lower right picture: Xiadu Ancient Road of Shanghang is the ancient post (commercial) road of Fujian and Guangdong, and Songyuan of Meixian County, which borders Xiadu. Since ancient times, it has been a famous border trade fair with prosperous commodity trading, material distribution and personnel flow along the border of Fujian, Guangdong and Jiangxi. Now the ancient road has few people. Photographed by Cui Jiannan

隘岭关位于古城镇大井村隘岭、长汀通往江西的古驿道上，建于宋嘉定元年（1208），明、清均有修葺。俗称罗坑隘，关隘占地面积1500平方米，高3米，关门内宽2.5米，长5米。周边商店、客栈的残垣断壁还历历可见。隘岭关往东边下坡到隘岭坑，过了拱门以西就属江西地界。

汀州大道指以长汀为中心，北达宁化、南至上杭的通衢大路。这条大路蜿蜒于丘陵山谷之间，地势相对平坦；同时，大道往四向延伸，东北往清流、明溪、将乐后接入延平，东南出永定后通往漳州，西南出武平后可往广东，又东往连城，西通江西瑞金，四通八达，打造出长汀这一汀州首府的中心枢纽地位。

上杭关隘的修建，主要集中在明代的早中期。如明弘治元年（1488）设水归、吊钟岩、驴子岭、牛皮、佛祖高、白鹏、双髻山、通桥等8隘；明弘治六年（1493），巡抚都御史金泽设狗闷岭、新长岭、寒陂隔、径石矶、桃牌岭、羊蹄岭等6隘；嘉靖十九年（1540），设濑溪口、胡卢岗、兴化岗、柯树岗、虎岗、上南坪、庐丰、檀岭、鲜水塘、银子凹、郭公口、军营前、彩眉山、板寮等14隘。关隘之外，还有为数不少的大小山寨，如梅溪、雷公、石壁、武婆（即摩陀寨）、王家、丁光围、狮子、西天、天宝、古塘、郑坑、老虎、石城、凭风、鸡冠等寨。

武平的石径岭又名“云梯山”，海拔947米。“石径云梯”是武平古八景之一。其雄俊奇险闻名闽粤赣边界，民谣：云梯山，离天三尺三。石径岭悬崖壁立，古树参天，陡峭的石阶直上山顶，是当年粤东闽西赣南通衢的古驿道。五坊大道位于武东乡五坊村，民间称之为“汀州大道”，是上杭县经由武平县通往汀州府的主要陆路通道。此古道在县境内长约 30 公里，现存最完整的五坊古道完整段长 500 米，宽在 1~1.55 米之间，由不规则的块石砌成，沿途有凉亭数个。现存的凉亭有晏然亭、越荫亭。

晏然亭位于武平县武东乡川坊村。建于清代，坐东南向西北，通面阔 5.3 米，通进深 9.6 米，建筑面积 46 平方米。砖木结构，平面呈方形。抬梁式、硬山顶。石砌门框，镶嵌一石匾，阴刻“晏然亭”三字，旁有浮雕花卉图案。

越荫亭位于武平县五坊村狐狸凹山上。建于清光绪贰拾柒年（1901）。坐南朝北，砖木结构，平面呈方形，通面阔 4 米，通进深 7 米，面积 28 平方米。抬梁式、硬山顶。石砌门框，镶嵌一石匾，阴刻“越荫亭”三字，旁有浮雕花卉图案。中梁墨书“大清光绪贰拾柒年岁次辛丑仲冬月众姓立”。亭东侧开一方形窗，西侧墙壁内镶嵌“建造越荫亭题捐诸公各位碑”三通。

左　图：武平桃溪镇小澜村古道最乐亭　阮任艺　摄
右　图：武平桃溪镇古道亭　崔建楠　摄
The left picture: Zuile Pavilion on the Ancient Road in Xiaolan Village, Taoxi Town, Wuping. Photographed by Ruan Renyi

The right picture: Ancient Road Pavilion in Taoxi Town, Wuping. Photographed by Cui Jiannan

左　图：汀州古道上有多个供行人歇脚的凉亭。图为上杭往汀州府古道上的晏然亭
崔建楠 摄
右　图：建于清代的越荫亭是古时上杭到长汀驿道上的路亭
崔建楠 摄

The left picture: There are many pavilions for pedestrians to rest on the ancient Tingzhou Road. The picture shows Yanran Pavilion on the ancient road from Shanghang to Tingzhou Capital. Photographed by Cui Jiannan

The right picture: Yueyin Pavilion, built in the Qing Dynasty, is a road pavilion on the post road from Shanghang to Changting in ancient times. Photographed by Cui Jiannan

Ancient Roads in Tingjiang River Basin

The Tingjiang River was once the only navigable river in Fujian. Most of this area belongs to Hakkas, of which Ninghua County is the ancestral land of Hakkas and Changting County is called the capital of Hakkas. This area takes Changting as the center of the area, and the road networks around the area are connected by post stations. Judging from the conditions of the road itself, although there are also some ridge roads that cross the mountains, most of them are still along the flat ground of the river valley. At the same time, because it mainly connects Tingzhou with Jianzhou and Fuzhou, it is also the main passage from Hakka region to central Fujian, Jiangsu and Zhejiang provinces and the Central Plains.

Changting County is located in the south of Wuyi Mountain and is called "Fujian West Gate". The Tingjiang River has a long history of water transportation. Changting is navigable to Shanghang County, Yongding County, Chaozhou City and Shantou City. Since Song Ci, magistrate of Changting County, opened up the shipping of Tingjiang River in 1236, the waterway traffic has been busy, with the number of ships going back and forth on the waterway reaching "up to 3000, down to 800".

In terms of land transportation, from the Song Dynasty to the Qing Dynasty, Changting County has built three post stations, Linting, Guanqian and Sanzhou, with a total of five post roads. Tingzhou Avenue takes Changting County as the center, reaching Ninghua County in the north and Shanghang County in the south. This avenue lies between the valleys and the terrain is relatively flat. At the same time, the avenue extends in four directions and is accessible from all directions, creating the central hub position of Changting, the capital of Tingzhou.

中南鸟道，千山飞渡

中南区鸟道主要指穿行于闽江以南、介于东部平缓丘陵与西部山区谷地之间的闽中大山带道路。从行政区划看，介于延平府、汀州府、泉州府、漳州府及广东潮梅之间，主要有南面龙岩的新罗与漳平、中部的大田与德化、北部的尤溪，以及永定（主要指永定河及以东区域）、平和、诏安、南靖、华安、长泰、安溪、永春、仙游、莆田、福清、永泰、闽清等县的山区部分。这一区域万山绵延，交通极不发达，但却有着丰富的山水资源和各类矿藏。河流主要是汀江以及漳州九龙江、泉州晋江等河流的上游地带，源出于山势险峻的闽中大山，坡陡水急，河段极少可通航。历经千辛万苦铺砌的大路，虽然已经用卵石砌成，但窄径陡梯，同样艰险异常。

如清代蓝鼎元在《福建全省总图说》中称所述，“如由汀州陆路至漳州，须经上杭、永定，则岭高路险，与福宁羊肠鸟道相仿佛。”闽中大山带从东北向西南纵贯福建全境，横亘在汀州与漳泉之间的戴云山、博平岭高耸延绵，有“闽中屋脊”之称。

中南区道路的形成，与明代汀漳南道的设立有一定的对应关系。洪武二十年（1387），福建分设福宁、建宁二道以总辖全境，其中福、兴、泉、漳道隶福宁，建、延、邵、汀道隶建宁。但漳、汀之界多高山，林木蓊郁，幽遐瑰诡，艰于往来，掌福宁者巡止漳州，掌建宁者巡止汀州，二郡之不

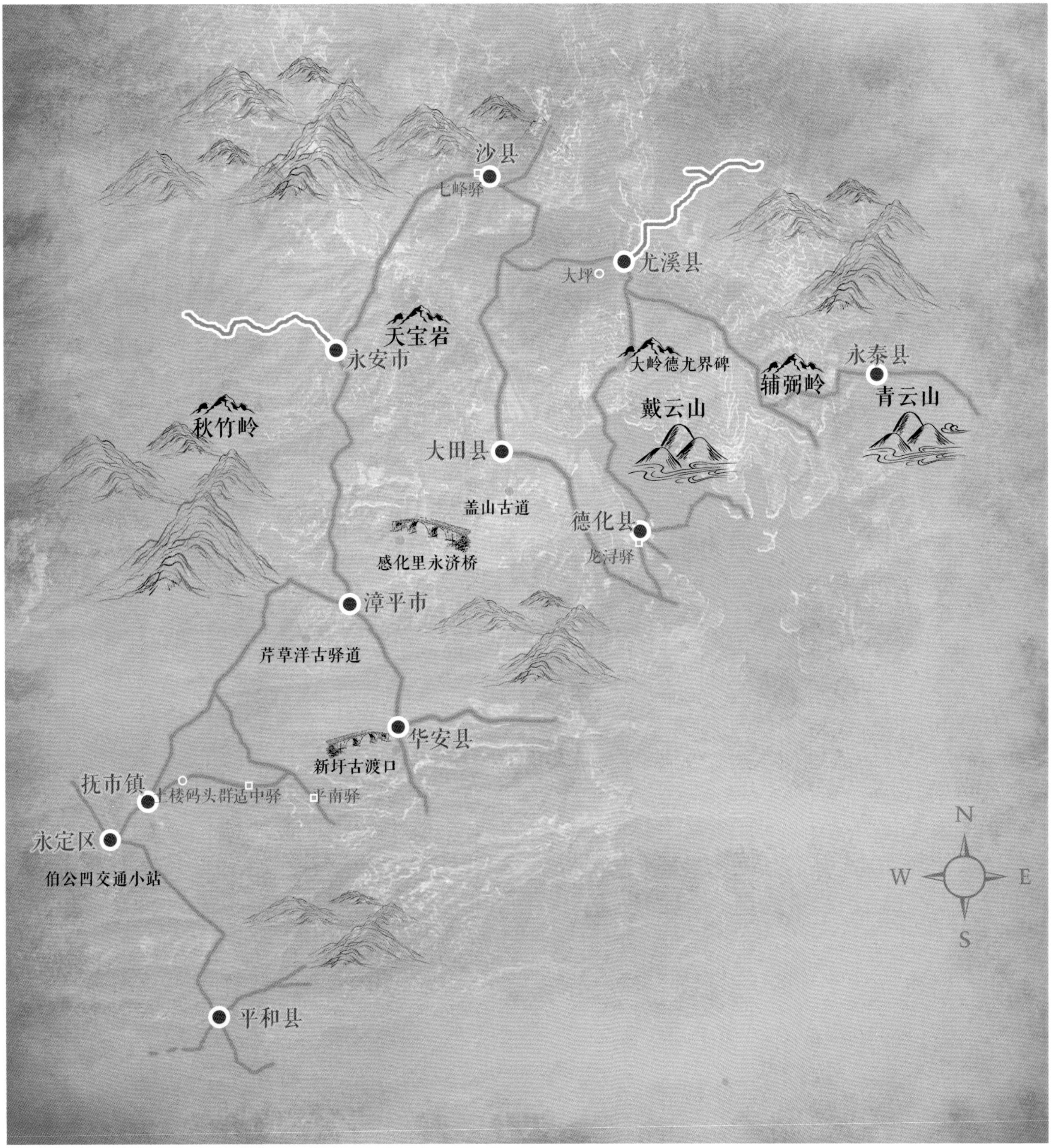

中南鸟道主要穿行于闽江以南，这一区域万山绵延，交通极不发达，历经千辛万苦铺设的古道，艰险异常

Zhongnan Bird Road mainly passes through the south of Minjiang River. This area is stretched with mountains and traffic is extremely underdeveloped. The ancient road paved through hardships is extremely dangerous and unusual

通如手足之痿痺，气之不贯也。故成化六年（1470），因顺天府治中岩人邱昂之奏请，添设一道，为漳南道，独莅二郡。漳南道成，既连贯漳、汀两地，更为粤东北的物流北赴闽中开拓了全新的通道。同时，漳州、泉州、莆田等沿海地区为了便捷出省，往往需要穿行闽中大山，直通延平等闽西北大路。闽中大山带之间的道路虽然险峻，但毕竟打通了千百年来始终横亘于福建中、南部之间的苍莽群山，也使福建东南沿海与西北晋京通道之间建立起更为直接的路径通连。

明嘉靖十九年（1540)，巡道侯廷训摒弃“永地为闽之绝域”的传统观念，认为永定路通汀赣、漳泉、潮惠，是闽粤赣边区的要冲。为充分发挥永定地理位置的作用，特将原来设在上杭县东小板池边的西平驿迁至本县凤城的府馆，由永定知县和驿主分掌其政。按《永定开路记》（明·田汝成）：“汀、漳岩郡也，介于万山，鸟道盘纡，毒草蒙密，为暴客逋薮。……成化中，立漳南于上杭，以领辖汀、漳二郡，始相联络。复立永定于西偏，去上杭百余里。自漳入汀者，东由龙岩，西由永定。东路险远，不若西路便，而驿传舖舍俱从东偏。故东为孔道，而舆夫之费、跋涉之劳盖有年矣。……汀、漳比邻之国也，缓急相援，往来之道非近易不可；且令永定新民频觐官府，习法令仪度，不若开西路便。……刈芟草木，堕高堙庳，而两山之阻夷为大途，改西平驿附县治，以空廨当鬻，旧驿以建御史行台，迁舖舍于抚溪、太平、白沙、炉坪，连延布置，以给传送，比之东路减其远三之一，又少险阻，既近且易，行者安之。”

闽中南山区道路开拓艰难，可以称得上是福建境内最为艰险的通道。图为戴云山脉 刘建波 摄

It is difficult to develop roads in the southern mountain area of central Fujian, which can be called the most dangerous passage in Fujian. The picture shows Daiyun Mountain Range. Photographed by Liu Jianbo

福建沿海低海拔地区面积较小，横跨戴云山脉的多数县份以山脉边坡为界，形成东西不同的两类地形。如永春境内以蓬壶、马跳为界，西部多山，系戴云山脉主体部分，海拔千米以上山峰58座；东部地势呈阶梯状，以丘陵和河谷为主，沿桃溪散布着串珠状的山间小盆地，成为重要的经济文化带。安溪也有内外之分，其东南部靠近同安、南安的丘陵地带习惯上称为外安溪，例如官桥、龙门、虎丘、西坪、县城、湖头；靠近北部、西北部山地区域称为内安溪，例如祥华、剑斗、长坑、蓝田。自然地形的巨大差异，也使得东南区与中南区之间的道路形态与管理方式等差别较大。

闽中南的山区道路开拓艰难，县际通道相对较少，主要是出于贯通福建南部左右方向以及纵贯粤东北山区至福州、延平的通道需求。福建中南部属于极险峻的山区地形，各地开发较晚，但元明之际矿盗频发，之后又倭患严重，出于地方治理的需要，永安、大田、漳平、平和、永定等县治陆续成立，县际之间的驿铺设置也随之完善。从路况的好坏以及亭、桥等附属道路建筑而言，中南区的道路无疑可以称得上是福建境内最为艰险的通道。这一片区的水路交通亦有，部分河段可通木帆船和木、竹排，但河床坡降大、险滩暗礁多，故有“有路莫坐船”之说。

左　图：20世纪10年代，福建德化古驿道挑夫，他们肩挑装着蘑菇的竹筐。这里地处永春境内一座山岭的关隘，边上有几间屋，往来于此的挑货脚夫和行人可停留歇脚

右　图：福建永春县界内，德化古驿道上的指路碑：“上去德化下去苏坑”

The left picture: In the 1910's, porters on the ancient post road in Dehua, Fujian, carried bamboo baskets with mushrooms on their shoulders. It is located in a mountain pass in Yongchun. There are several houses on the side. Pickers and pedestrians who come and go here can stop and rest

The right picture:Within the boundary of Yongchun County, Fujian Province, the road guide tablet on the ancient post road of Dehua reads: "Go up to Dehua and go down to Sukeng"

左　图：德化凤山古道　楼建龙 摄
右上图：连城白石岭古道与上杭交界的松荫亭　崔建楠 摄
右下图：永定是中央苏区红色交通线中的重要一段，从广东青溪摆渡汀江到陆路入闽第一站永定伯公凹交通小站，这条古驿道成为当年中央苏区输送情报的重要通道　阮任艺 摄

The left picture: Fengshan Ancient Road of Dehua. Photographed by Lou Jianlong

The upper right picture: Songyin Pavilion at the junction of Baishiling Ancient Road in Liancheng and Shanghang. Photographed by Cui Jiannan

The lower right picture: Yongding is an important section of the Red Traffic Line in the Central Soviet Area. From Qingxi in Guangdong, ferrying across the Tingjiang River to Bogongwa Traffic Station in Yongding, the first stop to enter Fujian. This ancient post road became an important channel for the Central Soviet Area to transport information in those years. Photographed by Ruan Renyi

清代单德谟的《汀行笔记》（《汀州府志》·艺文三），对闽西南的交通有所描述："乾隆辛未年五月既望，汀属之宁化、清流、归化三邑，猝逢水患，赤子颠连，几无更生庆。余于廿六日闻报，即轻骑简从，兼程而赴，闰五月十一日至宁（化）……（六月）廿九日，由汀返漳。七月朔，过上杭之紫金山。……初十日，至水潮之半月泉。次日，欲登鹅峰顶祈梦，而山势逼直，又夜雨泥泞难行，遂登舟而之署。"单德谟当时署理汀漳龙道，即便是"轻骑简从，兼程而赴"，从漳州至宁化也用了半个月的时间，处理完宁清归三邑事务后，由汀返漳，又用了12天之久。当时跨越福建南部博平岭大山，来回汀州与漳州之间的行程之艰辛，显见于此。

在这片广袤的闽中南山区，因为不属于交通要道，所以宋元以来一直未有官方正式驿站的设置。虽然明代一度将西平驿从上杭迁至永定，但也仅此一驿而已。

以龙岩新罗为中心，主要有三个方向的铺递。一往东北，通往漳平，再往永安，可接沙县，通往延平方向；一往东南，通往南靖、漳州方向；一往西南，通往永定，由永定再西通上杭，或东往平和、诏安，南出省境至梅县。

与其他四处古道有着相对明确的主次道路走向不同，西南通道的通往方向相对较为散漫。从各处县际道路看，南北通向的，主要有起于上杭、永定、平和、诏安等与广东相邻边界处，经由连城、新罗、漳平通往永安、尤溪、沙县的古道；以及由东南沿海地区的漳州、泉州、莆田，穿越闽中大山，通往延平以至中原的"通京大道"；此外，还有由汀州通往漳州、漳浦，或由新罗、永安、大田等内陆地区通往泉州、莆田的大小道路等。这些通行于县与县之间的主要道路，有的设有铺递，但多数减省，改为"立庵以管理"。

以上道路，主要有：1、起于诏安、云霄、漳浦，经九峰（原平和县治），往永定，再分别通往上杭、长汀与新罗、永安方向；2、起于漳州，往华安，通漳平，接于永安；3、起于同安，经安溪接永春，以及起于泉州府，经南安接永春，再由永春出发，或经大田往沙县，或经德化往尤溪；4、起于仙游、莆田、福清，由永泰嵩口，通尤溪，最后抵延平。因此，穿行于闽中南山区的这些道路，其主要目的就是为了连通被大山阻隔的东西向及南北向交通，以相对便捷的途径，实现各地方由延平至中原、由福州往闽东的物资转移与人员流动。

德化承泽隘门 楼建龙 摄

Chengze Pass Gate of Dehua. Photographed by Lou Jianlong

DANGEROUS ROADS IN CENTRAL AND SOUTHERN AREA, FLYING ACROSS THOUSANDS OF MOUNTAINS

The ancient road in central and southern Fujian lies between the gentle hills in the east and the mountainous valleys in the west, mainly including Xinluo and Zhangping of Longyan in the south, Datian and Dehua in the middle, Youxi in the north, as well as the mountainous parts of Yongding, Pinghe, Zhao'an, Nanjing, Hua'an, Changtai, Anxi, Yongchun, Xianyou, Putian, Fuqing, Yongtai and Minqing counties. This area has continuous mountains and extremely underdeveloped transportation, but it is rich in landscape resources and various mineral resources. The rivers in this area are mainly the upper reaches of Tingjiang River, Jiulong River in Zhangzhou, Jinjiang River in Quanzhou and other rivers, which flow through the steep mountains in central Fujian, with steep slopes and sharp water, and are navigable with very few reaches. Although the ancient road has been built of pebbles, it is narrow and steep, which is also very dangerous.

The formation of roads in the central and southern districts of Fujian is directly related to the establishment of Tingzhang South Road in the Ming Dynasty. The completion of Tingzhang Ancient Road connected Zhangzhou and Tingzhou, and also opened up a new channel for the connection between northern Guangdong and Fujian. Meanwhile, in order to get out of the province conveniently, Zhangzhou, Quanzhou, Putian and other coastal areas often need to cross the mountains in central Fujian and go straight to the main roads in northwest Fujiansuch as Yanping District. The mountain belt in central Fujian connects the southeast coast of Fujian with The passage from northwest Fujian to Beijing.

The ancient road in this area takes Xinluo District of Longyan City as the center and extends in three directions. Northeast direction: leading to Zhangping, then to Yongan, accessible to Sha County, and leading to Yanping direction; Southeast Direction: leading to Nanjing and Zhangzhou; Southwest direction: leading to Yongding, and then leading to Shanghang in the west from Yongding, leading to Pinghe and Zhao'an in the east, and leading to Mei County of Guangdong Province in the south.

There are mainly the following roads in the central and southern regions:

漳龙古驿道

新罗境内多山，自古只有小道通邻县，虽有雁石溪、万安溪等，但滩多水浅，只能分段行驶小型木船，运输多靠肩挑。

古道多有铺石，陡坡砌台阶，每隔五至十里设一凉亭，供行人避雨小憩。古道多为好义乐善的乡人捐资修筑，但境内多崇山峻岭，山路崎岖，险仄不平；溪涧之桥，多属独木，下临深渊，殊为可畏。加之有些旧路年久失修，依山的多崩塌，傍水的多被冲决，在田间的多为耕人侵削，凡抬轿、骑马、行走、挑担负重的，身履其地、无不慨叹行路之维艰。

按清乾隆三年（1738）的《龙岩州志》，知州张廷球曾倡议修路。自硿溪修至漳平舅姑岭，经三峰岭至宁洋；通往溪口的胡营；去漳州的黄涂硿、

万安溪、雁石溪两大溪流在新罗区汇合 朱晨辉 严硕 摄

Wan'an Creek and Yanshi Creek meet in Xinluo District. Photographed by Zhu Chenhui and Yan Shuo

崎濑、马坑大路；大吉隔至硿溪桥等处的古道。依山傍溪崩塌者，加以修复，无法修复的改道；侵削田间道路的，按路宽三尺六寸为标准，责令填复。经数月，各路竣工，当时可称康庄大道。

洋东漳龙驿道位于新罗区适中镇洋东村，建于清代。为南北走向，全长约30公里。从南靖和溪经过适中的林田、内田、前林，过马石山至孟头。再经蓝田、山坪头、三井，由百重坪出三坑至合溪去龙岩。其中在林田至前林路段最为险要，途中一凉亭，称“穿心亭”，现已残缺，路面为鹅卵石铺砌。

THE ROAD CONNECTING ZHANGZHOU TO LONGYAN

There are many mountains in Xinluo District. Since ancient times, only small roads have led to neighboring counties and the transportation mostly depends on Manual Materials handling.

Longyan County was transferred from Tingzhou to Zhangzhou in the Tang Dynasty because it was connected with Zhangzhou by Jiulong River. Since then, Xinluo District of Longyan has been classified into the southern Fujian region and the southern Fujian culture.

Yangdong Zhanglong Post Road is located in Yangdong Village, Moderate Town, Xinluo District. It was built in the Qing Dynasty and runs from north to south with a total length of about 30 kilometers. This post road has always been an important passage from Longyan to Zhangzhou in the history.

新罗洋东漳龙驿道 楼建龙 摄

Zhanglong Post Road in Yangdong Village, Xinluo County. Photographed by Lou Jianlong

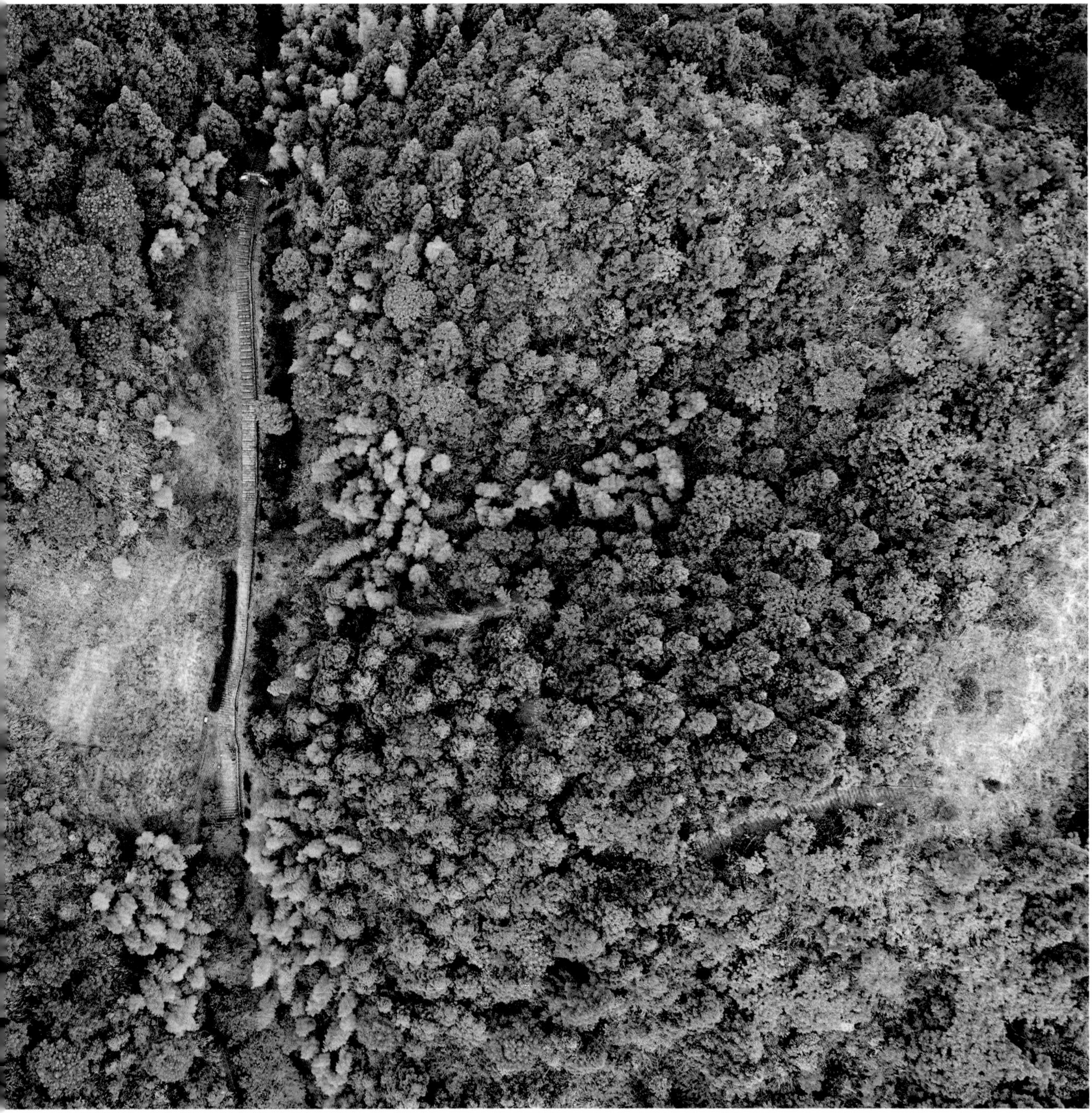

漳平华安道

漳平地处戴云山、玳瑁山和博平岭三大山脉结合部，位于九龙江（北溪）上游，名取“邑居漳水上流，千山之中，此地独平”之意，是闽西的东大门。漳平于明成化七年（1471）置县。九龙江北溪横切中部，将漳平分成南北两半，地势由南、北向中部河谷倾斜，呈马鞍形。中部沿江两岸为漳平市地势较为平缓的河谷、丘陵地带，其余为博平岭山脉所盘踞，地势高峻，形成平均海拔750米左右的永福山间盆地。

按《徐霞客游记》所记漳平至华安之山路。“时旭日将中，万峰若引镜照面。回望上岭，已不可睹，而下方众岫骈列，无不献形履下。盖马山绝顶，峰峦自相亏蔽，至此始廓然为南标。询之土人，宁洋未设县时，此犹属永安；今则岭北水俱北者属延平，岭南水俱南者属漳州。随山奠川，

开辟于唐代的漳平九龙江古航道　陈龙林 提供

The Ancient Waterway of Jiulong River in Zhangping opened in the Tang Dynasty. Photographed by Chen Longlin

上　图：漳平通往安溪、永春、泉州古道上的感化里永济桥　陈龙林 摄
左下图：漳平九龙江古渡口　陈龙林 提供
右下图：漳平县城通往漳州的文昌古浮桥　陈龙林 提供

The upper picture: Yongji Bridge of Ganhua Lane on the Ancient Road from Zhangping to Anxi, Yongchun and Quanzhou. Photographed by Chen Longlin

The lower left picture: Jiulong River Ancient Ferry in Zhangping. Photographed by Chen Longlin

The lower right picture: Wenchang Ancient Floating Bridge from Zhangping County to Zhangzhou. Photographed by Chen Longlin

固当如此建置也。……下华封舟。行数里，山势复合，重滩叠溜，若建溪之太平、黯淡者，不胜数也。六十里，抵华封，北溪至此皆从白脊悬泻，舟楫不能过，遂舍舟逾岭。”

芹草洋古驿道位于拱桥镇上界村芹草洋自然村，是清末以前漳平出龙岩、通永福的驿道。明清时称此驿道为龙岩、永福、上界上下十八乡的风水宝地。芹草洋古驿道原十分繁荣，现仅存古驿道和溜马场遗址。古驿道宽约 1 米，长约 300 米，依弯就曲，青石铺筑，凹凸不平。

半岭亭古驿道位于双洋镇坑源村半岭亭山腰，是古代永安至宁洋的交通要道，驿道路面由河石铺砌而成，两旁是茂盛的竹林，驿道左侧一石壁上刻有“界碑：下去坑源路界，上去亚田坑坪路界。乾隆二十三年三月”。

天台山古道位于赤水镇香寮村天台山，是古时宁洋县（今漳平市双洋镇赤水镇）通往永安县的交通要道，也是村民到天台山的步行必经之路。古道路面由河石铺砌而成。长满青苔，宽约 2 米，两旁是茂密的树林，现存石阶仅剩 300 米左右。

驿道所处的香寮村为明代大航海家王景弘故里。凌云桥位于天台山上，建于明代，为石构单孔拱桥，呈西北至东南走向，全长 15.5 米，宽 3.1 米，高 4.8 米。桥基为石块垒迭，桥面由大块河卵石铺成。

左　图：漳平芹草洋古驿道　陈秀容 摄

中　图：漳平芹草洋古驿道旁的水槽　陈秀容 摄

右　图：漳平芹草洋古道在清末前曾是繁忙的交通要道　陈秀容 摄

The left picture: Qincaoyang Ancient Post Road in Zhangping. Photographed by Chen Xiurong

The middle picture: The water tank beside Qincaoyang Ancient Post Road in Zhangping. Photographed by Chen Xiurong

The right picture: The Qincaoyang Ancient Road in Zhangping was a busy traffic artery before the end of the Qing Dynasty. Photographed by Chen Xiurong

THE ROAD CONNECTING ZHANGPING AND HUA'AN

Zhangping is situated at the junction of Daiyun Mountain, Hawksbill Mountain and Boping Ridge, which is located in the upper reaches of Jiulong River and is also the eastern gate of western Fujian. Zhangping was established as a county in the 7th year of Chenghua in the Ming Dynasty (1471). The North Stream of Jiulong River cuts across the central part, dividing Zhangping into two halves, north and south, with a saddle-shaped terrain. The middle part is a relatively gentle valley and hilly area in Zhangping, while the rest is high and steep, forming Yongfu Mountain Basin with an average altitude of 750 meters.

Qincaoyang Ancient Post Road is located in Qincaoyang Village, Shangjie Village, Gongqiao Town, which was the post road from Longyan to Yongfu in Zhangping before the end of Qing Dynasty. QincaoyangAncient Post Road was originally very prosperous, but now only the ruins of the ancient post road and the horse-walking farm remain. The ancient post road is about 1 meter wide and 300 meters long, paved with bluestones, which is uneven and windig.

Banlingting Ancient Post Road is located on the mountainside of Banlingting in Kengyuan Village, Shuangyang Town, which was the only traffic artery from ancient Yongan to Ningyang (now Chishui Town, Shuangyang Town, Zhangping City). The post road is about 2 to 3 meters wide with the road surface paved with river stones.

Tiantaishan Ancient Road is located in Tiantai Mountain, Xiangliao Village, Chishui Town, which was the main traffic artery from Ningyang County (now Chishui Town, Shuangyang Town, Zhangping City) to Yong'an County in ancient times, and also the only way for villagers to walk to Tiantai Mountain. The road surface of the post road is about 2 meters wide, and Xiangliao Village passed by is the hometown of Wang Jinghong, the great navigator of the Ming Dynasty.

左　图：半岭亭古驿道是古代延平至永安的重要交通要道　陈秀容 摄

右上图：明代著名航海家王景弘故里　陈秀容 摄

右下图：半岭亭古驿道石壁上的界碑　陈秀容 摄

The left picture: Banlingting ancient post road is an important traffic route from Yanping to Yong'an in ancient times. Photographed by Chen Xiurong

The upper right picture: Hometown of Wang Jinghong, a famous navigator in the Ming Dynasty. Photographed by Chen Xiurong

The lower right picture: The boundary monument on the rock wall of the Ancient Post Road in Banlingting. Photographed by Chen Xiurong

左上图：漳平通往永安的古驿道 陈秀容 摄
右上图：漳平赤水镇香寮村天台山凌云桥 朱裕深 摄
下 图：漳平天台山古驿道 陈秀容 摄

The upper left picture: The Ancient Post Road from Zhangping to Yong'an. Photographed by Chen Xiurong

The upper right picture: Lingyun Bridge in Tiantai Mountain, Xiangliao Village, Chishui Town, Zhangping. Photographed by Zhu Yushen

The lower picture: Ancient Post Road of Tiantai Mountain in Zhangping. Photographed by Chen Xiurong

德化戴云路

德化历史上交通落后，北宋有剑州（南平）驿道过境，经元、明、清相继修筑，有驿道、县际大道和乡村小道沟通全县。水路除铲溪等流域的下游两岸有少量木材、毛竹放排流往闽江、晋江外，运输靠肩挑，行旅靠步行。小道穿山越岭，有的数十里无人烟，自古以来，都有人修建路亭（雨亭），供行人憩息乘凉、避风躲雨。

虎豹关，位于德化三班镇锦山村与永春吾峰镇之间的天马山山口。因古道所经，德化以及闽西闽中的山货自此挑往永春，转运南安、泉州等地；沿海的食盐等生活用品、则由此挑往大山之内。官府在此设立关隘，派员屯兵驻守，防敌御寇，检查行旅，征收关税。

虎豹关地势险要，控扼两县，古来为兵家必争之地。“虎豹关”始建于何时，邑志记载不详。《明史》地理志中有记：德化“东南有虎豹关”。此地以“虎豹”为名，正寓其凶险。古代从德化南往永春、泉州，是条重要官道。清朝雍正十二年（1734），永春升为直隶州，德化、大田二县划归其辖。因此该界碑当在建永春州之后。

锦山湖山驿站位于德化至永春古道上，建筑面积66平方米，方向60度，现存一间小房间，墙壁靠古道，门左侧墙为土墙筑成，右侧墙为石块垒成，屋顶青瓦铺盖，屋内有一石碑，惜年代久远，部分字迹漫漶不清，依稀辨出为清光绪十一年九月十一日立的告示。

凤永古道位于盖德乡凤山村，建于明代，该古道东西走向，计有一千二百个台阶，石块砌成，台阶宽0.6~1米，长约1.5公里，是凤山村通往永春的交通要道。

上　图：1910年前后，福建德化古驿道上挑食盐、手工业品的脚夫

下　图：1910年前后福建德化古驿道上往来的挑夫

The upper picture: In the 1910's, porters carrying salt and handicraft products on the ancient post road in Dehua, Fujian.

The lower picture: Porters on the Ancient Post Road in Dehua, Fujian around 1910

左　图：德化虎豹关古道地势险要，为历代兵家必争之地　楼建龙 摄
右上图：德化虎豹关古道是德化往永春、泉州的重要官道　楼建龙 摄
右下图：虎豹关古道上留下的为挑夫歇脚的柱窝　楼建龙 摄

The left picture: The ancient road of Hubao Pass in Dehua has a dangerous terrain and was a place for military strategists of all ages to contend for. Photographed by Lou Jianlong

The upper right picture: The ancient road of Hubao Pass in Dehua was an important official road from Dehua to Yongchun and Quanzhou. Photographed by Lou Jianlong

The lower right picture: The pillar nest left on the ancient road of Hubao Pass for porters to rest on. Photographed by Lou Jianlong

左上图：德化出产的瓷器大多通过古道运往永春，再由永春经水陆运往海外。图为道光二年(1822)驶往爪哇途中触礁沉没的"泰兴号"沉船出水瓷器

左下图：德化是我国古代重要的外销瓷产地。图为宋元时代的德化屈斗宫窑址

右　图：明代何朝宗制作的德化瓷器《渡海观音》 崔建楠 摄

The upper left picture: Most of the porcelain produced in Dehua was transported to Yongchun through ancient roads and then to overseas by land and water from Yongchun. The picture shows the porcelain from the sunken ship Taixing, which hit rocks and sank on its way to Java in the second year of Daoguang's regin (1822)

The lower left picture: Dehua was an important export porcelain producing area in ancient China. The picture shows the kiln site of Qudou Palace of Dehua in the Song and Yuan Dynasties

The right picture: The Dehua porcelain "The Goddess of Mercy crossing the sea" made by He Chaozong in the Ming Dynasty. Photographed by Cui Jiannan

德永界碑位于凤山村与永春县交界处。明万历元年（1573）八月德化知县事秦霑立，该碑高2.03米，厚0.23米，宽0.91米，大字字径39~44厘米，阴刻小字字径3~5厘米。离此界碑十四米处有一块清光绪元年（1875）十月“永春知州同德化知县合立”的界碑，该碑高80厘米，宽30厘米，厚65厘米，大字字径8~10厘米，小字字径4~6厘米。此二块碑刻说明，在明代德化与永春就已划出界线，析分各自的行政区域。

仙昆古道位于德化县水口镇毛厝村岐山脚下。该古道东南西北走向，由石块铺成，长约5公里，宽50~80厘米，该古道是仙游、永泰与德化水口镇昆坂村旧的古道。

大岭德尤界碑位于葛坑乡大岭村安龟仑，系清光绪捌年（1883）伍月德化县同尤溪县正堂合立。碑文有些文字已模糊，露地面高134厘米，宽44厘米，厚5厘米。据介绍，北汉乾祐元年（948），尤溪与德化争议县界，互约二县县官相向步行，至大岭脚相遇，于此，立德、尤石刻界碑，遂称“大官岭”。

The Road Connecting Dehua County and Yongchun County

Dehua County is surrounded by mountains, and its traffic was backward in history. In the Northern Song Dynasty, there was a post road crossing Jianzhou (now Nanping). After successively built by Yuan, Ming and Qing Dynasties, post roads, inter-county roads and village roads connected the whole county.

Hubao Pass is an important gateway to Dehua and has always been a military fortress. It is located at the Tianmashan Pass between Jinshan Village, Sanban Town, Dehua County, and Wufeng Town, Yongchun County. From then on, the mountain products of Dehua County, western Fujian and central Fujian were transported to Yongchun and then transferred to Nan’an, Quanzhou and other places; Salt and other daily necessities along the coast are thus carried into the mountains. The governments of various dynasties set up passes here and sent troops to garrison them.

步瀛塔曾经是古道上供人休息的一个驿站 赖小兵 摄

Buying Pagoda used to be a post station for people to rest on the ancient road. Photographed by Lai Xiaobing

东南间道，桥渡相济

福州往广东方向的驿道形成较早，属于福州南向主通道。该道起于闽粤交界处，由汾水关过诏安、漳浦，从漳、泉、兴化一路直达省城，虽有坡岭，不通舟楫，但福建只此一途较为平坦。同时，这一路也是福建自然条件相对优越、经济较为发达地区，沿途的莆田、泉州、漳州与福州号称“下四府”，与发展最早、同属闽江流域的建宁、延平、邵武、汀州等“上四府”先并驾齐驱，再后来者居上。

该路驿铺北起福州三山驿，往南经福清宏路驿、莆田莆阳驿、仙游枫亭驿、惠安锦田驿、晋江晋安驿、南安康店驿、同安大轮驿、龙溪江东驿、漳浦临漳驿、云霄驿、诏安南诏驿等，出省至广东饶平县。从福州经泉州至厦门的详细行程可参考黄叔璥的《南征纪程》：第一天出福州南门，经福州台江区“万寿桥”过闽江，晚宿南台岛上的福州仓山区三角埕；第二天渡乌龙江，晚宿福州闽侯县青口镇坊口村；第三天过闽侯县青口镇东台村“相思岭”，晚宿福清市渔溪镇；第四天过福清新厝镇蒜岭村，渡木兰溪，晚宿莆田市荔城区“兴化府考院”；第五天过木兰溪上游的“濑溪桥”，宿泉州泉港区涂岭镇；第六天过惠安县城螺城镇，中午经“万安桥”（又名“洛阳桥”）过洛阳江，入泉州城，宿“泉州府试院”；第七天经泉州晋江市磁灶镇五龙村，越大盈岭、小盈岭，行人“往来如织”，晚宿厦门翔安区内厝镇前垵村；第八天经厦门新店镇刘五店，乘船30里渡海，至厦门五通登岸。

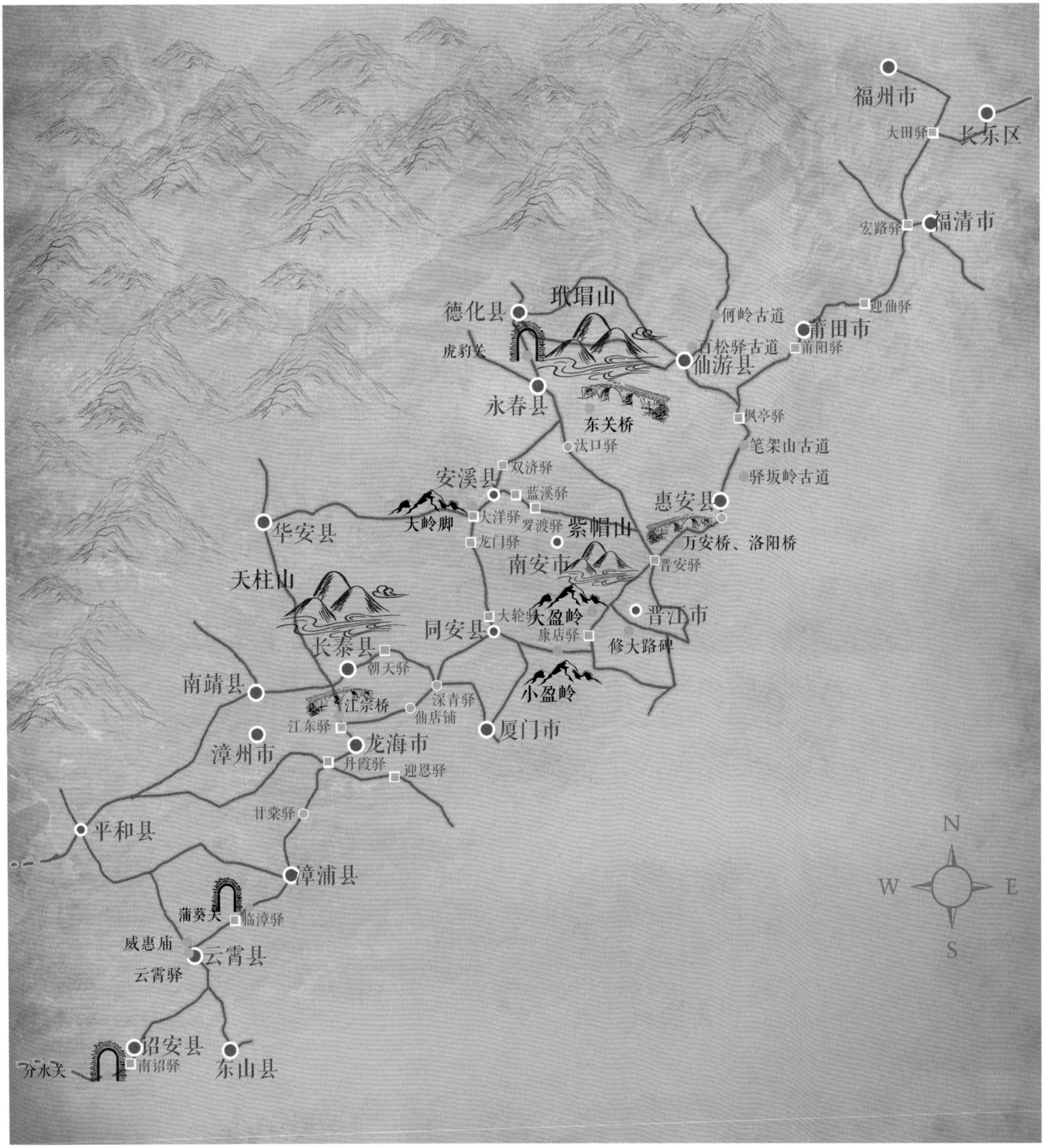

通往广东方向的东南间道，成形较早，这一路是福建自然条件相对优越，经济较为发达地区

The southeast road leading to Guangdong took shape earlier. This road is a region with relatively superior natural conditions and relatively developed economy in Fujian

上　图：20 世纪初的福州台江码头和万寿桥，船只林立，一派繁忙景象

下　图：福州解放大桥原名万寿桥，始建于宋佑八年，最早为浮桥，元代改建为石桥，即“万寿桥”，是闽江上最早的跨江大石桥。1971 年对万寿桥进行全面的增高拓宽，1996 年重建为目前这座现代大桥　阮任艺 摄

The upper picture: At the beginning of the 20th century, Fuzhou's Taijiang Wharf and Wanshou Bridge were full of boats

The lower picture: Fuzhou Jiefang Bridge, formerly known as Wanshou Bridge, was built in the 8th year of the Emperor Songyou reign. It was originally a floating bridge and was converted into a stone bridge in the Yuan Dynasty, namely, "Wanshou Bridge", which is the earliest large stone bridge across the Minjiang River. Wanshou Bridge was fully elevated and widened in 1971 and rebuilt into the current modern bridge in 1996. Photographed by Ruan Renyi

左上图：金斗桥是福州安泰河上的一座古桥，是唐代罗城金斗门外跨越护城河的桥梁 崔建楠 摄

右上图：驿里巷内河的观音桥 朱晨辉 摄

下　图：驿里巷内河桥 朱晨辉 摄

The upper left picture: Jindou Bridge is an ancient bridge on the Antai River in Fuzhou. It was a bridge across the moat outside Jindou Gate in Luocheng in the Tang Dynasty. Photographed by Cui Jianna

The upper right picture: Guanyin Bridge in waterway of Yili Lane. Photographed by Zhu Chenhui

The lower picture:Neihe Bridge in Yili Lane. Photographed by Zhu Chenhui

闽粤驿道福建段全长 1030 里，约合 593 公里，全线共设 17 驿又 2 处“塘驿”，沿途须跨越闽江、福清龙江、莆田萩芦溪、木兰溪、仙游枫慈溪、惠安洛阳江、泉州晋江、晋江安海港、同安东西溪、漳州九龙江、漳浦鹿溪、云霄漳江、诏安东溪等大小河流、港湾，翻越福清与莆田之间的蒜岭、仙游与惠安之间的白水岭、南安与同安之间的大小盈岭、龙海的九龙岭、漳浦与云霄之间的盘陀岭、云霄与诏安之间的油柑岭，以及闽粤交界之处的黄石山等。虽然路途维艰，但客观来说，在清代闽地出省的 5 条官道中，闽粤驿道是最好走、最安全的一条；部分路段宽度达 4 米，可供舆马并行。

依地形，东南区的道路以漳州的九龙江口的江东桥为界，大致分为南北两区。北面路途坦夷，沿海驿路相对平坦，但途中需要跨越多处大江大河，虽有渡口，但水流凶险，多处需要绕道上游方可过渡，殊属不便。最难的一处，就是福州往南的方山渡，在不到 200 年间，数次变易。但北宋之后沿海地区众多石梁桥的架设，渡口成通途，大大改善了沿海通道的通行状况。

左上图：昔日繁华乌龙江古渡口，现在偶有村民在此洗衣　黄景业 摄

右上图：福州城门镇峡北村的乌龙江渡口遗留的“龙江飞渡”石刻　阮任艺 摄

左下图：乌龙江渡口在今仓山区城门镇峡北村，是福州南驿道的重要古渡口　阮任艺 摄

右下图：福州仓山区城门镇林浦渡口古塔，古时为闽江水运的一个航标塔　阮任艺 摄

The upper left picture: The ancient ferry crossing of Wulong River used to be prosperous, but now occasionally villagers wash clothes here. Photographed by Haung Jingye

The upper right picture: Stone Carvings of "Longjiang Feidu" left over from Wulong River Ferry in Xiabei Village, Chengmen Town, Fuzhou. Photographed by Ruan Renyi

The lower left picture: Wulong River Ferry is located in Xiabei Village, Chengmen Town, Cangshan District today, which is an important ancient ferry on Fuzhou South Post Road. Photographed by Ruan Renyi

The lower right picture: The ancient pagoda of Linpu Ferry in Chengmen Town, Cangshan District, Fuzhou was a navigation mark tower for water transportation of the Minjiang River in ancient times. Photographed by Ruan Renyi

上　图：福清市新厝镇蒜岭全景　阮任艺 摄
左下图：相思岭（尤木臭）古驿道　崔建楠 摄
中下图：江兜朱熹书院旧址　崔建楠 摄
右下图：福州市闽侯县青口镇前洋村穆岭古道是宋代以后一条由闽南到福州的重要驿道　阮任艺 摄

The upper picture: Panorama of Suanling Mountain, Xincuo Town, Fuqing City. Photographed by Ruan Renyi

The lower left picture: Xiangsi Ridge (Youmuchou) Ancient Post Road. Photographed by Cui Jiannan

The lower middle picture: Former Site of Zhu Xi Academy in Jiangdou. Photographed by Cui Jiannan

The lower right picture: Muling Ancient Road in Qianyang Village, Qingkou Town, Minhou County, Fuzhou City is an important post road from southern Fujian to Fuzhou after the Song Dynasty. Photographed by Ruan Renyi

孝

左上图：位于莆田市黄石镇桥兜村的宁海桥，古为宁海渡 阮任艺 摄
右上图：莆田江兜土地庙，古人行旅至此地便可以望见湄洲湾的大海 崔建楠 摄
下 图：福州闽侯尤木臬古驿道全景 阮任艺 摄

The upper left picture: Ninghai Bridge, located in Qiaodou Village, Huangshi Town, Putian City, was originally Ninghaidu at ancient times. Photographed by Ruan Renyi

The upper right picture: Jiangdou Land Temple of Putian, the ancients traveled here to see the sea of Meizhou Bay. Photographed by Cui Jiannan

The lower picture: Panorama of Yumuchou Ancient Post Road in Minhou, Fuzhou. Photographed by Ruan Renyi

以莆田的福兴泉驿道为例，唐宋时因河海阻隔，大路由莆田城关乌石街北出，经泗华至白杜（溪白村）。南宋建炎年间（1127 ~ 1130），延寿桥建成，改由莆田城关拱辰门出，经上林、白杜、后卓、枫林（西天尾镇）、东宫、东田入迎仙驿（江口观后村），过迎仙桥，穿过溪东山后，经大岭村翻福莆岭与福清蒜岭铺相接。南宋江口桥建成，元明时期驿道直接由福清县入江口桥进莆境，经涵江、新港、四亭、三亭、头亭至莆田城关。

江东桥往南，虽然途经漳州平原，但很快就进入连绵不断的山岭。行人稀少，路远驿疏，行旅艰辛。《读史方舆纪要》曰："梁山，一名高昌山，高千仞，盘亘百里，有九十九峰。亦名梁岳。……山之中，纡折回旋，有田、有村、有溪。溪之名，有长源溪、锦溪、万顷溪、仙溪、盛溪、锦石溪、垂玉溪、龙潭溪，分流洒道，互相萦绕。……山之西，接盘陀岭，丛薄崎峻，盘亘可十里，岭盖即宋葵冈岭，汉时为南越蒲葵关，闽粤通道也。"在陈元光开漳之前，梁山至潮梅之间的大片区域为蛮獠所据，陈政南征，但"志未酬而身先死"；陈元光临危受命，与潮梅地区汛息往来，相互驰援。平叛之后，继续设置行台加以有效管理；入宋之后，驿站始成。

按漳州《旧正德志》中记述："……路远驿疏，行人无所依靠，当时守郡往往酌量道里之中，随铺立庵，命僧守之，以待过客，且置田赡僧，卑守庵焉。于是南路十有三庵。又东出漳境为泉州同安界，有鱼孚庵等（共四庵）。北路至长泰县有武安馆、使星馆，未闻设庵，非要道也。"这是宋代对路远驿站少的要道采取随铺立庵，置田赡养僧侣，以便利驿运的一个好办法。

闽粤古道路途艰险，重山阻隔。图为云霄县梁山全景 阮任艺 摄

The ancient road between Fujian and Guangdong is difficult and dangerous, with heavy mountains blocking it. The picture shows a panoramic view of Liangshan in Yunxiao County. Photographed by Ruan Renyi

The upper picture: The ancient road of Pantuo Ridge between Zhangpu and Yunxiao is an important section of the ancient post road in Fujian and Guangdong. The road is rugged. Photographed by Ruan Renyi

The lower picture: Jiangdong Bridge of Zhangzhou is located on the north stream of Jiulong River, which is one of the ten famous bridges in ancient China and the largest and most reconstructed stone beam bridge in the world. It was once the only way to pass the ancient road between Fujian and Guangdong. Photographed by Ruan Renyi

上　图：漳浦与云霄之间的盘陀岭古道是闽粤古驿路重要的一段，道路崎岖　阮任艺 摄

下　图：漳州江东桥位于九龙江北溪水道之上，是中国古代十大名桥之一，世界最大最重构件的石梁桥，曾是闽粤古道的必经之路　阮任艺 摄

THE REMOTE ROAD IN THE SOUTHEAST, BRIDGES AND FERRIES COORDINATE WITH EACH OTHER

The post road from Fuzhou to Guangdong was formed earlier and belongs to the main passage from Fuzhou to the south. Although there are mountains on the way, only this ancient post road in Fujian is relatively flat. Along the post road is an area with relatively superior natural conditions and relatively developed economy in Fujian. Putian, Quanzhou, Zhangzhou and Fuzhou along the way are called the "lower four prefectures", which are in line with the "upper four prefectures" such as Jianning, Yanping, Shaowu and Tingzhou, which developed earliest and belong to Minjiang River Basin.

莆田延寿村延寿桥 阮任艺 摄

Yanshou Bridge in Yanshou Village, Putian. Photographed by Ruan Ren Yi

The northern starting point of the ancient post road is Sanshan Posthouse in Fuzhou. All the way south, it passes through Honglu Posthouse of Fuqing, Puyang Posthouse of Putian, Fengting Posthouse of Xianyou, Jintian Posthouse of Hui'an, Jin'an Posthouse of Jinjiang, Kangdian Posthouse of Nan'an, Dalun Posthouse of Tong'an, Jiangdong Posthouse of Longxi, Linzhang Posthouse of Zhangpu, Yunxiao Posthouse, Nanzhao Posthouse of Zhao'an, etc., and then leaves the province to reach Raoping County of Guangdong Province. The detailed itinerary from Fuzhou to Xiamen via Quanzhou can be referred to Huang Shujing's "Journey to the South" in the Qing Dynasty: on the first day, leaving the south gate of Fuzhou, crossing Minjiang River via Wanshou Bridge in Taijiang District of Fuzhou, and staying at the Sanjiaocheng of Cangshan District of Fuzhou on Nantai Island at night; on the second day, crossing Wulong River and staying at Fangkou Village, Qingkou Town, Minhou County, Fuzhou; on the third day, passing through Xiangsi Ridge in Dongtai Village, Qingkou Town, Minhou County, and staying in Yuxi Town, Fuqing City at night; on the fourth day, passing Suanling Village, Xincuo Town, Fuqing, crossing Mulan River, and staying at Xinghua Prefecture Examination Institute in Licheng District, Putian City; on the fifth day, crossing Laixi Bridge on the upper reaches of Mulan

River and staying in Tuling Town, Quangang District, Quanzhou; on the sixth day, passing Luocheng Town in Hui'an County, crossing Luoyang River via Wan'an Bridge (also known as Luoyang Bridge) at noon, entering Quanzhou City, and staying in Quanzhou Prefecture Test Institute; on the seventh day, passing through Wulong Village, Cizao Town, Jinjiang City, Quanzhou, crossing Dayingling and Xiaoyingling, and staying in Qian'ai Village, Neicuo Town, Xiang'an District, Xiamen at night; on the eighth day, passing through Liuwudian, Xindian Town, Xiamen, and taking a boat 30 miles across the sea to reach Wutong Wharf of Xiamen.

The Fujian section of this Fujian-Guangdong post road is 1030 miles long. about 593 kilometres, with a total of 17 post stations and 2 "pond post stations" set up along the whole line. Along the way, we must cross Minjiang River, Longjiang River of Fuqing, Hagilu River of Putian, Mulan River, Fengcixi River of Xianyou, Luoyang River of Hui'an, Jinjiang of Quanzhou, Anhai Port of Jinjiang, Dongxi River of Tong'an, Jiulong River of Zhangzhou, Luxi River of Zhangpu, Zhangjiang River of Yunxiao, Dongxi River of Zhao'anand other large and small rivers and harbors, then climbing over Suanling between Fuqing and Putian, Baishuiling between Xianyou and Hui'an, Dayingling and Xiaoyingling between Nan'an and Tong'an, Jiulong Ridge in Longhai, Pantuo Ridge between Zhangpu and Yunxiao, Yougan Ridge between Yunxiao and Zhao'an, and Huangshi Mountain at the junction of Fujian and Guangdong. Although the journey was tough, among the five official post roads that Fujian left the province in the Qing Dynasty, Fujian-Guangdong post road was the best and safest one. Some sections have a width of 4 meters and can be used for chariots and horses to run in parallel.

According to the topography, the roads in southeast Fujian are divided into two regions, north and south, with Jiangdong Bridge at the mouth of Jiulong River in Zhangzhou as the boundary. The road to the north is smooth, but it needs to cross many big rivers on the way, with dangerouswater flow, and many places need detours to cross safely. One of the most difficult places is Fangshan Ferry to the south of Fuzhou, which has changed several times in less than 200 years. After the Northern Song Dynasty, many stone beam bridges were built in Fujian coastal areas, greatly improving the traffic conditions of this coastal passage.

漳诏万松分水

唐代，随着闽粤古道辟为驿道，漳州成为闽东南的交通中心，北至同安，南达漳浦，西通龙岩。宋代，以漳州城区为中心向四方辐射的驿道网已具雏形：东路，第一铺在朝天门外，向东经鹤鸣铺、江东铺、管桥铺、龙江亭，抵今厦门同安区界；西路，宋称“平南驿道”，第一铺在安丰门外，向西经京元铺、越岭铺、金山铺、和溪铺至今龙岩地界；南路，第一铺在南门外，经木棉铺，南行经今漳浦、云霄、诏安，出分水关，抵广东潮州；北路，出东城门，经郭坑渡头、半岭亭（五里亭）至长泰县城，再顺朝京路抵今同安灌口，北上泉州。

南宋，东架虎渡桥，南筑薛公桥；铺砌石路，设铺、立馆，于要道上随铺立庵，赡僧待客，方便商旅。明代，增辟沟通沿海的东南驿路，县乡道路有较大发展，驿铺设置较为完善。迨至清代，官方大路基本稳定，城乡之间道路交织。

万松关位于龙文区蓝田镇梧浦村岐山与鹤鸣山之间。明正统间，龙溪人陈克聪在岐山路段“植松夹道，连荫十里”，故称万松岭；明崇祯二年（1629）在岭上建关，称万松关，山势险峻，为渡江必经之地。关城左右两山夹峙，雄伟坚实，巍然威镇隘塞，古人形容为“麟蹲凤翔，襟带川原”。关上城墙，全部用工整的长方形花岗石砌成，高 25 米，宽 7 米，全长 100 米。高大的城门关上，嵌着一块青石横匾，镌“天宝维垣”四个大字。在万松关东南侧保存有两方碑记，一通为清光绪十二年（1886）元月“张公司马德政去思碑”；另一通为清同治四年（1865）的左宗棠题刻。梧浦贞节坊，四柱三间石枋，额枋上刻：“龙溪故监生蔡朝宗妻黄氏暨男故生正薰妻林氏坊”。

The upper left picture: After the opening of Zhangzhou in the Tang Dynasty, a main road from Zhangzhou to the capital and the provincial capital was set up between Qishan and Heming Mountain, named "Fuqi Road". Now it has become a mountain path. Photographed by Ruan Renyi

The lower left picture: Wansong Pass has gone through many wars, and the remains of the pass and historic sites can be remembered by future generations. Photographed by Cui Jiannan

The right picture: Wansong Pass of Zhangzhou is an ancient traffic fortress and a place that military strategists must contend for. Photographed by Ruan Renyi

左上图：唐朝开漳之后，在岐山和鹤鸣山之间辟出一条漳州通往京都、省城的要道，取名“福岐路”。如今已变成山间小路 阮任艺 摄

左下图：万松关历经多次战火，遗存的关隘古迹可供后人缅怀 崔建楠 摄

右 图：漳州万松关是古代的交通要塞，又是历来兵家必争之地 阮任艺 摄

The upper picture: The stele of "*Notes of Dianlong Mountain*" on Shuimoling Ancient Road in Zhangpu was written by Zhu Tianqiu, minister of public works in the Ming Dynasty. Photographed by Ruan Renyi

The lower left picture: The stone inscription of "Dangpingling Road" on Shuimoling Ancient Road in Zhangpu. Photographed by Ruan Renyi

The lower right picture: Shuangjie Memorial Archway from Shuimoling to Changqiao Ancient Road in Zhangpu. Photographed by Ruan Renyi

上　图：漳浦水磨岭古道《奠龙脉记》碑，为明代工部尚书朱天球所撰　阮任艺 摄
左下图：漳浦水磨岭古道“荡平岭路”石刻　阮任艺 摄
右下图：漳浦水磨岭至长桥古道边双节牌坊　阮任艺 摄

左上图：云霄县火田镇后埔村与佳园村交界处的黄斗桥 阮任艺 摄
左下图：云霄威惠庙是开漳圣王陈元光祖庙，在两岸及海外影响巨大 崔建楠 摄
右　图：蒲葵关关隘遗存 崔建楠 摄

The upper left picture: Huangdou Bridge at the junction of Houpu village and Jiayuan village, Huotian town, Yunxiao county. Photographed by Ruan Renyi

The lower left picture: Weihui Temple of Yunxiao is the ancestral temple of Chen Yuanguang, the holy emperor for the opening of Zhangzhou, and has great influence on both sides of the Taiwan Strait and overseas. Photographed by Cui Jiannan

The right picture: Remains of Pukuiguan pass. Photographed by Cui Jiannan

诏安县地处福建省南端闽粤交界处，素有“福建南大门”之称。宋代，诏安的梅岭港为泉州港和广州港之间的中继站。明清时期，官马大路穿境而过。清嘉庆间，有船行 10 多家，拥有大帆船 100 多艘，通航国内各大港口及东南亚一带，是海运业的鼎盛时期。

分水关位于诏安县西南境，离诏安县城 13 公里，是福建、广东两省的交界。关墙两侧群山屏列，明洪武年间，漳潮巡检司在山上建筑石城。嘉靖年间，诏安知县李尚理和龙溪知县林松建立“闽粤之交”石牌楼。天启年间，诏安知县周立扩建关城。清同治年间，诏安知县杨庆容又扩建石门关，并在关门上题署“漳南第一关”。“功罩闽粤”坊位于分水关的长乐寺东侧，是明崇祯期间福建、广东两省官员士绅为褒扬时任南澳副总兵郑芝龙而立。坊为花岗岩仿木结构，东北至西南走向。占地面积 12 平方米。四柱三间三楼，歇山顶，通高 9.6 米，宽 7.49 米，东北面书“功罩闽粤”，西南面书“声震华夷”。大额坊署“福建广东乡晋绅士为大总戎都督郑芝龙立”。

左上图：诏安分水关前的“闽粤之交”石牌楼 楼建龙 摄

右上图：诏安东溪是境内最大河流，明清时期，内河航运繁忙，可停泊百吨船只 崔建楠 摄

下 图：诏安分水关全景 阮任艺 摄

The upper left picture: The stone pailou of "the Intersection of Fujian and Guangdong" in front of the Fenshui Pass in Zhao'an. Photographed by Lou Jianlong

The upper right picture: Dongxi river of Zhao'an is the largest river in China. During the Ming and Qing Dynasties, inland watrer transport was busy and could berth 100-ton ships. Photographed by Cui Jiannan

The lower picture: Panorama of Zhao'an Fenshui Pass. Photographed by Ruan Renyi

上　图：诏安古街上的五谷神庙　崔建楠 摄

下　图：诏安古街间绵延 700 多米的古建筑群坐落着至少 7 座以上的明清石牌坊，均由花岗岩石雕凿榫而成，雕刻技艺精湛，可见当初这条古街的繁荣　赖小兵 摄

The upper picture: The Grain Temple on Zhao'an Ancient Street. Photographed by Cui Jiannan

The lower picture: The 700-meter-long ancient buildings between Zhao'an Ancient Street are located with at least 7 stone archways of the Ming and Qing Dynasties, all of which are made of granite stone carved with tenons. The exquisite carving skills show the prosperity of this ancient street at the beginning. Photographed by Lai Xiaobing

The left picture: Four-sided Buddha of the Ancient Pagoda at the East Gate of Xuanzhong Ancient City of Zhao'an. Photographed by Ruan Renyi

The upper right picture: The ancient city of Xuanzhong is located in Nanmen Village, the southernmost part of Meiling Town, Zhao'an County, which was a military fortress against Japanese pirates in the Ming Dynasty. The statue of Guandi enshrined in Guan Yu Temple in the ancient city and the statue of Guan Yu in the Guan Yu Temple in Dongshan are carved with the same piece of wood, so pilgrims come in an endless stream and incense is flourishing. Photographed by Ruan Renyi

The lower right picture: Legend has it that the former ancient road passed under the ancient pagoda. Photographed by Cui Jiannan

左　图：诏安悬钟古城东门古塔四面佛　阮任艺 摄

右上图：悬钟古城位于诏安县梅岭镇最南端的南门村，是明朝抗击倭寇的军事要塞。古城内的关帝庙供奉的关帝神像和东山关帝庙的关帝神像是同一段木头所雕，故香客络绎不绝，香火鼎盛　阮任艺 摄

右下图：传说昔日的古道就从古塔下面经过　崔建楠 摄

THE ANCIENT ROAD CONNECTING ZHANGZHOU CITY AND ZHAO'AN COUNTY

In the Tang Dynasty, Zhangzhou became the transportation center of the ancient road in southeast Fujian, reaching Tong'an in the north, Zhangpu in the south and Longyan in the west. In the Song Dynasty, the post road network with Zhangzhou city as the center and radiating to all directions took shape. In the Southern Song Dynasty, Zhangzhou paved stone roads, set up shops and restaurants, and set up temples on major traffic arteries, mainly to entertain monks and guests passing by. In the Ming Dynasty, the southeast post road connecting the coast was opened, and the roads of counties and villages also developed greatly. In the Qing Dynasty, Zhangzhou's official roads were basically stable, with roads interwoven between urban and rural areas.

Zhao'an County is located at the junction of Fujian and Guangdong at the southern end of Fujian and is called the "South Gate of Fujian". In the Song Dynasty, Meiling Port in Zhao'an was the transit point between Quanzhou Port and Guangzhou Port. During the Ming and Qing Dynasties, The Official Avenue passed through the border. During the reigns of Emperor Jiaqing of the Qing Dynasty, there were more than 10 shipping lines and more than 100 large sailing boats, which were navigable to major domestic ports and Southeast Asia. It was the heyday of the shipping industry.

左　图：云霄与漳浦交界处的盘陀岭蒲葵关皇帝井，相传南宋少帝赵昺南逃时，曾于此休息　崔建楠 摄

右　图：诏安古街遗存的石狮头　阮任艺 摄

The left picture: At the junction of Yunxiao and Zhangpu, the Emperor Well of Pukui Pass in Pantuo Ridge. It is said that Zhao Bing, the little emperor of the Southern Song Dynasty, had a rest here when he fled to the south. Photographed by Cui Jiannan

The right picture: The remains of the head of the stone lion from Zhao'an Ancient Street. Photographed by Ruan Renyi

泉厦大小盈岭

漳泉古道同安段境内保留着多丰富的文物古迹，同安区大同道凤山文笔塔公园内的甘露亭，古代同安通往泉州古道上往来官驻足憩息之所　崔建楠 摄

There are many rich cultural relics and historic sites in Tong'an section of Zhangquan ancient road. Ganlu Pavilion in Wenbi Pagoda Park Fengshan Mountain Datong Street, Tong'an District is the place where officials from ancient Tong'an to Quanzhou stop and re Photographed by Cui Jiannan

小盈岭关隘地处南安与同安交界，在漳泉古驿道上。南明永历五年（1651），郑成功率军攻漳州，清福建提督杨名高率部驰援，两军战于小盈岭，清军大败。

关隘所在岭口形如漏斗，东北风长驱直入，古代沙溪一带民田苦为风沙所害，曾有一句谚语“沙溪七里口，无风沙自走”，故南宋绍兴二十三年（1153）朱熹任同安主薄时，建造“同民安”石坊于岭上，寓意“以坊补缺，安定斯民”。清雍正十二年（1734）石坊塌圮。乾隆三十三年（1768）马巷秀才林应龙等呈请倡捐，就原址将坊改建为同安通往泉州之关隘。现存石砌关隘为东西向，南北拱门通道，长8.60米，高3.56米，拱门高2.44米，宽2.38米。关隘拱门上留用朱熹所题“同民安”石匾，东侧石匾残，南侧石匾高0.5米，长1.63米，落款“朱熹书”。关隘东侧立石碑，以原坊脊改成，碑中直书：“小盈岭南同交界碑”，碑刻四周小字为同安知县吴镛撰写《改坊为关记》，字迹已漫漶不清，碑高1.9米，宽0.58米，厚0.1~0.2米。

除同安东南一片可走小盈岭驿道外，也有走十八弯这条古道。古道起自南安罗田，经十八弯、古宅、后埔、行宫至同安城关，再经乌涂、新塘埔、南山岭、苎溪、安民、鱼孚、深青、仙店铺入漳州。全长110公里，宽不足2米，鹅卵石路面，其中部分为官道。元迄清末，先后设有驿铺12个。古宅十八弯这条古道，也是当时北同安一带读书人参加科举，上京求取功名的必经捷径。在接近寨仔尾村的大埔路旁，原有南宋景定元年（1260）石碑一方，高0.35米，宽0.38米，上面镌刻八行字：“郑公祥化忌经，并

“绩光铜柱”坊横跨在漳（州）泉（州）古驿道中，是康熙五十六年(1717)为纪念统一台湾的施琅将军而立的，也是目前厦门地区规模最大、保存最好的清代石牌坊 崔建楠 摄

The "Jiguang Bronze Pillar"Archway, which straddles the ancient post road of Zhang (Zhou) and Quan (Zhou), was set up in 1717 in memory of General Shi Lang, who unified Taiwan. It is also the largest and best preserved stone archway in the Qing Dynasty in Xiamen. Photographed by Cui Jiannan

The Pass of Tong'an in Xiamen

Xiaoyingling Pass is located at the junction of Nan'an and Tong'an. In 1651, Zheng Chenggong led the army to invade Zhangzhou, and Yang Minggao, commander-in-chief of Fujian Province in the Qing Dynasty, led the troops to rush to the rescue. The two armies fought on Xiaoyingling. Finally, the army of Qing dynasty suffered a heavy defeat.

左　图：同安文笔塔为光绪末年(1905~1908)重建，砖木结构，七级八面，每级4个拱门，中有旋梯。塔下有曲池、拱桥。“夕照塔影”为文笔胜景。文笔塔位于东西溪的交汇处，山下在古代甚至近代都有码头。文笔塔位于凤山之巅，巍然耸立，非常醒目，海上归来的船只习惯性的将其视为入港的航标　阮任艺 摄

右　图：古道旁遗留下的两个染坑遗址，诉说着同安往昔商旅麇集、货肆星罗的染坊文化　崔建楠 摄

The left picture: Wenbi Tower of Tọng'an was rebuilt in the late Guangxu period (1905-1908). It has a brick and wood structure with seven levels and eight sides, four arches in each level and a spiral ladder in it. There are curved pools and arch bridges under the tower. "The setting sun and the tower shadow" is a beautiful scene for writing. Wenbi Tower is located at the junction of East and West Streams. There were docks at the foot of the mountain in ancient and even modern times. Wenbi Tower is located at the top of Fengshan Mountain, which stands tall and is striking. Ships returning from the sea habitually regard it as a navigation mark for entering the harbor. Photographed by Ruan Renyi

The right picture: The ruins of the two dye pits left behind by the ancient road tell of the dye house culture of Tongan in the past when business travelers gathered and goods were sold in Xingluo. Photographed by Cui Jiannan

上　图：同安故里古道边苏颂故里碑：位于甘露亭旁边，是清光绪六年同安知县八十四(字寿征)为北宋丞相苏颂所立。碑上镌有阴刻字“宋熙宁三舍人丞相正简苏公故里”　阮任艺 摄

下　图：同安古城墙遗址南门　阮任艺 摄

The upper picture: Su Song's Hometown Monument on the Ancient Road of Tong'an Hometown: Located next to Ganlu Pavilion, it was erected by Su Song, Prime Minister of the Northern Song Dynasty, in the 6th year of the Guangxu regin of the Qing Dynasty. The tablet is inscribed with the inscription "Hometown of Su Song, the Prime Minister of the Xining Regin of the Song Dynasty". Photographed by Ruan Renyi

The lower picture: South Gate of Tongan Ancient City Wall Site. Photographed by Ruan Renyi

施琅

（1627~1696），字尊侯，号琢公，晋江衙口人。他原来是郑成功部将，先后在同安有7年的活动时间。

康熙二十二年（1683）六月，施琅领兵自东山出发，在澎湖击败郑军统帅刘国轩，一举解决了台湾统一问题。中秋佳节捷报传到京城，龙颜大悦，随即钦赐龙袍御衣并褒锡诗章，赞扬施琅统一台湾的功绩。施琅逝世后，福建巡抚、学台、布政使，道、府、厅、县等地方官员，为他在厦门同安建造了『绩光铜柱』坊以纪念施琅将军的功绩。

Shi Lang (1627-1696), styled himself Zunhou, with an alternative name of Zhuogong, a native of Yakou, Jingjia. He turned out to be the military officer of Zheng Chenggong's command and had seven years of activities in Tong'an.

In June of the 22nd year of Kangxi's reign (1683), Shi Lang led his troops from Dongshan and defeated Zheng Jun's commander Liu Guoxuan in Penghu, thus solving the Taiwan reunification problem at one stroke. When the good news of the Mid-Autumn Festival reached the capital, the emperor was greatly pleased. Immediately, he gave the dragon robe and royal clothing and praised with poems, praising Shi Lang's achievements in unifying Taiwan. After Shi Lang's death, Fujian Governor, educational inspector, secretary for proclamation, Taoist, government, department, county and other local officials built the memorial arch named "Ji Guang Tong Zhu" in Tong'an to commemorate the exploits of General Shi Lang.

苏颂

（1020~1101），字子容，汉族，福建同安人。宋代天文学家、天文机械制造家、药物学家。

苏颂幼承家教，勤于攻读，深通经史百家，学识渊博，举凡图纬、阴阳、五行、星历、山经、本草无不钻研。庆历二年（1042）中进士。

苏颂亦是同安历史长河中独具代表性的人物，他创制的『水运仪象台』号称『时钟之祖』，英国著名科技史学家李约瑟称赞他是『中国古代和中世纪最伟大的博物学家和科学家之一』。

Su Song (1020-1101), styled himself Zirong, the Han natinaolity, a native of Tong'an, Fujian. He was an stronomer, astromechanic, pharmacist in the Song dynasty. Su Song adhered to family education since childhood, and was diligent in studying. He had a deep knowledge of hundreds of classics and history, with a large stock of information. He has studied all kinds of charts, Yin and Yang, Five Elements, Ephemeris, Mountain Classics and Materia Medica. In the second year of the Qingli regin (1042), he was a successful candidate in the highest imperial examinations.

Su Song is also a unique representative figure in Tong'an's long history. His "Astronomical Clock Tower" is known as "the ancestor of the clock". Joseph Needham, a famous British historian of science and technology, praised him as "one of the greatest naturalists and scientists in ancient and medieval China".

自舍，又僧妙谦十千，足以（钱）乙伯贯足，铺修此路，计八百余丈，以济往来。景定元年记。”文字寥寥仅40字，但却是一块完整的记事牌，讲述郑祥化和僧人妙谦为方便往来旅人，合力捐款修路800余丈之事。从石块的不加雕琢及文字的简朴无华来看，这是一条民间自发铺修的古道，石碑现收藏在同安博物馆。

同安半岭古道位于汀溪镇半岭村半岭自然村至前格村五里林自然村。古道建成于宋代，是同安北面经汀溪、古坑、西源、半岭，翻越东岭往安溪东南部龙门和南安西部翔云一带的主要道路。古道上端的半岭自然村内有古厝、客栈等房舍多座；古道下端在前格村五里林北边300米二十四阶下，旧时五里林因古道而富有，开有数家客栈、点心店。半岭村至五里林的古道遗迹保存尚好，长达5里，古道由不规则、石面光滑的石块铺设成石阶和小道，宽1~1.5米，坡度较平缓，局部石阶衔接。半岭古道是古同安通向北部安溪、南安山区的主要商旅古道，通过古道运送进山的是粮食、食盐、日用杂货、海产等，由山区运往同安的是茶叶、土纸、粽叶、竹器、草席等，由于运送货物常常借助驴骡牲畜驮运，翻山越岭，因此也是古代同安北部运送货物的重要“茶马古道”。

越尾山古道位于灌口镇双岭村西北越尾山上，又称“小岭路”。建于清代，由双岭村大厝自然村至长泰县山重薛厝，全长14千米。现存古道分成上、下两段，下半段长约800米，由新建的越尾山庄至越尾山半山腰，土路石路相间，保存状况一般；上半段长约100米，由半山腰至山顶与山重的薛厝交界处，多用石块铺筑，宽0.5~1.5米，山顶建有安泰祠，祠前立有清光绪十三年（1887）重修小岭路石碑。碑宽0.41米，高0.64米，碑镌“厦门庵长社 薛评观捐英艮陆拾大员 薛涉观捐英艮肆大员 山重薛林众社助小工弍仟工 光绪丁亥重修小岭路”。

The upper left picture: At the junction of Nan'an and Tong'an-Xiaoyingling Mountain, Zhu Xi wrote "Tong Min an" here. Photographed by Ruan Renyi

The upper right picture: The boundary monument at the intersection of Nan'an and Tong'an in Xiaoyingling Mountain. Photographed by Ruan Renyi

The lower picture: Banling Ancient Road in Tong'an. Photographed by Lou Jianlong

左上图：南安与同安的交界——小盈岭，朱熹在此写下“同民安” 阮任艺 摄
右上图：小盈岭南安与同安交界碑 阮任艺 摄
下 图：同安半岭古道 楼建龙 摄

泉州朋山古道

泉州驿道以泉州府城为中心，通往京城和邻省的有3条：1、经福州进京驿道。唐至北宋初，万安桥（洛阳桥）未建造前，泉州至京城长安的驿道是出城北朝天门，过白虹山左面至仙游、福州。北宋皇祐五年（1053）万安桥建成后，进京的驿道改出仁风门过万安桥，经惠安锦田驿、仙游枫亭驿至福州。2、经剑州进京驿道从泉州城西义成门出发，经南安汰口驿、永春桃源驿、德化龙浔驿、上壅驿入尤溪到剑州，再经建州至浙江。3、往广东驿道，形成于唐代，是总章二年（669）归德将军陈政所开，至宋代正式辟为驿道。

朋山岭观音宫古道在双阳街道新岭社区朋山岭半岭。古道从朋山岭岭脚沿山麓向南过岭直达泉州北门，现此路多已无存，惟留朋山岭一段，总长约5公里。古道多由不规则石头铺砌，宽约1米，两边草木茂盛。观音

1926年，泉州西街开元寺门口驿道上的行人

Pedestrians on the post road at the gate of Kaiyuan Temple in Quanzhou West Street in 1926

上　图：驿坂古道明清时期“北通省会，南抵漳泉”，是官马古驿道上重要的古驿站。图为当年遗存的涂岭古驿站　崔建楠 摄

左下图：驿坂古道上涂岭古街古驿站　阮任艺 摄

右下图：涂岭古驿站具有典型的闽南建筑结构　崔建楠 摄

The upper picture: During the Ming and Qing Dynasties, Yiban Ancient Road "connected the provincial capital in the north and reaches Zhang zhou and Quanzhou in the south". It is an important ancient post station on the ancient official post road .The picture shows the Tuling ancient post station of left over from that year. Photographed by Cui Jiannan

The lower left picture: Ancient Post Station on Tuling Ancient Street on Yiban Ancient Road. Photographed by Ruan Renyi

The lower right picture: The ancient post station in Tuling has a typical architectural structure in southern Fujian. Photographed by Cui Jiannan

宫在朋山岭古道边，相传宋代即有此宫，现宫系近代在原址重建，前有四角凉亭 1 座，惟六根石柱为旧构，上刻有“乾隆壬申年”“隆庆五年辛末九月立”“隆□五年”等字样；宫北约 30 米处原有石坊一座，现仅存坊两边的石柱。

驿坂古道位于涂岭镇驿坂村大雾山，距村委会约 6.5 公里。现存古道始于驿坂村大雾山林场。林场坐落于大雾山麓，古道直达山顶部，约 6.5 公里，基本是上坡。沿路均为石阶，只小部分为土路，石阶砌筑较规整，呈不规则形石面。路宽约 1 米，两边林木成荫，甚为幽邃。此地临古港口不远，是泉州货物流转的重要枢纽。修路碑立于大雾山半山腰古道旁，为摩崖。碑坐西北向东南，刻高 98 厘米，宽 53 厘米。碑状作圭首，上刻：温陵里捨路乙百丈 / 至正乙丑九月日誌，字楷。大字径 13 × 10 厘米，小字径 9 × 7 厘米。碑字工整，遒劲有力。

笔架山古道位于涂岭镇黄田行政村笔架山上。据传该路是为避倭患而辟，至晚始于明代。古道上承惠安紫山半岭，长约 10 公里，下接仙游枫圆庄。傍山而筑，一边依山坡，另一边临溪涧，由不规则山石铺砌，宽约 1–1.5 米，石块基本保留。路口有土地庙，俗称险宫。

The left picture:Dade Bridge on Yiban Ancient Road is located in Yiban Street, Yiban Village, streches across Yiban Creek, which was built in the Song Dynasty and is still well preserved. It is still a major traffic route in the countryside. Photographed by Ruan Renyi

The right picture: There was a "Wuliang bridge" built on the ancient post road in Yiban, which was the only place for officers and soldiers, merchants, literati and the common people to pass through at that time. There was an endless stream of boats and cars, and it was very lively. Photographed by Ruan Renyi

左　图：驿坂古道上的大德桥位于驿板村驿坂街，横跨驿板溪，始建于宋代，现保存尚好，仍为乡间交通要道　阮任艺 摄

右　图：驿坂古驿道上建有一座“无量桥”，是当时官兵、商贾、文人、百姓的必经之地，舟车穿行，络绎不绝，热闹非凡　阮任艺 摄

南安的西华万衣岭道位于丰州镇西华村董埔后山南坡，其走向基本为从南往北，依山坡而上，为泉州通往永春、德化的古道，始建于隋唐，历有修缮。该古道由石块铺砌而成，陡坡处铺成台阶，较平缓的地方平铺。古道宽约 2 米，残长约 1000 米。清顺治二年（1645）郑成功率军攻泉州，过此遇雨，军士将衣服披晒于山坡。后人将此岭取名“万衣岭”。路上有“万衣岭”碑。碑刻于清乾隆五十一年（1786），方首抹角，高 1.1 米，宽 0.58 米，厚 0.14 米，正中刻楷书“万衣岭”三字，字径 0.28×0.2 米。款识“乾隆丙午年（1786）桂月曹廷莲、谢宗安重修”。碑边有一座小土地庙，庙内有龛，刻有“福德正神，宣统四年”。

QUANZHOU ANCIENT POST ROAD

Quanzhou Post Road takes Fucheng Town of Quanzhou as the center , with a total of 3 roads leading to the capital and neighboring provinces. Guanyin Palace Ancient Road on Pengshanling is located in the half ridge of pengshanling, Xinling Community, Shuangyang Street, which passes from the foot of Pengshanling to the south along the foothills to the north gate of Quanzhou. It was the main traffic route from Quanzhou to Fuzhou in ancient times.

左　图：南安万衣岭古道上的石碑　陈小阳 摄

右　图：万衣岭古道流传着郑成功征战的传奇故事　陈小阳 摄

The left picture: The stone tablet on the Ancient Road of Wanyiling in Nan'an. Photographed by Chen Xiaoyang

The right picture: The legendary story of Zheng Chenggong's going on an expedition is circulating along the ancient road of Wanyiling. Photographed by Chen Xiaoyang

仙游古道

仙游地处闽中，倚山临海，水陆交通兼备。木兰溪航道民国时期成为全县唯一的交通运输线，溪运盛极一时。海运在宋代就颇为兴盛，枫亭港是仙游海运的主要港口。福泉驿道在仙游境内路段 14 余公里，沿途设长岭铺、沙溪铺、枫亭铺等。

百松古驿道位于仙游县西北部的书峰乡，原名书坑，因林氏定居此山峰后，以诗书为训，改称书峰。古驿道长约 4 公里，两旁有三百多棵古松，其中树龄百年以上的就有 135 棵。道旁的松树是北宋蔡襄倡导种植的“夹道松”的遗迹。蔡襄倡议官吏，发动百姓，在福州大义至泉州、漳州 700 余里大道旁栽植松树，荫庇大道。有民谣歌颂道：“夹道松……行人六月不知暑，千古万古摇清风”。这条驿道是西乡民众（大济、度尾、西苑等）通往仙游县城必经之路，也是祖辈进京赶考之路。

驿道中间留有一块“民国”三年（1913）的摩崖石刻。石刻长 1.17 米，宽 0.5 米，竖刻隶书，直下计 18 行，满行 8 字，全文共 135 字。石刻内容主要记载驿道两旁百年松柏为村财，村民不得乱砍。

仙游至永福（今永泰）之路于宋代开辟。路出东门，经林碑、洋尾、灵山、上乾、赤荷、仙水、何岭头、三角埕、马铺、双峰、游洋、寨前、潼关至永泰县梧桐尾，全长 60 公里；另一通道由何岭头分岔经石力、潭头、石苍、田坑、粗溪、霞湖、老山至永泰县境。

何岭古道位于仙游县城东北约 20 公里的榜头镇岭下村，是仙游最长的古道之一，汉以前号“虎岭”，因山顶一巨石似虎而得名。汉代何氏九兄弟往九鲤湖隐居，登上虎岭，故改称为“何岭”。在当地，何岭的莆仙话

The upper left picture: Heling Ancient Road, which began in the Song Dynasty, is the ancient road from Xianyou to Yongtai. Photographed by Ruan Renyi

The lower left picture: On the Heling Ancient Road from Xianyou to Yongtai, there is still an ancient pass. Photographed by Ruan Renyi

The right picture: Ma Yangqi Tombstone, Commander-in-chief of jockeys of the Qing Dynasty in Meiling, Fengting Ancient Town, Xianyou County, Putian. Photographed by Ruan Renyi

左上图：始于宋代的何岭古道是仙游通往永泰的古道 阮任艺 摄

左下图：仙游通往永泰的何岭古道，依旧留存的古隘口 阮任艺 摄

右 图：莆田仙游县枫亭古镇梅岭清朝骁骑师提督马仰齐神道碑 阮任艺 摄

发音类似“虎岭”。何岭现存石阶4045级，全长5公里，岭道两旁，松枫古树挺拔苍翠，路亭和摩崖点缀其间，原每隔一弯曲处有一座路亭，计18亭，现仅存5座。何岭从前是仙游通往古田、永泰、福州、尤溪等地的关隘，地势险要，自古以来为兵家必争要地。岭顶有座高耸的古建筑——何岭关。关上石额“何岭关”三个大字，是清咸丰五年（1855）仲夏知县铨庆所书，在关口还有小古塔、土地庙等古建筑。

何岭摩崖石刻位于何岭古道处，现存10多处，主要有：1、“何岭关”石刻，宋陈说书，楷书，字径0.35米；2、“忠孝”石刻，行楷，字径0.40米；3、“剑气破山裂……天与一关雄”石刻，民国吴威书，行楷，字径0.4米；4、“一卷”石刻，楷书，字径0.5米；5、清光绪十九年（1893）的禁止砍伐森林令：“仙游县正堂王示……”石刻，楷书，字径0.15米。

何岭古道起于榜头岭下村，止于钟山何岭关，古道地形险要，气势雄伟，曲折长达五公里，自宋代起，铺砌石阶，便于行人登涉，现存石阶4045级、5座古亭 崔建楠 摄

Heling Ancient Road starts from Bangtou in Lingxia Village and ends at He Ling Pass in Zhongshan. The ancient roadis dangerous and majestic, twisting for 5 kilometers. Since the Song Dynasty, stone steps have been paved to facilitate pedestrians to climb and wade. There are currently 4045 stone steps and 5 ancient pavilions. Photographed by Cui Jiannan

左　图：何岭古道上禁止砍伐的通告石刻
　　　　崔建楠 摄
右上图：何岭古道与摩崖石刻　崔建楠 摄
右下图：苍松古道摩崖石刻　崔建楠 摄

The left picture: Notification stone carvings prohibiting felling on Heling Ancient Road. Photographed by Cui Jiannan

The upper right picture:Heling Ancient Road and Cliff Stone Carvings. Photographed by Cui Jiannan

The lower right picture: Cliff Stone Carvings in Cangsong Ancient Road. Photographed by Cui Jiannan

THE CHANNEL OF XIANYOU

Xianyou is located in the central region of Fujian, leaning on mountains and facing the sea, with both land and water transportation. During the Republic of China, the waterway of Mulanxi River became the only transportation line in the county. In the Song Dynasty, Xianyou's shipping was quite prosperous, and Fengting Port was Xianyou's main shipping port.

东北岭道，山高路峻

东北岭道是指起于浙闽之间，从福鼎至福安、柘荣、寿宁一线关隘通往福州的各条通道。从区域上，大致可以分为北面的长溪流域，含福鼎、柘荣、寿宁、福安、周宁、霞浦；中部的霍童溪流域，包括上游的周宁、屏南、古田大东山区以及蕉城；南部的鳌江流域，主要有连江、罗源以及福州北部山区等。这一区域最为重要的古道，是沿着闽东近海一线行走的"福温古道"，也包括从政和、建瓯、古田等处经由周宁、屏南等县通往福安、宁德，汇于福温古道后通往福州、浙江的道路。因为多数路段都是穿行于崇山峻岭之间，攀山越岭，上下盘旋而山岭连续不断，故多以"岭道"相称。

闽东北地处鹫峰山脉的腹地与东坡，东西方向坡降极大，而南北方向则山谷纵横切割，通达条件极差。有《募建庾岭头亭序》（清·李毓姬）详之："自下抵巅，各距十余里，仅于二村附近，各见一亭。舟车不通，往来贸易，悉任肩荷。游客、殷商，优游者无论已，若乃遥程负重，气索神疲，欲登反却，血沸鼻烟，度阜越陵，蜿蜒层折，矫首白云之端。"

东北岭道的开通不会早于唐代。在此之前的文献所记，由这个方向入闽的，基本全为"海道"；而陆路艰难，"难于上青天"，所以多有"蜀道无以过"的感叹！福温古道的起修时间应该是唐代，至五代完善，又称"福

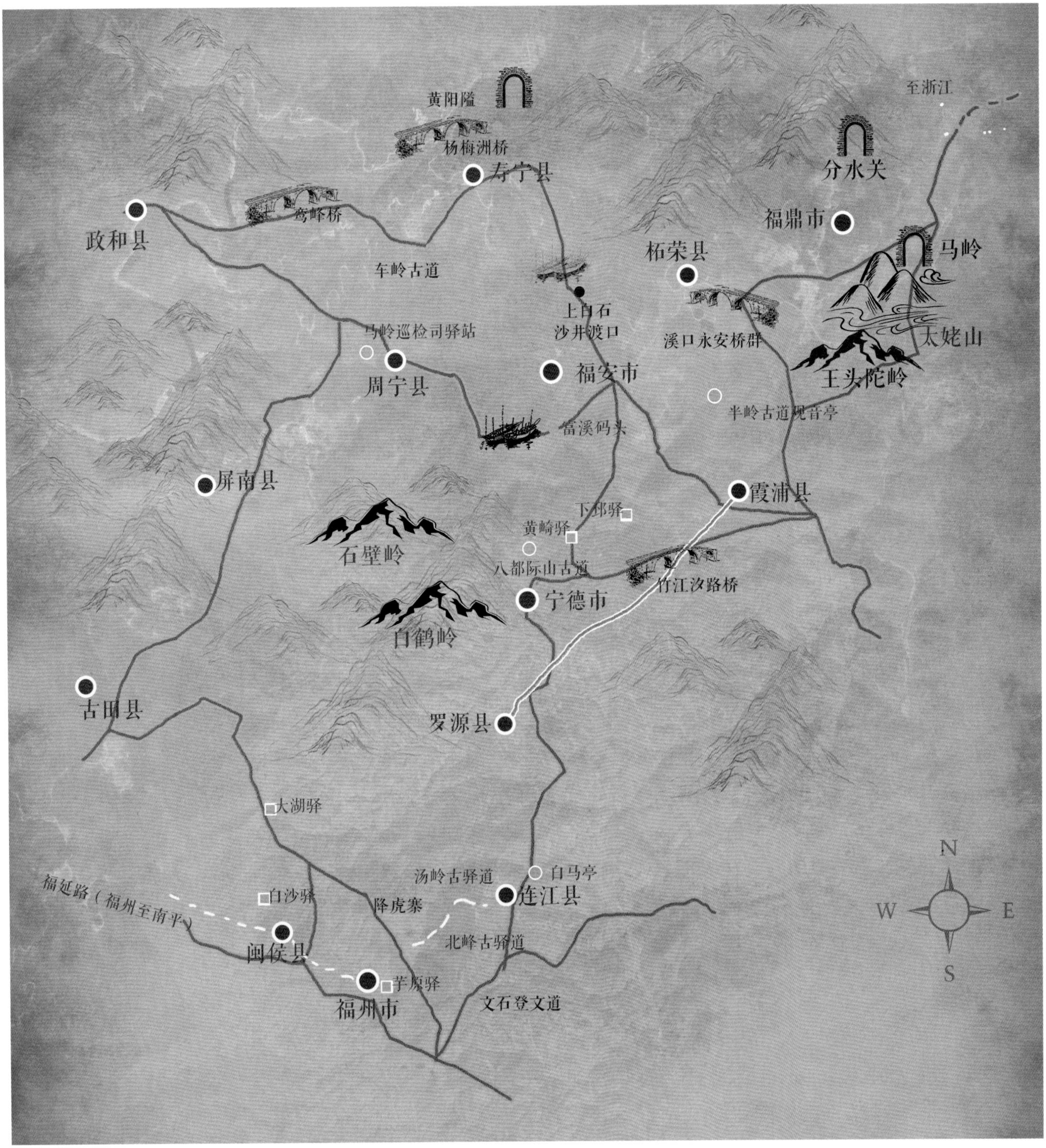

东北岭道是闽东地区的通道，起于闽浙之间的福鼎分水关，止于福州。多数路段穿行于崇山峻岭之间，攀山越岭，路途艰难

Dongbei Ridge Road is a passage in eastern Fujian, starting from Fuding Fenshui Pass between Fujian and Zhejiang and ending in Fuzhou. Most of the road sections travel between high mountains, climbing mountains and crossing mountains is difficult

建北驿道”“温州路”。至迟于北宋熙宁七年（1074）始设驿站，驿道路线从福州井楼门上行，经北岭、汤岭、连江潘渡、罗源四明至宁德飞泉（后移至焦门颊），乘船过官井洋到长溪县盐田。而后陆行至县治（今松城镇），再经天台岭、倒流溪（今属水门乡）、饭溪（今属牙城镇），入今福鼎县属白琳、桐山、分水岭至温州平阳县境。南宋绍兴三十年（1160），因官井洋行船危险，废焦门颊至盐田船渡，改陆行至宁德宁川驿，经双岩岭、黄崎镇、下盃（今均属福安）过渡到盐田。明代恢复官渡，改从宁德飞鸾乘船至盐田，其余路线基本不变。明弘治十八年（1505），驿废，改设铺递，显示出这条官道在经历了宋代的辉煌后，在沟通地方与中央的重要性方面已经逐渐下降。

宋以前，在宁德县城西南群山中，已有宁德、罗源边界民众自行踩踏而形成狭窄的区间小道，称“白鹤之岭”。南宋绍兴二十八年（1158）任宁德县主簿的陆游在所作《宁德县重修城隍庙记》中就有“宁德为邑，带山负海，双岩、白鹤之岭，其高摩天，其险立壁，负者股栗，乘者心惮”之说。宋宝庆时（1225~1227），宁德县主簿丁大全废朱溪路，另辟白鹤岭路接罗源，经宁德县城、七都，过福安县境的大获、衡阳、下白石、湾坞、溪尾到盐田接原路。除福温官路上的白鹤岭道外，还有飞鸾岭道、霍童岭道、石壁岭道、隐仙岭道、亲母岭道等。

《福温古道路引》中有一段话形象地描述了这段宁德通往罗源的主要通道：“宁德出城西门宫，白鹤山岭十里长；全条岭中亭三座，白鹤岭头观音亭。直行岭头一歇气，再行五里是塆亭，界首叠石隔十里，中间一观名半天。”

乾隆二十四年（1759），李拔任福宁知府，重修宁德至分水关的道路。并在分水关题额，曰“分水雄关”。

左上图：福鼎白琳镇尚书岭古茶道，北上可通县城和闽浙交界的分水关，如今古道上依旧有茶农在此耕作 赖小兵 摄

右上图：福鼎白琳镇尚书岭古道偶有挑夫经过 赖小兵 摄

下　图：福鼎风水关 朱晨辉 摄

The upper left picture: The ancient shangshuling tea road in Bailin Town, Fuding, goes north to the Fenshui Pass at the junction of the county seat and Fujian and Zhejiang. Today, tea farmers still work here on the ancient road. Photographed by Lai Xiaobing

The upper right picture: Porters occasionally pass by Shangshuling Ancient Road in Bailin Town, Fuding. Photographed by Lai Xiaobing

The lower picture: Fuding Fengshui Pass. Photographed by Zhu Chenhui

崇山峻岭中的车岭古道，悬崖飞瀑直泻百丈 赖小兵 摄

On the Cheling Ancient Road in high mountains, the cliff waterfall goes straightdown thousands of meters. Photographed by Lai Xiaobing

福温古道之外，从沿海往内陆山区的道路，设置铺递的，主要有从宁德往周宁至政和，从霞浦往福安至寿宁、政和，以及从霞浦经行柘荣通往福鼎的各条道路。这些道路随着重要性的下降，其路面、路况也相应变差。最主要的原因，在于路况的维护之艰以及地形变化起伏的剧烈。如明代时任寿宁知县的冯梦龙在其亲撰的《寿宁待志》中所记：“新坑口至东峰一路，险峻非常，除本县外，别无官府往来。余每赴府，预先行牌传谕，令诛茅辟径，全然不理。一遭天雨，寸步登天，亦付之无可奈何矣！”

这片区域的道路大多垂直于河流，而这些河流又多数位于高山之间的谷底，不仅无法借助于水流之利，不同季节的山洪变幻，使架桥的难度也远胜于沿海地区。由此，在闽东北道路之间，发展出极具特色的木拱廊桥和石拱桥、石梁柱桥、碇步桥以及与桥梁相与配建的大小庙宇，成为东北岭道之间的亮丽风景。

The left picture: Yangmeizhou bridge in Kengdi Township of Shouning is the main road leading to Zhejiang. Photographed by Yan Shuo

The right picture: Dengyun Bridge in Shouning, built in the Song Dynasty, is always used to celebrate every time a student succeeds in the government examination. Photographed by Lai Xiaobing

左　图：寿宁坑底乡的杨梅洲桥，是通往浙江的要道　严硕 摄

右　图：建于宋代的寿宁登云桥，每逢学子金榜题名，必登此桥庆贺　赖小兵 摄

NORTHEAST RIDGE ROAD, WITH HIGH MOUNTAINS AND DANGEROUS ROAD

The ancient road in the northeast region of Fujian refers to the passages from Fuding to Fu'an, Zherong and Shouning to Fuzhou originating between Zhejiang and Fujian. Regionally, it can be roughly divided into Changxi River Basin in the north, including Fuding, Zherong, Shouning, Fu'an, Zhouning and Xiapu; the Huotong River Basin in the middle includes Zhouning, Pingnan, Dadong Mountain in Gutian and Jiaocheng in the upper reaches, the Aojiang River Basin in the south mainly includes Lianjiang, Luoyuan and the mountainous areas in northern Fuzhou. The most important ancient road in this area is the Fuwen Ancient Road, and most of the sections are between loft mountains and high hills, and need to climb.

The mountains in northeast Fujian have great slopes in the east and west directions, and the valleys are cut vertically and horizontallyin the north and south directions, with extremely poor access conditions. The initial building time of Fuwen Ancient Road should be in the Tang Dynasty and the perfection in the Five Dynasties. According to archaeological discoveries, the time for Fuwen Ancient Road to set up post stations should not exceed 1074 at the latest.

Before the Song Dynasty, people on the border between Ningde and Luoyuan trampled on their own to form a narrow interval path, which was called "White Crane Ridge". In addition to Baihe Ridge Road on Fuwen Guan Road, there are Feiluan Ridge Road, Huo Tong Ridge Road, Shek Pik Ridge Road, Yi Ridge Road, Yin Xian Ridge Road, Qin Mu Ridge Road, etc.

Outside the Fuwen Ancient Road, the roads from the coast to the inland mountainous areas with post stations are mainly the roads from Ningde to Zhouning to Zhenghe, from Xiapu to Fu'an to Shouning and Zhenghe, and from Xiapu to Zherong to Fuding.

Most of the roads in this area are perpendicular to the rivers, and most of these rivers are located at the bottom of the valleys between high mountains, which not only cannot benefit from the flow of water, but also increases the difficulty of traveling and building bridges. Among these roads, wooden-arched corridor bridges, stone arch bridges and various temple buildings corresponding to the bridges have developed with great characteristics, which have become the beautiful scenery between Dongbei Ridge Road.

车岭古道平氛关段　赖小兵 摄

Pingfenguan Section of Cheling Ancient Road. Photographed by Lai Xiaobing

福温分水

福鼎古代的官马大道有两条：一条称“福建北驿道”，起自福州，经连江、宁德、霞浦，入福鼎蒋阳，经五蒲岭、白琳、点头至县城，再延伸到万古亭、贯岭，越分水关达浙江苍南、平阳、瑞安、温州；另一条由寿宁入福安，经柘荣，过管阳、金钗溪、唐阳、柯岭，达县城。宋代，北驿道共设11驿，在福鼎境内有两驿，一在白琳天王寺，一在桐山栖林寺。古代驿道原为军事和政治所需而设，置县后，设县前总铺，下辖11铺。

福鼎分水关始建于五代十国时期，乃闽国（909~945）为防吴越国入侵而建。明弘治《八闽通志》卷八十“古迹”载：“分水岭关，与温州平阳县接境，今犹号军营。叠石关。上二关在州东廉江里，伪闽立，以备吴越。”明万历《福宁州志》卷五“古关”亦云：“分水岭 与温州平阳交界。叠山关在十八都，与分水岭皆闽王立以防吴越之侵。”分水关遗迹包括古城墙、古道、灶台等，其中城墙遗迹包括关门、石城墙、敌台、跑马道、窝铺等。

与此同时，吴越国也在分水山（岭）北麓驻兵设防。清顾祖禹《读史方舆纪要》有云：“分水山（泰顺）县南二百里，与平阳县西南之松山相接。泉发陇上，东西分流，以限闽浙，山下地名平水，达前仓江，可通舟楫。吴越尝守此，以与闽人相拒。”

左　图：福鼎风水关是南宋时期，福州北取温州驿道的重要驿站　朱晨辉 摄

中　图：福鼎风水关纪念石碑　朱晨辉 摄

右　图：福鼎栖林寺始建于五代，寺院曾是福温古道上的驿站，也是南来北往的旅人休憩歇脚的客栈　朱晨辉 摄

The left picture: Fuding Fengshui Pass was an important post station in the Southern Song Dynasty when Fuzhou took the Wenzhou post road to the north. Photographed by Zhu Chenhui

The middle picture: Monument of Fengshui pass in Fuding. Photographed by Zhu Chenhui

The right picture: Qilin Temple of Fuding was built in the Five Dynasties. The temple was once a post station on the ancient Fuwen Road and an inn for travelers from south to north to rest. Photographed by Zhu Chenhui

FUWEN FENSHUI PASS

There are two ancient official avenues in Fuding County: one is called "Fujian North Post Road", which starts from Fuzhou, passes through Lianjiang, Ningde and Xiapu, enters Jiangyang in Fuding, passes through Wupuling, Bailin andDiantou to the county town, then extends to Wangu Pavilion and Guanling, and reaches Cangnan, Pingyang, Ruian and Wenzhou in Zhejiang through Fenshui Pass; the other one goes from Shouning to Fu'an, passes through Zherong, Guanyang, Jinchaixi, Tangyang and Keling, and reaches the county town. In the Song Dynasty, there were 11 post stations in the North Post Road, two in Fuding, one in Bailin Tianwang Temple and the other in Qilin Temple in Tongshan. The ancient post road was originally set up for military and political needs. After the county was set up, the county's front general shop was set up, with 11 shops under its jurisdiction.

The Fuwen Ancient Road starts from Fuzhou, through Xindian and Beifengover the ridge, by way of Lianjiang, Luoyuan and Ningde counties, and then enter Zhejiang through passes in Fuding, Shouning and other places.

Fuding Fenshui Pass was founded in the period of Five Dynasties and Ten Kingdoms. During the Southern Song Dynasty, Fenshui Pass was an important post station for Fuzhou to take Wenzhou post road to the north. Fuding Fenshui Pass borders Pingyang in Wenzhou. The existing relics of Fenshui Pass include ancient city walls, ancient roads, hearths, etc. Among them, the relics of city walls include the door of the strategic pass, stone city walls, lookout towers, bridle paths, shelters, etc.

左　图：尚书岭古道上的隘口　朱晨辉 摄
中　图：尚书岭古道　赖小兵 摄
右　图：福鼎白琳镇境内的寺庙驿站　赖小兵 摄

南宋时期，分水关是福州往温州驿道的重要驿站。南宋淳熙《三山志》卷五《驿铺》对该驿道有详细的记载，其中福鼎境内有："桐山驿，去泗洲驿二十五里，今废，只憩栖林院。骆驼岭、平阳，二十里，泗洲院。过分水岭。"由此进入浙江平阳县，继达温州府，"虽非孔道，实闽浙豫广往来便道也。"据明万历《福宁州志》卷三"舍铺"，该驿道为南宋乾道年间（1165~1173）设，至元朝初废。

霞浦王头陀岭简称"头陀岭"或"王陀岭"，民间有人叫做"驼驼岭"。它位于钱大王村至王头陀岭头垭口（俗称破亭岔）之间，系五代时王头陀砌造路面而得名。在郡城东北七十里，崎岖峻峭难行，王头陀于此开路。宋嘉定十四年（1221）长溪县令杨志又用石甃平之。南宋状元王十朋在赴任泉州与返回乐清均经这条古道，途经王头陀岭时，赋诗二首。《宿饭溪驿》："门拥千峰翠，溪无一点尘。松风清入耳，山月自随人。"《自泉返至王头陀岭》："凌晨饱饭渡秦溪，要上青云九级梯。不使瓯闽隔人世，头陀力与五丁齐。"因此，王头陀岭又被称为"状元路"。

The left picture: The Pass on the Ancient Road of Shangshuling. Photographed by Zhu Chenhui

The middle picture: Shangshuling Ancient Road. Photographed by Lai Xiaobing

The right picture: Temple Post Stations in Bailin Town of Fuding. Photographed by Lai Xiaobing

左上图：福鼎挑矾古道的隘口 赖小兵 摄

右上图：数百年来，明矾作为工业品的输出，全赖于人力，因此形成了矾山至前岐镇的 4 条挑矾古道，再由这 4 个港口集镇中转至国内外销售。其中，矾山至前岐是历史最为悠久的一条挑矾古道，终点皆在前岐妈祖庙 赖小兵 摄

下　图：福鼎挑矾古道全景 朱晨辉 摄

The upper left picture: The Pass of Alum Picking Ancient Road in Fuding. Photographed by Lai Xiaobing

The upper right picture: For hundreds of years, alum, as an industrial product, has been exported entirely by manpower, thus forming four ancient alum picking roads from Fanshan to Qianqi Town, which are then transferred from these four port towns to domestic and foreign sales. Among them, from Fanshan to Qianqi is the oldest ancient road to pick alum, and the end point is Mazu Temple in Qianqi. Photographed by Lai Xiaobing

The lower picture: Panorama of Alum Picking Ancient Road in Fuding. Photographed by Zhu Chenhui

福鼎挑矾古道曾是浙闽古驿道。浙江苍南县矾山镇盛产明矾，是名副其实的矾都。从清代中期开始，矾矿的开采规模逐渐扩大，运输就成为发展的一大问题。矾矿地处山区，路窄途远，舟车不便，依靠的是人力挑运。根据出海口不同，逐渐形成了不同的运输路线 赖小兵 摄

Alum Picking Ancient Road in Fuding was once an ancient post road in Zhejiang and Fujian. Fanshan Town, Cangnan County, Zhejiang Province, is rich in alum and is truly the alum capital. Since the middle of the Qing Dynasty, the mining scale of alum mines has gradually expanded, and transportation has become a major problem in development. Alumminesare located in a mountainous area, with narrow roads and long distances, and inconvenient transportation, which relies on manpower to carry. Different transportation routes have gradually been formed according to different outlets to the sea. Photographed by Lai Xiaobing

车岭古道

车岭古道确切的修筑时间无法稽考，但最早记载“车岭”的是明朝崇祯十年（1637）冯梦龙撰的《寿宁待志》。《寿宁待志》载：“车岭关即车岭头，去县二十五里，一线千仞，仰关者无所措足。东南路第一险峻处，有匾曰‘南门锁钥’”。

明万历二十一年（1593），知县戴镗为防卫倭患，在此设立“车岭关”，建石砌关门，称“隘门”。沿岭有4亭2泉，岭边遍植枫松，大者高达30 ~ 40米。以一条长岭，四座古亭，山高岭峻取胜，岭头亭边有嘉庆十七年（1812）郭宜魁题的“岭峻云深”摩崖石刻，每字两尺见方。

清朝雍正十二年（1734），寿宁县改隶福宁府。自此，寿宁行政重心南移，逐步形成了以“车岭”为标志的，从寿宁县城经斜滩往福安至福宁府的官道。来往货物全靠人扛肩挑。民谣云：“千年扁担万年筐，压得背驼腰又弯。磨烂两肩流尽汗，工钱不够饱三餐”。

车岭古道斜滩段依峭壁而建，极为险峻；因山脚以上无一节平路，素有“车岭车到天”之说。车岭古道全长约10公里，山石随地形铺就，路宽约1米到2米之间，自斜滩蜿蜒而上，相对高差658米，酷似一条天梯直上霄汉，有“去天五尺”之称，为斜滩通往县城的必经之路。

上　图：寿宁车岭古道，山以形称，岭以山名，名车岭。明中叶（1450~1460）修建，全岭除岭亭引道稍平缓，无一节平路　赖小兵 摄

下　图：寿宁下党乡的鸾峰桥，清嘉庆五年造，是寿宁木拱廊桥中最为壮观的一座。是全国单拱跨最长的贯木拱廊桥　赖小兵 摄

The upper picture: Cheling Ancient Road in Shouning, the mountain is named after the shape, the ridge is named after the mountain, so it is named Cheling. In the middle of the Ming Dynasty (1450 ~ 1460), except for the approach road of the ridge pavilion, there is no flat road in the whole ridge. Photographed by Lai Xiaobing

The lower picture: Luanfeng Bridge in Xiadang Township of Shouning, built in the fifth year of the Jiaqing regin of the Qing Dynasty, is the most spectacular wooden arcade bridge in Shouning. It is a through wooden arcade bridge with the longest single arch span in the country. Photographed by Lai Xiaobing

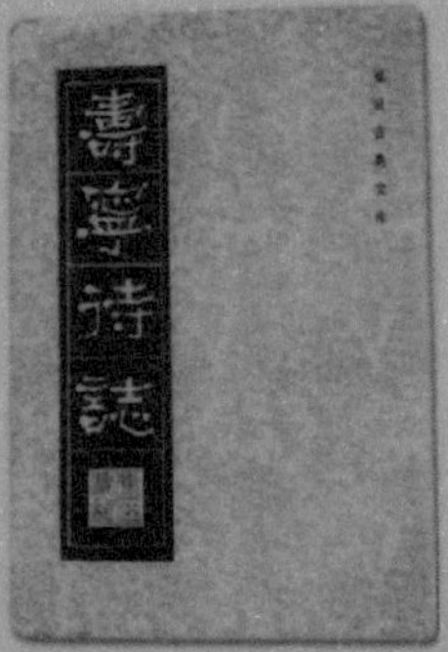

《寿宁待志》

冯梦龙（1574~1646），字犹龙，又字子犹，公鱼，号龙子犹、墨憨斋主人等，南直隶苏州府长洲县（今江苏省苏州市）人，是我国著名通俗文学家。

《寿宁待志》是中国第一部私家志书。明崇祯七年八月至十一年（1634~1638）冯梦龙任寿宁知县。任内他对寿宁风俗民情处处留意，深入调查研究，搜集了不少轶事逸闻，涉笔记录在案，写成了这部『以待其人』『以待其时』的地方志书《寿宁待志》。其内容除记载寿宁县的历史、地理、政治、经济与风土人情外，还以大量篇幅记录他宦游寿宁时的施政设想和治理活动。

Uncompleted Notes of Shouning

Feng Menglong (1574-1646), styled himself Youlong, also tyled himself Ziyou and Gongyu, with alternative names of Long Ziyou, Master of mohan house, etc. He was native of Changting county, Suzhou prefecture, Nanzhi (now Suzhou of Jiangsu province).

Uncompleted Notes of Shouning——China's first private chronicles. Feng Menglong, a famous popular writer in China, was appointed magistrate of Shouning County from August in the7th yearto the 11st year of the Chongzhen regin in the Ming Dynasty (1634-1638). During his term of office, he paid attention to the customs and people's feelings of Shouning everywhere, conducted in-depth investigations and studies, collected many anecdotes and anecdotes, and put them on record, thus he wrote a local chronicle book "*Uncompleted Notes of Shouning*" which "waits for the person" and "waits for the time". Its content not only records the history, geography, politics, economy and local conditions and customs of Shouning County, but also records his administrative ideas and activities during his official visit to Shouning with much writing.

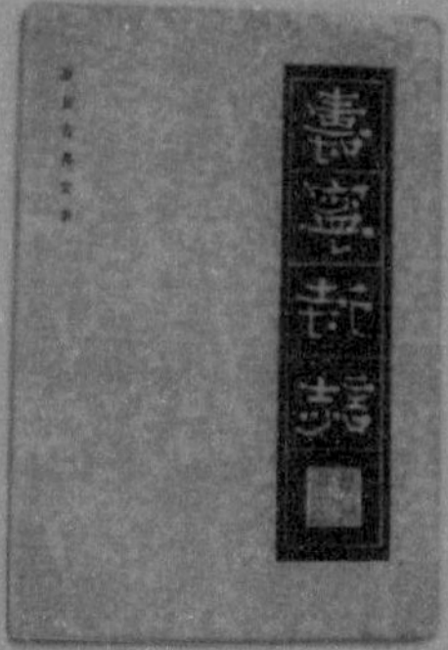

《寿宁待志》

冯梦龙（1574~1646），字犹龙，又字子犹，公鱼，号龙子犹，墨憨斋主人等，南直隶苏州府长洲县（今江苏省苏州市）人，是我国著名通俗文学家。

《寿宁待志》是中国第一部私家志书。明崇祯七年八月至十一年（1634~1638）冯梦龙任寿宁知县。任内他对寿宁风俗民情处处留意，深入调查研究，搜集了不少轶事遗闻，逐笔记录在案，写成了这部一以待其人一以待其时的地方志书《寿宁待志》。其内容除记载寿宁县的历史、地理、政治、经济与风土人情外，还以大量篇幅记录他宦游寿宁时的施政设想和治理活动。

Uncompleted Notes of Shouning

Feng Menglong (1574-1646), styled himself Youlong, also tyled himself Ziyou and Gongyu, with alternative names of Long Ziyou, Master of mohan house, etc. He was native of Changting county, Suzhou prefecture, Nanzhi (now Suzhou of Jiangsu province).

Uncompleted Notes of Shouning——China's first private chronicles. Feng Menglong, a famous popular writer in China, was appointed magistrate of Shouning County from August in the7th yearto the 11st year of the Chongzhen regin in the Ming Dynasty (1634-1638). During his term of office, he paid attention to the customs and people's feelings of Shouning everywhere, conducted in-depth investigations and studies, collected many anecdotes and anecdotes, and put them on record, thus he wrote a local chronicle book "*Uncompleted Notes of Shouning*" which "waits for the person" and "waits for the time". Its content not only records the history, geography, politics, economy and local conditions and customs of Shouning County, but also records his administrative ideas and activities during his official visit to Shouning with much writing.

车岭古道上的隘口　赖小兵 摄

The pass on Cheling Ancient Road.

Photographed by Lai Xiaobing

CHELING ANCIENT ROAD

Cheling Ancient Road is located 20 kilometers south of Shouning County in Fujian Province, between Shantian Village in Xietan Town and Yangwei Village in Qingyuan Township, which was the only way to lead the ancient town Xietan to the county town in the past.

The exact construction time of Cheling Ancient Road cannot be investigated, but there were records of "Cheling" during the Wanli period of Ming Dynasty.

In the 12th year of the Yongzheng period in Qing Dynasty (1734), Shouning County was transferred to Funing Prefecture. Since then, the administrative center of Shouninghas moved southward, forming an official avenue marked by "Cheling" from Shouning County to Fu'an to Funing Prefecture via Xietan Town.

The Xietan section of Cheling Ancient Road is built on cliffs and is very steep. The Cheling Ancient Road has a total length of about 10 kilometers and a road width of about 1 to 2 meters, with a relative height difference of 658 meters, just like a ladder straight up the sky.

左 图：车岭古道山路险峻，素有“车岭车到天”之说 赖小兵 摄
右 图：车岭古道上的驿亭 赖小兵 摄

The left picture: The ancient Cheling Road has steep mountain roads, which is known as "Cheling to the sky". Photographed by Lai Xiaobing

The right picture: The posthouse on Cheling Ancient Road. Photographed by Lai Xiaobing

白鹤石壁

宁德境内山峦叠嶂，古代陆路交通极为不便，正如明嘉靖版《宁德县志》中所说："宁德（今蕉城区）处闽东北，摄乎福宁、福安、政和、古田、怀安、罗源之间，连山亘北，大海入南，水陆俱阻，货利不通。盖闽之穷邑也。"

在白鹤岭古驿道开辟之前，由宁德通往省城福州的主通道为"南路二道"。其一"飞鸾岭道"，需先经宁德二都飞鸾村，上飞鸾岭，过南阳楼村、南靖关、护国乡蒋店，才到达罗源城，虽山道较为平缓，但路程太长；其二"朱溪岭道"，需攀登在宁德二都村内二百余丈高的福源山川（今主峰海拔 1048 米的凤凰山延脉），道途艰险难行。至宋室南渡，宁德户籍人口大量增加，经济、文化进一步发展，原本崎岖难行的"南路二路"，已阻碍了官府政令的颁布实施、文化教育的传播和商品经济的流通。

左　图：从白鹤岭古道望去，蕉城区尽收眼底　朱晨辉 摄

右上图：民国时期的著名历史人物许世英在白鹤岭古官道上留下了"白鹤"二字　朱晨辉 摄

右下图：白鹤岭古道对当时经济贸易、文化交流都起到了积极的作用，历代文人墨客、达官贵人在这条古官道上留下诗篇和题刻，这是清乾隆范宜恒题书"仰观俯察"　朱晨辉 摄

The left picture: Looking from the ancient Baiheling Road, it has a panoramic view of Jiaocheng District. Photographed by Zhu Chenhui

The upper right picture: Xu Shiying, a famous historical figure in the period of "Republic of China", left the word "White Crane" on the ancient official road of Baihe Ridge. Photographed by Zhu Chenhui

The lower right picture: The ancient Baiheling Road played a positive role in the economic, trade and cultural exchanges at that time. Literati and dignitaries of all ages left poems and inscriptions on this ancient road. This is the inscription "Yang Guan Fu Cha" inscribed by Fan Yiheng of the Qianlong regin in the Qing Dynasty. Photographed by Zhu Chenhui

白鹤岭古道是古代宁德通衢南北的重要陆路通道，也是福温古道的重要组成部分 朱晨辉 摄

Baiheling ancient road is an important land route between the north and south of Ningde thoroughfare in ancient times, which is also an important part of Fuwen ancient road. Photographed by Zhu Chenhui

南宋宝庆年间（1225~1227），为顺应民众需求，时任宁德县主簿丁大全经实地勘察，决定废“南路二道”，开辟新的通往省城福州路途较近、较为平缓的道路。经过二三年的辛勤劳作，终于在“石壁峭削，上连烟霄”的白鹤山间铺设出一条二十里长的驿道。白鹤岭道开凿工程浩大，尤其是铺设岭头隘门的白鹤岭一段，其工程之艰险至今令人难以想象。白鹤岭古道以险峻、秀丽著称，历经千年沧桑，大部分仍完整保存于（在）宁德城西“悬崖峭壁，架阁如削”“秀拔千仞，形如翔鹤”的白鹤山中。

石壁岭官道则是古代宁德县城通往西乡（洋中、石后、虎贝的统称）以及古田、屏南、上府（闽北地区）等地的咽喉要道。据乾隆《宁德县志》记载，这条路的起点始于金涵，离城六十里与古田县交界，离城一百四十里与屏南交界。

上　图：石壁岭沿途山峰险峻，风光独特　朱晨辉 摄
左下图：石壁岭古道上的“山高水长”摩崖石刻　黄景业 摄
中下图：石壁岭古道岭路崎岖，行走不便，只有户外行旅者到此　黄景业 摄
右下图：石壁岭古道岭道崎岖，路途艰难　朱晨辉 摄

The upper picture: The way along Shibi Ridge has steep peaks and unique scenery. Photographed by Zhu Chenhui

The lower left picture: The cliff stone carving "High Mountains and Long Rivers" on Shibiling Ancient Road. Photographed by Huang Jingye

The lower middle picture: The road of Shibi Ridge Ancient is rugged and inconvenient to walk. Only outdoor travelers can come here. Photographed by Huang Jingye

The lower right picture: The road of Shibi Ridge Ancient is rugged and difficult. Photographed by Zhu Chenhui

石壁岭以其山体如石壁般笔直陡峭而得名。明嘉靖十七年版《宁德县志》载："石壁岭，在四都。与石钟山相连，上有石壁峭拔，盖岭之最高者也。"清康熙之前，石壁岭陡峭的山壁之上，仅有羊肠小道，行人至此步步难行，需手足并用方可攀爬而上。

石壁岭官道的开辟时间史无稽考，最迟应不晚于南宋时期。官道沿途山峰险峻，古木荫翳，风光独特。明进士林保童途经此处，惊叹岭道险峻，有诗曰："绝壁藤萝绕，行人上下攀。欠身苏力倦，举目使心酸。谁信闽山险，无殊蜀道难。始知平地上，步步得身安。"嘉靖四年（1525），王阳明的学生聂豹任福建道监察御史，过岭亦留有《度石壁岭喜晴》七律一首："孤骢岁晚按遐方，萍梗年来只异乡。仆马饱淹山雨滑，巾袍偏湿野云香。缘江春意先桃柳，隔水禽言问瑟簧。一道晴风开霁色，阴霾何处更茫茫。"

清康熙四十五年（1706），邑人王天行苦于"岭道崎岖，不便通行，劝募垦辟"，采用火烧水攻之法，利用热胀冷缩的原理烧裂石壁，"遂成通途"。他还在岭道两旁栽种树木，以荫行人。今岭头余有一株柳杉，树龄在300年以上。

左 图：石壁岭古道的残存遗迹 黄景业 摄
右 图：旧时的石壁岭古道清晰可见 朱晨辉 摄

The left picture: The remains of Shibiling ancient road. Photographed by Huang Jingye

The right picture: The old Shibiling ancient road is clearly visible. Photographed by Zhu Chenhui

BAIHESTONE WALL

Ningde is covered with mountains, and its land transportation was very inconvenient in ancient times. Before the opening of Baiheling Ancient Post Road inNingde, the main passage from Ningde to Fuzhou, the provincial capital, was two roads to the south, one of which was relatively flat but the distance was very long,the other one is very dangerous.

The inconvenience of transportation seriously restricted the economic and cultural development at that time and was not conducive to the government's management. During the Southern Song Dynasty, the government opened up the ancient official avenue of Baiheling.

Baiheling Ancient Road can enter Zhejiang from the north to Fuding Fenshui Pass, and can reach Fuzhou through Luoyuan in the south. It is an important land route from ancient Ningde to the north and south, and is also an important part of Fuwen Ancient Road.

Shibiling official avenue is the key junction from ancient Ningde County to Xixiang (collectively referred to as Yangzhong, Shihou and Hubei) and Gutian, Pingnan and Shangfu (northern Fujian). The starting point of this road starts from Jinhan, 60 miles from the county town to the border with Gutian County and 140 miles from the county town to the border with Pingnan.

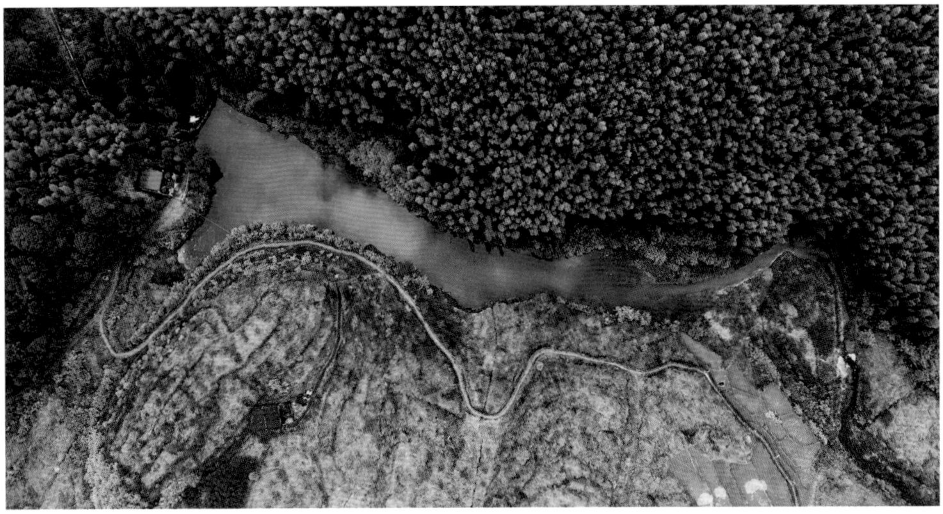

大北岭道

据清《连江县志》，宋嘉祐三年（1058）怀安知县樊纪募造大北岭道。自福州井楼门向北经大北岭关寨至连江境内，经贵安、潘渡、陀市、朱公、丹阳等地进入罗源、闽东。古驿道宽 0.8~1.8 米，多用乱石铺设。

贵安位于连江西北角，与福州仅一山之隔，这里山峦叠嶂，溪水潺潺，温泉丰沛，风光迷人。从福州宦溪镇的降虎寨东寨门出，有一条蜿蜒于山间的下山古道，就是汤岭古驿道。据连江民国版县志记载："汤岭，一名云岭，赴省大路。旧属光临里。清光绪间，郑存里砌修，自茶亭至西溪桥上"。它联结福州至连江贵安的通道，全长五公里。

降虎寨，又名云漈关，在北峰宦溪乡降虎岭上。相传有一虎中药箭至岭上独觉庵前，若有所诉。僧法诠为其去镞，抚摩。虎去，数日痊愈，复来，遂相随，因以名。降虎寨地势十分险要，处于隘口之上，为古时福州北面的重要门户。山寨至迟建于明代，明王应山《闽都记》载："降虎岭有寨，置戍。"明嘉靖年间，戚继光曾率兵破寨，消灭了盘踞寨中的倭寇（一说此寨为戚继光所建）。

降虎寨的寨墙遗址犹存，前后两寨门至今仍屹立。面向连江的前寨门气势雄伟，古朴壮观。门系方石砌造，拱形，高 2.85 米，宽 1.92 米，厚 1.73 米；上有寨楼，已毁。后寨门为石构，高 2.47 米，宽 2.85 米，厚 1.17 米。前后寨门相距近百米，古道穿寨而过。降虎桥位处降虎村降虎寨前古驿道上，距降虎寨约 1000 米，双孔石梁，桥身东西走向，长 2.66 米，宽 1.23 米。桥面有"绍兴四年（1134）"题刻。

The upper picture: Dabeiling Road is located in the southeast of Xiangfeng Village, Wusi North Xiufeng Road, Xindian Town, which is a major passage connecting ancient Fuzhou to the mainland in the north and is relatively well preserved. Photographed by Yang Xin

The lower left picture: The post station on Dabei Ridge. Photographed by Yang Xin

The lower middle picture: Zhuangyuan Ridge is called Dabei Ridge in history. The starting point of the ancient road is Xiangfeng Village, Xindian Town, Fuzhou. Photographed by Yang Xin

The lower right picture:The Ancient Dabeiling Road in the sunset. Photographed by Yang Xin

上　图：大北岭道位于新店镇五四北秀峰路象峰村东南侧，是古代福州北向与内地连接的大通道，保存较为完整　杨欣 摄
左下图：大北岭上的驿站　杨欣 摄
中下图：状元岭史称大北岭，古道的起点在福州新店镇象峰村　杨欣 摄
右下图：夕阳下的大北岭古道　杨欣 摄

上　图：如今这条宋代古驿道与森林公园融为一体，成为市民休闲的怀古之路　朱晨辉 摄

左下图：福州森林公园内的宋代古驿道，古人晋京应试的脚步从这里开始　朱晨辉 摄

右下图：位于福州市森林公园内的宋古驿道　黄景业 摄

The upper picture: Today, this ancient post road in the Song Dynasty is integrated with the forest park and has become a road for citizens to meditate on the past for leisure. Photographed by Zhu Chenhui

The lower left picture: The ancient post road of the Song Dynasty in Fuzhou Forest Park started from here when the ancients went to the capital for examination. Photographed by Zhu Chenhui

The lower right picture: Songgu Post Road located in Fuzhou Forest Park. Photographed by Huang Jingye

牛山蹬道位处鼓山镇，牛山村和牛山顶飞炉庙之间一块长宽各 90 多米的巨石上，南北向，共凿蹬道计79级，长94米，宽1.1米左右。每级高0.06~0.15米，进深 0.35~3 米。山顶石门边有摩崖石刻记载：政和乙未年（1115）邑人萧邻为“使舩（船）海道并父母乞保平安，各延景福”而“开此石阶一条”。

沿着这条古驿道，可直达福州的北岭 朱晨辉 摄
Along this ancient post road, you can reach Beiling in Fuzhou directly. Photographed by Zhu Chenhui

Dabeiling Road

In the third year of the Jiayou period in Song Dynasty (1058), the government built Dabeiling Road. From Jinglou Gate in Fuzhou to Lianjiang via the pass camp of Dabeilingto the north, it enters Luoyuan and eastern Fujian via Gui'an, Pandu, Tuoshi, Zhugong and Danyang.

Guian is located in the northwest corner of Lianjiang River, separated from Fuzhou by a mountain, which is rich in forest and hot spring resources and has charming scenery. From the east gate of Jianghu Village in Huanxi Town, Fuzhou, you can go to Guian Village at the foot of the mountain along Tangling Ancient Post Road. Tangling Ancient Post Road is a small section of Fuzhou North Post Road, connecting Fuzhou to Guian in Lianjiang County, with a total length of 5 kilometers.

Dabeiling Road is located on the southeast side of Xiangfeng Village, Wusi North Xiufeng Road, Xindian Town, Fuzhou, which is a major passage connecting ancient Fuzhou to the mainland in the north and is relatively well preserved. Jianghu Village, also known as Yunji Pass, is located on Jianghu Ridge in Huanxi Township, Beifeng, near the border of Lianjiang County.

The site of the village wall of Jianghu Village remains to this day, and the front and rear gates of the village still stand erect in Jianghu Ridge. Facing Lianjiang, the front village gate is majestic and spectacular. The front and rear village gates are nearly 100 meters apart.

夕阳下的大北岭古道　赖小兵 摄

Dabeiling Ancient Road under the light of the sunset. Photographed by Lai Xiaobing

第三章

Chapter III

关隘寨亭 驿馆铺塘

PASSES AND VILLAGES
POSTHOUSES AND SHOPS

仙霞古道枫岭关关隘
赖小兵 摄
Fengling Pass on Xianxia Ancient Road. Photographed by Lai Xiaobing

在各处交通线上，除了关隘与驿站铺递，还有更多以官办或官倡民助、民办等方式陆续建成的路亭、桥梁、渡口等配套设施，为漫漫古道增添了动人风情，也记录了过往行旅的故事冷暖。

据民国版《福建通志》总卷十一之《邮驿传》记载，宋代的邮驿制度“凡铺有马递，有步递、有急递、有供申、有节级，有铺兵等若干人。又或设曹司、添厢军。随时随地增减不一也。”对铺兵、铺马则规定：“元丰六年（1083）……令每铺以十五人为额，内二名充急脚。皇祐元年（1049），减罢急脚兵士，改作马铺，剩数拨填厢军。……嘉祐二年（1057），知建州薛绾奏急脚兵士传送递角使命，经过州县，临时借马于人户，不无骚扰，乞每铺量置马匹，复罢急脚。”于是马递铺自行设置马匹，不再骚扰人户。

两宋时，福建全路设有44驿，以福州为总枢纽，分南、北、西3路：南通粤，北通浙，西北通浙赣。出福州南门，经兴化、泉州、漳州共18驿，而达广东；出福州北门，经闽东，共12驿，而至浙江温州；出福州西门，取南剑州、建州，共14驿，而通浙赣。上列3线驿站，有明确记载的只有古田水口至福州及邵武樵川两处是水驿，而驿路经过的渡口则有6处。这说明了两宋时，福建的水驿，仅是陆驿的补充。

元代仿照宋制，为“通达边情，布宣号令”，按10里、15里或25里的间距设急递铺，专司传递朝廷及郡邑往来文书。铺设铺长，有铺兵5名。元代福州路共设6个驿、18个铺和2个站。元代邮驿制度，主要有以下各点规定：元代驿传称为站赤，陆路用马、牛、驴，或用车；水路则用船。驿传隶属于通政院及中书兵部。

据《福建通志》：“（洪武二十六年）凡马驿设置马、骡不等；如冲要的地方设马八十匹、六十匹或三十匹；其余虽非冲要，亦系经行道路，则设马二十匹、十匹或五匹。凡水驿设船不等，如使客行正路，设船二十只、十五只或十只；其分行偏路，亦设船七只、五只。一般每船设水夫十名。凡递运所设置船只、水夫不等。急递铺，凡十里设一铺，每铺设铺长一名，铺兵要路十名，偏路五名或四名。每铺设十二时区晷一个，以验时刻。铺门前设置牌门一座，牌额齐全。常明灯烛一副，簿历二本。铺兵每名合置夹板一副，铃攀一副，缨枪一把，棍一根，回历一本。凡递送公文依照古法，一昼夜通一百刻，每三刻行一铺，昼夜须行三百里。但遇公文到铺，不问角数多少，须要随即递送，不分昼夜，鸣铃走递至前铺交收，于回历附写到铺时刻，以凭稽考。”

清代驿传掌于兵部，各地驿铺隶属于州县。驿设赡夫、递夫和兜夫，铺设铺兵。驿铺夫兵配置名额根据业务繁简有所不同。如驿一般配有赡夫五至一百十五人，递夫二至十四人，兜夫三至四十四人。次要的驿，只配赡夫六至四十人和递夫二至四人。个别驿只配兜夫十五人。全省配有板船与水手的只有三个驿，浦城小关驿，配赡夫一百零五人、递夫十二人，兜夫四十五人，板船八只，水手四十八人；古田水口驿配赡夫七十五人、递夫八人、兜夫四十人，板船四只，水手二十四人；侯官芋源驿配赡夫七十人、递夫十二人、兜夫三十人，板船六只，水手三十六人。至于铺则有府前铺、县前铺、州前铺之别，因其大小，配备的夫兵名额有所差别，自二至十人不等。

云际关是闽浙两省的重要关隘，地势险要。云际关西南属福建光泽县司前乡云际村；东北属江西的铅山县天柱山乡佛寨村 吴军 摄

Yunji Pass is an important pass in Fujian and Zhejiang provinces, with dangerous terrain. The southwest of Yunjiguan belongs to Yunji Village, Siqian Township, Guangze County, Fujian Province, and belongs to Fozhai Village, Tianzhushan Township, Qianshan County, Jiangxi Province in the northeast. Photographed by Wu Jun

In addition to passes and post stations, there are more road pavilions, bridges, ferries and other facilities built in succession by government or private means.

During the northern and southern Song dynasties, the whole road in Fujian had 44 post stations, with Fuzhou as the main hub, divided into three routes: access to Guangzhou in the south, access to Zhejiang in the north, access to Zhejiang and Jiangxi in the northeast. After leaving the south gate of Fuzhou and passing through 18 post stations in Xinghua, Quanzhou and Zhangzhou, thus arrive in Guangdong; After leaving the north gate of Fuzhou and passing through a total of 12 post stations in eastern Fujian,thus arrive in Wenzhou, Zhejiang; After leaving the west gate of Fuzhou and passing through a total of 14 post stations in Nanjianzhou and Jianzhou, they arrived at the junction of Zhejiang and Jiangxi. Of the above three post roads, only two were clearly recorded as water post roads, but there were six ferries through which the post roads pass. This shows that Fujian Water Post Roadin the northern and southern Song dynasties was only a supplement to land post roads.

The Yuan Dynasty imitated the system of the Song Dynasty and set up emergency posts in ancient times at intervals of 10, 15 or 25 miles, which were specially used to transfer documents between the imperial court and the counties and cities.

The postal delivery system in Qing Dynasty was under the management of the Ministry of War, while delivery stations in various places were under the management of states and counties. There aresuppliers, postmen, sedan bearers and soldiers in charge of delivering emergency documents in the delivery station. According to the records in *The chorography of Fujian*, the number of soldiers allocated in the post shop varies according to the complexity and simplicity of the business. There are only three post stations in the province equipped with board boats and sailors.

关隘寨堡，据险以设

清光绪年《邵武府志》云："言险要则有关隘，言声援则有驿递，言守御之法则寇警有备也，言巡察之方则保甲宜先也。"

为增强管控，官府在各处重要边界及道路沿线修筑有关、隘、寨、堡等。关、隘一般设置在道路所经的省、县分界的险要之处，是为了扼守大、小通道而设立的检查与守御设施。大口为关，小口为隘，均据险而设。其两翼筑墙或筑城以资坚固，当路设门，按时启闭，以司查验。关隘皆有驻兵，但驻关的守军要远远多于守隘的官兵，战时为军，平时担负检查与征收货税之责。与之相比，寨属于相对单纯的军事单位。寨、堡据险以守，但多数不在省、县分界处，而是设置在交通要道沿线或战略守备要地的附近。有的寨内设有巡检司，肩负管理职责；有的仅为战时的临时设置，接近于屯兵或驻军。如明嘉靖《清流县志·兵制》："磊石为寨，聚骁勇保守县境，寇不敢犯"，或临时"筑之，为民备寇"。

据《福建通志》记载，全省境内共设有89关、376隘、158寨，其中，仅与浙江、江西、广东三省交界的福鼎、柘荣、福安、寿宁、松溪、政和、浦城、崇安、光泽、邵武、泰宁、建宁、宁化、长汀、武平、上杭、永定、平和、诏安等19个县境，设置的关隘寨即达370座之多。从分布上看，大关主要位于西北方向官马大道的出省边界；通往西面江西的道路通行量较少，边界线上多数只是设置隘口；西南、中南方向道路错综复杂，所以多数设立寨堡以司巡查；东南路临海，沿途人口众多，卫所力量强大，因此只在省界以及平原进入山区的要道处设立关隘，路途以驿铺管理为主；东北路道路崎岖险峻而警汛尤多，因此关隘沿道路层层分设，防范最为紧密。

左上图：建宁县茱萸隘，关隘上的石碑记载 吴军 摄

左下图：邵武黄土关为古代闽赣界关，自古就是八闽重要军事要塞，又是古代闽赣两地重要的陆路商贸通道，东连邵武、南平、福州，西接黎川、南城，通过水路下赣江、入鄱阳湖、通达长江，是闽赣贸易的大动脉 阮任艺 摄

右 图：地处闽赣两省交界处山鞍部的建宁县茱萸隘，现还保存着一座石砌风雨亭，古道穿亭而过，亭外一侧立有闽赣两省界碑 吴军 摄

The upper left picture: Records of the stone tablet on Zhuyu Pass in Jianning County. Photographed by Wu Jun

The lower left picture: Huangtu Pass in Shaowu is the border between Fujian and Jiangxi in ancient times which has been an important military fortress in Fujian since ancient times. It is also an important land trade channel between Fujian and Jiangxi in ancient times, which connects Shaowu, Nanping and Fuzhou in the east, Lichuan and Nancheng in the west, goes down the Ganjiang River into Boyang Lake, thus reaches the Yangtze River by water. It is the major artery of Fujian and Jiangxi trade. Photographed by Ruan Renyi

The right picture: Zhuyu Pass in Jianning County, located at the mountain saddle of the junction of Fujian and Jiangxi provinces, still has a stone wind and rain pavilion. The ancient road passes through the pavilion, and the boundary monument of Fujian and Jiangxi provinces are erected on one side outside the pavilion. Photographed by Wu Jun

光泽杉关

光泽县西九十里，有杉关岭，置关其上，为江闽往来之通道。

杉关始建于唐广明元年（880），于垭口垒石为关，两侧山脊筑城墙。历代朝廷倚之为“天险可凭，有恃无恐”，频繁调兵遣将加防镇守。如宋韩世忠、元王溥等都奉命率部守关，明太祖朱元璋派遣征南将军胡廷瑞，亦由陆路督师入杉关而定闽中。明洪武三年（1370）又于山脊筑城垣，屏障闽赣之边界。明清之交的南明隆武二年亦即清顺治三年（1646），郑成功提出“据险控扼”等条陈，奉命进守光泽的杉关等关隘，以阻清军进逼。

Shanguan Pass in Guangze

Shanguan Ridge is located 90 miles west of Guangze County, which is the passage between Jiangxi and Fujian. The total length of Shanguan Pass preserved so far is 674.9 meters. Shanguan Pass was built in the 880th year of the Tang Dynasty, which is built with stones at the mountain pass, with city walls built on both sides of the ridge.

郑成功

（1624~1662），又名福松，字明俨、大木，福建泉州南安人，明末清初军事家，民族英雄。因蒙永历帝封延平王，称『郑延平』。

明隆武二年（1646）清军南下踞赣袭闽，明隆武帝驻跸延平，22岁的郑成功临危受命，亲自率师扼守杉关、铁牛关等隘口，阻拒由江西方向奔袭的清军。

Zheng Chenggong

(1624-1662), also known as Fusong, styled himself Mingyan, born in Nanan, Quanzhou, Fujian Province, was a military strategist and national hero in Late Ming and Early Qing Dynasties. Because he was named King Yanping by Emperor Yongli, he was called "Zheng Yanping".

In the second year of Longwu reign of the Ming dynasty (1646), the Qing army was stationed in Jiangxi and attacked Fujian. Emperor Longwu of the Ming Dynasty was stationed in Yanping. Zheng Chenggong, at the age of 22, was ordered to personally lead his troops to guard the passes such as Shanguan and Tieniu Pass in the face of danger to resist the Qing army rushing from Jiangxi.

郑成功

（1624~1662），又名福松，字明俨，大木，福建泉州南安人，明末清初军事家，民族英雄。因蒙永历帝封延平王，称「郑延平」。

明隆武二年（1646）清军南下据赣攻闽，明隆武帝驻跸延平，22岁的郑成功临危受命，亲自率师扼守杉关、铁牛关等隘口，阻拒由江西方向奔袭的清军。

Zheng Chenggong

(1624-1662), also known as Fusong, styled himself Mingyan, born in Nanan, Quanzhou, Fujian Province, was a military strategist and national hero in Late Ming and Early Qing Dynasties. Because he was named King Yanping by Emperor Yongli, he was called "Zheng Yanping".

In the second year of Longwu reign of the Ming dynasty (1646), the Qing army was stationed in Jiangxi and attacked Fujian. Emperor Longwu of the Ming Dynasty was stationed in Yanping. Zheng Chenggong, at the age of 22, was ordered to personally lead his troops to guard the passes such as Shanguan and Tieniu Pass in the face of danger to resist the Qing army rushing from Jiangxi.

The upper picture:Guangze County is located in the northwest of Fujian Province, in the upper reaches of Futun Creek in the Minjiang River. In the northern section of Wuyishan Mountains, mountains are continuous and mountains are high and valleys are deep. There is a saying that "The beach is ten feet high and Guangze is in the sky." Photographed by Ruan Renyi and Chen Yinghui

The lower picture: Today's Shanguan is still the main transportation route between Fujian and Jiangxi provinces, through which the famous Yangshan Highway and Liguang Highway pass. Photographed by Wu Jun

上　图：光泽县位于福建省西北部，闽江富屯溪上游，武夷山脉北段境内群山连绵，山高谷深，有“一滩高一丈，光泽在天上”之说　阮任艺 陈映辉 摄

下　图：今天的杉关，仍是闽赣两省的交通要道，著名的阳杉公路和黎光公路都通过这里　吴军 摄

上　图：立于光泽县境四面高山险道上的“九关十三隘”是八闽一绝，闻名遐迩，其中衫关最为著名。图为杉关遗留的石刻　崔建楠 摄

左下图：杉关经历了无数战火硝烟，记录着历史的变迁　沈少华 摄

右下图：1934 年修建的闽赣公路从杉关贯穿而过　吴军 摄

The upper picture: The "Nine Passes and Thirteen Passes", which stands on the high mountains and dangerous roads around Guangze County, is a unique skill in Fujian and is well known, of which Shirt Pass is the most famous. The picture shows stone carvings left over from Shanguan Pass. Photographed by Cui Jiannan

The lower left picture: Shanguan Pass has experienced numerous wars, recording historical changes. Photographed by Shen Shaohua

The lower right picture: The Fujian-Jiangxi highway built in 1934 runs through Shanguan Pass. Photographed by Wu Jun

杉关于元朝始置驿站，明设大寺寨巡检司。1956 年，因修筑鹰厦铁路装运大型机械之需要，拆除了关门两侧的部分关墙，但两翼城堞尚存。关门左墙上嵌乾隆己丑年“闽西第一关”石碑，右墙上嵌民国二十九年“杉关”石碑。保存至今的杉关总长达 674.9 米，宛如两条长龙蜿蜒伸展在隘口两侧山脊之上，夹峙关口，雄视闽赣！

杉关的南、北两侧城墙沿山脊蜿蜒而上，直插山峰顶部。北侧城墙在接近古道一侧沿山势做明显的弧形前凸，其目的是为了有效抵御进犯之敌对关门的侵犯。该处前凸式城墙高逾 6 米，内侧还有较为开阔的屯兵营地等。由该处城墙往北，城墙基本沿山脊而建，高度在 3~5 米之间，外侧女墙及内侧跑马道等大部保存完好。南侧城墙沿陡峭之山脊层叠而上，因山体极为陡峻，故城墙为迭落式构造，外侧女墙及内侧跑马道、上下蹬道等基本完整，城墙高度多在 5 米以上。

城墙向江西一侧筑有较为低矮的女墙，墙上开设多处射击孔。射击孔用石块垒砌，外小内大，基本是每间隔 2 米就有一处。城墙的内侧，分布有多处的圆形窝铺。窝铺是当时驻守杉关士兵的居住、休息场所，平时用作堆放军需武器，因此又称为“兵房”。杉关的窝铺面积较小，兼作登高瞭望的哨所，驻有哨兵做四时之警戒；如遇警讯，可以烟火等方式示警，故又兼具烽火台之作用。当地百姓以其地势高险，将其统称作“炮台”。

据现场勘察，杉关北侧建有三处窝铺，其中一处在中段城墙的内侧，另两处在城墙以北的高处峰顶；杉关南侧建有四处窝铺，除一处在中段城墙的内侧外，其余三处均分布在由低向高的几处峰顶。

窝铺外围均有壕沟相连，山顶的壕沟有的挖成环形，占据极好的位置，视野开阔，防御性极强。壕沟上宽下窄，宽度在 1.25~0.75 米之间，深度多数不足 1 米。

浦城毕岭关

毕岭关位于浦城县忠信镇村桥村与官路乡李处村之间的垭口，始建于明代。关上建有关城，内建毕峰亭和毕岭寺。东西关墙相距约 30 米，各自开门，为古道必经之处，东通忠信，西往官路，关门青石砌成，顶为半圆拱状。毕峰亭建于清乾隆三十一年（1766），保存完整。关内毕岭寺的脊檩下皮有墨书“大清乾隆叁拾壹年岁次丙戌孟冬月吉鼎兴建立”，上金檩墨书“钦赐文林郎知浦县事正常加三级记录三次”，毕峰亭南墙也嵌有当时捐造人的姓名及捐资数额的砖刻一方，显示出毕岭关及毕岭古道官民共建的历史事实。古道石阶保存完好，宽约 1.7~2 米，进深约 0.4~1 米。

Biling Pass in Pucheng

Biling Pass is located between Cunqiao Village of Zhongxin Town and Guanlu Lichu Village of Guanlu Township in Pucheng County, which was founded in Ming Dynasty. Close the construction of the relevant city, built in Bifeng Pavilion and Biling Temple. Where the ancient road must pass, it leads to loyalty in the east and official road in the west. The door is built of bluestone with a semi-circular arch top.

左　图：毕岭关上的毕峰亭　吴军　摄

右　图：毕岭寺内几多旅人祈愿路途平安　吴军　摄

The left picture: Bifeng Pavilion on the Biling Pass. Photographed by Wu Jun

The right picture: Many travelers in Biling Temple pray for a safe journey. Photographed by Wu Jun

左上图：毕岭关是福建浦城与浙江江山的界关之一 楼建龙 摄

右上图：横亘于闽浙两省之间的浦城县忠信镇福清山柘岭古道，山高险峻，早在隋朝以前，就是中原地区联系福建的主要通道，唐末黄巢义军在仙霞岭劈开山路七百里，从浙江突入福建。此后，仙霞岭古道成为入闽的主要通道，福清山柘岭古道自此衰落 吴军 摄

下 图：毕岭关是古道的必经之处 吴军 摄

The upper left picture: Biling Pass is one of the boundary pass between Pucheng in Fujian and Jiangshan in Zhejiang. Photographed by Lou Jianlong

The upper right picture: Zheling Ancient Road in Fuqing Mountain, Zhongxin Town, Pucheng County, which lies between Fujian and Zhejiang provinces, was the main channel connecting the Central Plains with Fujian as early as before the Sui Dynasty. At the end of the Tang Dynasty, the Huang Chao Rebel Army split the mountain road 700 miles in Xianxia Ridge and broke into Fujian from Zhejiang. Since then, Xianxialing Ancient Road has become the main passage into Fujian, and Zheling Ancient Road in Fuqing Mountain has declined since then. Photographed by Wu Jun

The lower picture: Biling Pass is the only place to pass through the ancient road. Photographed by Wu Jun

建宁卷亭隘

位于客坊乡湾坊村，古道由东向西从隘亭中间穿行而过，是当时通往江西的主要道路。石卷亭始建于清康熙四十四年(1705)，呈半圆拱形，通高3.8米，通面阔3.5米，通进深4.8米，石门宽1.6米，高2.43米，内拱顶至地面高2.95米，东西两侧石门上方阴刻亭名，亭内有从石墙上脱落的石碑。亭北10米处，有国务院1997年设立的闽赣两省分界石碑。

卷亭隘也叫风雨隘，峭壁巉岩，路若悬梯，上砌石亭，又名三祝亭，通广昌要冲。石门上方阴刻亭名的字迹虽然模糊，经拓片，还是可以看出“三祝亭”几个字的痕迹。由此证实，湾坊村的“石卷亭”就是“三祝亭”，“卷亭隘”就是“风雨隘”。

Juanting Pass in Jianning

Juanting Pass is also called FengyuPass, with a stone pavilion built on it, which is also called Sanzhu Pavilion. Located in Wanfang Village, Kefang Township, the ancient road passed through the middle of the pavilion from east to west and was the main road leading to Jiangxi at that time.

卷亭隘的垭口上有一石亭，当地人称石卷亭 吴军 摄

There is a stone pavilion on the pass of Juanting Pass, which is called Shijuan Pavilion by local people. Photographed by Wu Jun

左上图：卷亭隘的古道保存尚好，古道两边少有茅草和灌木 吴军 摄

右上图：从古道上回望湾坊村，千亩梯田依山就势盘旋于群山沟壑之间 吴军 摄

左下图：通往卷亭隘的驿道是闽赣的通道之一 吴军 摄

右下图：300 多年的卷亭隘虽历经风雨，但依然完整 吴军 摄

The upper left picture: The ancient road of Juanting Pass is well preserved, and there are few thatches and shrubs on both sides of the ancient road. Photographed by Wu Jun

The upper right picture: Looking back at Wanfang Village from the ancient road, thousands of terraced fields circled between the mountains and ravines. Photographed by Wu Jun

The lower left picture: The post road leading to Juanting Pass is one of the passages between Fujian and Jiangxi. Photographed by Wu Jun

The lower right picture: Although the 300-year-old Juanting Pass has gone through wind and rain, it is still complete. Photographed by Wu Jun

建瓯曹岩堡

建瓯历为郡、州、府、都、路、道治所，是闽北的政治、经济与文化中心，古道较多。县际主驿道分向而往，其东往政和浦湾，西至建阳黄口，南至南平大横，北达浦城南岸，东南至古田筹岭顶，西南至顺昌白岸，东北至松溪西溪，西北至建阳由源。清代十里一铺，四十里一驿，在县内设有叶坊、城西、太平三处驿站，其中西向由叶坊达中横，与建阳接；南向由太平达大横，与南平连接。

曹岩古堡位于房道镇曹岩村西北侧约 1 公里的龙门山上。堡墙南北横跨山谷走向，门呈拱单孔石砌，上以土夯建山墙，开三扇窗门，古堡上宽下窄，分上下两层，一楼为通道，二楼为城楼。龙门四周群山环绕，堡前古道自拱门由南向北通往曹岩村。

左　图：建瓯房道镇曹岩村堡门　吴军 摄

右　图：建瓯房道镇曹岩村古驿道，通过龙门——西门（清朝时期有东西南北四个城门）可进入曹岩村　吴军 摄

The left picture: The castle gate, Caoyan Village, Fangdao Town, Jian'ou. Photographed by Wu Jun

The right picture: The ancient post road of Caoyan Village, Fangdao Town, Jian'ou, can enter Caoyan Village through Longmen- West gate (there were four gates in the east, west, north and south during the Qing Dynasty). Photographed by Wu Jun

Caoyan Fortress in Jian'ou

Jian'ou is the political, economic and cultural center in northern Fujian, with many ancient roads. In the Qing Dynasty, there was one shop every ten milesand one post station every forty miles. There were three post stations in the county: Yefang, Chengxi and Taiping.

Caoyan Ancient Fortress is located on Longmen Mountain, about 1km northwest of Caoyan Village in Fangdao Town. The fortress is divided into upper and lower floors, the first floor is the passage and the second floor is the gate tower. The ancient road in front of the fortress leads from south to north from the arch to Caoyan Village.

延平岩头堡

南平地处八闽喉襟，是闽中大谷地的最低处，也是闽江上游建溪、沙溪、富屯溪的汇合处，四周峰峦环绕，丘陵蜿蜒。历史上，南平曾是州、军、路、道、府所在地，为“八闽锁钥之处”，有“铜南平，铁邵武，豆腐建宁府，纸糊福州城”之说。

南平地处交通要冲，溯西溪而上可达杉关，为赣东孔道；沿东溪北上可抵仙霞岭，为入浙要冲。双溪蜿蜒各数百里，至南平汇集成闽江，顺流直通省会福州。唐元和二年（807）福建观察使陆庶修官路由福州至南平，宋天圣二年（1024）剑州郡守刘滋开凿黯淡滩航道，使南平成为“舟车辐辏，物阜人彩，省门以北，无与为比”的内陆港埠，商旅日见繁盛。

三千八百坎位于茫荡镇筠竹村南1公里处，属赣闽古道。因古道北侧为金山，南侧为银山，故有传说，称“三千八百坎，坎坎出黄金”；西侧有一条小溪，从山顶流向山下的筠竹村。

岩头堡址位于三千八佰坎终点的山顶处，平面呈椭圆形，占地面积约1000平方米。堡墙以鹅卵石垒筑，长37米，宽2.5米，高约5.2米。开有东、西拱门。东门高3.23米，宽2.46米，进深1.5米；西门高2.53米，宽2.01米，进深1.7米。

岩头堡往下约300坎处，在古道之旁立有一块萨镇冰题刻石碑，石碑高1.8米，宽0.8米，厚0.12米。石碑上竖刻楷书3行，中部大字为“义声载道”。两侧小字左侧为：中华民国十七年十二月 萨镇冰题。右侧为：王善士堂选捐金修路劳费不辞颂德者遍道左爰为勤石以志不朽。

上　图：三千八百坎旧制图

下　图：古道旁的“义声载道”碑为曾任福建省省长得萨镇冰所题　楼建龙 摄

The upper picture: Old drawing of three thousand eight hundred holes

The lower picture: The monument "Yi Sheng Zai Dao" beside the ancient road was inscribed by De Sabing, a former governor of Fujian Province. Photographed by Lou Jianlong

YANTOU FORTRESSIN YANPING

Nanping is the lowest place in the Great Valley in central Fujian and the confluence of JianxiCreek, ShaxiCreek and Futun Creek in the upper reaches of Minjiang River. In history, Nanping was once the seat of the state, the army, the road, the avenue and the prefecture, and was "the strategic gateway of the ancient Fujian".

3800 Ridge is located 1 kilometer south of Yunzhu Village in Mangdang Town, connecting Jiangxi and Fujian. Yantou Fortress is located at the top of the mountain at the end of 3800 Ridge.

左上图：遗存至今的三千八百坎古堡 赖小兵 摄

右上图：瑞龙桥是茫荡山古廊桥群的代表，1646 年郑成功率部往杉关守关，多次经过该桥 赖小兵 摄

下 图：三千八百坎云海

The upper left picture: The Castle of three thousand eight hundred holes remains to date. Photographed by Lai Xiaobing

The upper right picture: Ruilong Bridge is the representative of the ancient covered bridges in Mangdang Mountain. In 1646, Zheng Chenggong went to Shanguan Pass to guard the bridge and passed it many times. Photographed by Lai Xiaobing

The lower picture: The seas of clouds of three thousand eight hundred holes

福鼎分水关

福鼎分水关蜿蜒于片山、五老山之间的山坡上，山上有泉水分流于南北两坡，分别注入福鼎河和苍南的横阳支江，故称分水。分水山属浙南雁荡山支脉，西自浙江泰顺来，东北跨浙江苍南，东南跨福建福鼎，东连松山。

分水关作为闽浙分界线，是两省客旅的中转站。历史上，许多文人慨叹分水关之地理、环境和历史，吟诗以抒惜别、思乡、感世之情，这是分水关人文的重要体现。北宋元祐进士、浙江瑞安人许景衡《分水关》诗曰：“再岁闽中多险阻，却寻归路思悠哉。三江九岭都行尽，平水松山人望来。”南宋绍兴进士、莆田人黄公度《分水岭》诗曰：“鸣咽泉流万仞峰，断肠从此各西东。谁知不作多时别，依旧相逢沧海中。”清学者俞樾由浙江德清往霞浦省亲，过此留题曰：“岭上岩岩分水关，令人回首故乡山。归途倘践山灵约，雁荡天台咫尺间。”明莆田进士林万潮《度分水关》诗曰：“北极星辰迥，南溟道路遥，栖迟淹日月，攸忽动凉飚，越峤临关尽，吴天入望饶，征途浩无极，何日返渔樵？”清赵治《分水关》诗曰：“连山行到顶，便作异乡人。流水分南北，征途判浙闽。殊音难共语，僮仆自相亲。长日崎岖路，翻怜老病身。”清代盘江逋客的《分水关》诗曰：“一道泉分两道泉，层层松栝翠参天。鹧鸪声里山无数，合向谁家草阁眠。”清末举人、诗人杜琨诗曰：“乱

Fenshui Pass

左上图：福鼎分水关防御墙 朱晨辉 摄
左下图：福鼎分水关是闽浙分界关 朱晨辉 摄
右 图：昔日的福鼎分水关，如今成为闽浙交通的分水岭 朱晨辉 摄

The upper left picture: Defense Wall of Fenshui Pass in Fuding. Photographed by Zhu Chenhui

The lower left picture: Fenshui Pass in Fuding is the boundary between Fujian and Zhejiang. Photographed by Zhu Chenhui

The right picture: The former Fenshui Pass in Fuding has now become a watershed of the transportation between Fujian and Zhejiang. Photographed by Zhu Chenhui

Fenshui Pass in Fuding was the product that the King of Min State occupied to prevent Wu and Yue states during the Five Dynasties and Ten Kingdoms. By the time the North and South were unified in the Northern Song Dynasty, its main function had evolved from military fortification to the boundary of Fujian-Zhejiang and the main road of frontier passes. In the Southern Song Dynasty, FenshuiPasswas an important post station from Fuzhou to Wenzhou. In history, many literati lamented the geography, environment and history of FenshuiPass, which is an important embodiment of FenshuiPass's humanity.

左　图：得益于古道交通的发展，福鼎白琳镇成为商贸繁荣的集散地。图为建于清乾隆十年（1745 年）的翠郊古民居。就单体建筑而言，可谓江南第一大古民居　朱晨辉 摄

中　图：福鼎前岐镇的挑矾古道，曾经繁华的交通要道，如今已人烟稀少　朱晨辉 摄

右　图：福鼎产茶历史悠久，精致的白琳功夫红茶，早在民国时期就销往欧洲各地　赖小兵 摄

The left picture: Thanks to the development of ancient road traffic, Bailin Town in Fuding has become a distribution center for commercial prosperity. The picture shows the ancient Cuijiao dwellings built in the 10th year of the Qianlong regin of the Qing dynasty (1745). As far as single building is concerned, it can be described as the largest ancient residence in Jiangnan. Photographed by Zhu Chenhui

The middle picture: The ancient road in Qianqi Town of Fuding, the former prosperous traffic thoroughfare is now sparsely populated. Photographed by Zhu Chenhui

The right picture: Fuding has a long history of tea production, delicate Bailin Kung Fu black tea was sold to all parts of Europe as early as the Republic of China. Photographed by Lai Xiaobing

山中断定龙蛇，遥控闽东百万家。一自烽烟过上国，更无士成到天涯。西风故垒迷秋草，落日平沙起暮鸦。不尽市朝今昔感，关门徒倚几停车。”

福鼎分水关是五代十国时期闽王据之以防吴越的产物，至北宋南北一统，其主要作用就由军事设防而演变为闽浙界线、关防要道。南宋时，分水关是福州北往温州的重要驿站。2004年7~9月，省考古所对分水关北段城墙进行的考古发掘，发现第四层为人工夯打的跑马道遗迹，内含物仅有南宋青瓷碗残片，说明北段城墙在南宋时期确有维修或增修。

虽然元代废分水关驿站，但明清时期仍设有分水铺、分水关铺，以传递公文；并设有分水关塘汛，“所以察奸宄，资守望也。无事则往来巡缉，有事则联络声援。”（清嘉庆《福鼎县志》）。与此同时，通过分水关的闽浙商旅逐渐增多，“虽非孔道，实闽浙豫广往来便道也。”（明万历《福宁州志》卷三）又如明嘉靖十七年（1538）福宁知州谢廷举所奏：“近来，浙江一带人知温州有路通本州，切近本省，多从此路而来，是本州道路之通达，又非昔年比矣。”（明万历《福宁州志》卷十四“艺文志”之奏疏《乞恩分处驿传奏》）

明嘉靖年间，福宁知州黄良材造隘房，并派福宁卫军守卫，以防倭寇。崇祯甲申年（1664）进士福安人刘仲藻为抵御清兵入闽，征召民工重修分水关，并扩建关口左右城垣数百米。

寿宁三关十六隘

寿宁位居闽浙两省交界，素有“两省门户，五界通衢”之称。县境之内山高岭长，行旅跋涉，渐成古道。明景泰六年（1455）建县，分别与福建省的政和、福安及浙江省的泰顺、景宁、庆元相邻。明嘉靖年间（1522~1566）倭寇猖獗，于各处分别设三关十六隘。另据统计，有岭路194条，以车岭、九岭、乌石岭、双岗岭、北山岭、檀香岭为著；路亭307座，以五里亭、铜坑亭、浪荡亭、百岁亭有名。

明弘治中期（1490~1500），朝廷在寿宁全县边境险要道口设隘。守隘之兵，称弓兵，亦称机兵，编额200名。编制百人为一队，队设总甲、小甲各一名，

Three Passes and Sixteen Passes in Shouning

Shouning is located at the junction of Fujian and Zhejiang provinces and is known as "the gateway to the two provinces and the thoroughfare of the five boundaries". Established in 1455, the county is adjacent to Zhenghe and Fu'an in Fujian Province and Taishun, Jingning and Qingyuan in Zhejiang Province. From 1522 to 1566, Japanese pirates were rampant and set up three passes and sixteen passes everywhere. According to statistics, there are 194 ridge roads, famous for Cheling Ridge, JiulingRidge, WushiRidge, Shuanggang Ridge, Beishan Ridge and Tanxiang Ridge; There are 307 road pavilions, famous for Wuli Pavilion, Tongkeng Pavilion, Langdang Pavilion and Baisui Pavilion.

寿宁坑底乡，地处闽浙二省，寿宁、庆元、景宁、泰顺四县交界地，古时即为交通要道 朱晨辉 摄

Kengdi Township of Shouning is located in Fujian and Zhejiang provinces. The junction of Shouning, Qingyuan, Jingning and Taishun are the four counties was the main traffic route in ancient times. Photographed by Zhu Chenhui

由巡捕管理，县令统摄。此外，还在全县主要村落及通道要口设置堡、寨。各堡由乡丁民壮把守，一乡有事，四方联防。县城外围屯兵之所，称为寨，隶属巡 检司。守寨者皆为弓兵。

明嘉靖二十四年（1545），知县张鹤年正民间疆里，根据自然地形，依山脉、分水划定界线，在黄阳隘、院洋隘、碑坑隘、伏际隘、上下党隘等全县边境隘口设立界碑，碑正面刻“寿宁县界”，左首小字“嘉靖□年□月”，右下落款“知县事贵州普安张鹤年”，反面刻“□□隘”和东南西北至何处。

冯梦龙在其著《寿宁待志·城隘篇》中写道：“（寿宁）有三关十六隘。隘之界庆元者十：曰佛际，曰青田、曰碑坑、曰峡头、曰榧子栏、曰杨婆墓、曰箬坑、曰双港、曰下党、曰杉坑。其界政和者曰石门。界福安者曰院洋。

□□□□曰武曲。界景宁者曰黄阳、曰青草。界政和、宁德之间者曰葡萄洋”。“各隘扼要而居，山径尺许阔，高下曲折，非用武之地。虽有长枪大戟，无所用之。守隘之具，铳第一，弩次之，虽弓矢亦不逮也。多蓄硝磺，此最紧着。”并强调“闽防在海，而福安正海艘登陆之地，昔年倭寇亦从此道。故（车岭、绝险、铁关、院洋隘）四隘特为要害”。

黄阳隘位于坑底乡长岭村铜坑亭1.5公里处，海拔897米。隘口东西走向，两边为小山，以山水流向为闽浙分界（离泰顺城关罗阳镇5公里）。隘口下半部乱毛石垒砌基础，上半部块石错缝交错发券，隘门用石拱形成拱门，门宽3米，拱高2.9米，总高约3.9米，从1.6米处起拱，隘口进深6.3米；隘口过道北面石墙中砌有一龛，龛高0.5米，宽0.82米，深0.32米，过道两旁有供人歇息的石凳。隘碑原立隘口，现为寿宁县博物馆收藏。碑高1.4米，宽0.68米，厚1.5米，青石素面，碑首呈半圆形。正面中刻“寿宁县界”，右刻“嘉靖贰拾肆□□□□”，左刻“知县事普安□□□□”，背面中刻“黄阳隘”，右边刻“东至□田，南至本土山”，左边刻“西至人行路，北至分水界”。

清末，乱弹声腔在南方地区得到广泛传播，江西与浙江同处于福建的边界，随着人员往来和交通的便捷，闽、浙、赣地方文化也逐步演变融合，盛行于杭州的温州杂剧也带到福建，形成了福建乱弹并产生了上路班、下路班、北路班、南路班等戏班，其中以北路班最为强盛，活跃在闽东北一带，北路戏即由此而得名，至今已有300多年的历史 赖小兵 摄

建于清代的杨梅州桥，是寿宁通往浙西南地区的要道，周边的杨梅洲风景区怪石嶙峋，风景独特 赖小兵 摄

Yangmeizhou Bridge, built in the Qing Dynasty, is the main road from Shouning to Southwest Zhejiang. The surrounding Yangmeizhou Scenic Area has jagged rocks and unique scenery. Photographed by Lai Xiaobing

上　图：始建于明代的寿宁大宝桥，是通往县城和浙江的交通要道　赖小兵 摄

下　图：黄阳隘为寿宁与泰顺的闽浙分界隘口，嘉靖二十四年（1545）知县事张鹤年在此立有“寿宁县界”碑
赖小兵 摄

The upper picture: Dabao Bridge in Shouning, which was built in the Ming Dynasty, is the main traffic route leading to the county seat and Zhejiang Province. Photographed by Lai Xiaobing

The lower picture: Huangyang Pass is the border pass of Shouning and Taishun between Fujian and Zhejiang. In the 24th year of the Jiajing regin (1545), Zhang Henian, magistrate of a county, set up a monument here entitled "Shouning County Boundary". Photographed by Lai Xiaobing

PASSES AND VILLAGESWERE SET UP DEPENDING ON THE STRATEGICAL LOCATION

In order to strengthen control, the government has built passes and villages along various important borders and roads. Passes are generally set up at the boundaries of provinces and counties through which roads pass, which are inspection and guarding facilities set up to guard large and small passages. The big mouth is the close, the small mouth is the pass. They are usually built with walls or cities on both sides, and doors are set up on the roads which opened and closed on time. There are troops stationed in the pass, but the garrison stationed in the pass is far more than the officers and soldiers guarding the pass. When there is a war, they are soldiers. At ordinary times, they are responsible for inspecting and collecting goods taxes. In contrast, the village belongs to a relatively simple military organization. Most of the villages and forts are not located at the boundaries of provinces and counties, but are located along major traffic arteries or near strategic garrison sites. Some villages have inspection departments, which shoulder management responsibilities; Some are only temporary settings during the war.

According to records in *The chorography of Fujian*, there are 89 passes, 376 strategic passes and 158 villages in Fujian. Among them, there are 370 passes and villages in 19 counties, including Fuding, Zherong, Fu'an, Shouning, Songxi, Zhenghe and Pucheng, which border Zhejiang, Jiangxi and Guangdong provinces. From the distribution point of view,great passesare mainly located at the provincial boundary of Official Avenue in the northwest; The traffic volume of roads leading to Jiangxi in the west is relatively small, and most of the boundary lines are only equipped with passes; The roads in the southwest and south-central directions are complicated, so most of them set up villages to inspect; Road in the southeast face the sea, with a large population along the way and a strong garrison, therefore, only passes are set up at the provincial boundary and the main roads from the plain to the mountain area; The road is mainly managed by post shops; The roadsin the northeast are winding and steep, so the pass is set up layer by layer along the road, which is the most closely guarded.

At the end of the Qing Dynasty, general term for Chinese opera melodies was widely spread in the southern region. Jiangxi and Zhejiang are on the sameborder of Fujian. With the convenience of personnel and transportation, the local cultures of Fujian, Zhejiang and Jiangxi also gradually evolved and merged. Poetic drama of Wenzhou, which prevailed in Hangzhou, also brought to Fujian, forming the general term for Chinese opera melodies in Fujian and producing Shanglu, Xialu, Beilu and Nanlu troupes. Among them, Beilu troupe is the most powerful and active in the northeast of Fujian. Beilu troupe is named from this and has a history of more than 300 years. Photographed by Lai Xiaobing

驿馆铺递，置廪传食

自古置驿以传食，置邮以传命。据《三山志》记载："宋之崇韶驿在南门内西，旧置，梁开平中翁承赞册闽王王审知于登庸门内，是时已有驿。"《福建通志》也说："宋承唐制，三十里有驿，非通途大道则曰馆"。又据明《弘治兴化志》记载："宋之迎仙驿即唐之待宾馆；太平驿即枫亭馆。"说明唐朝和五代已有驿馆的设置。

按明制，驿路十里为铺，铺兵五人，专用传檄；五十里为驿，驿以廪食。至清朝，传檄之所曰"十里铺"，其制：外为门，榜之以名，曰"急递"；门之内为亭，亭之后为堂；两房置厢，以届执事于铺者，缭之以垣，可以暂就栖息也。有的驿距过远，也可在两驿之间增设腰站、馆舍。后来，因铺递与步递的速度慢，清康熙八年（1669）发展出专递军情的马递机构—塘（汛）递，文职送文件到铺传递，武职照会发摆塘，各路每一二十公里设驿站（称兼站），三四十公里设宿站。

浦城县仙阳镇渔梁村，为古代中原入闽的第一驿站。自唐代设驿，延至明清，是商贾仕宦北上中原，或南下入闽出洋必经之地　赖小兵 摄

Yuliang Village, Xianyang Town, Pucheng County, was the first post station for the ancient Central Plains to enter Fujian. The post set uo in the Tang Dynasty, extended to the Ming and Qing Dynasties, was the only place for merchants and officials to go north to the Central Plains or south to Fujian and go abroad. Photographed by Lai Xiaobing

POSTHOUSES AND SHOPS WERE SET UP FOR GRAINS

Since ancient times, China has set up post stations to deliver materials and set up mail stations to deliver decrees and documents. According to "The chorographyof Xinghua during the reign of Hongzhi" in the Ming Dynasty, "Yingxian Post in the Song Dynasty is a posthouse for entertaining guests in the Tang Dynasty; Taiping Post is Fengting Pavilion."which shows that in the Tang Dynasty and the Five Dynasties of China have already set up posthouses.

浦城渔梁驿

YULIANG POST IN PUCHENG

如今，仙霞古道浦城境内还保留有深坑古道、小关、飞桥、渔梁驿、揖仙桥、朴树桥、夕阳岭古道等史迹，但它们所承载的历史使命已经完全发生了改变。

渔梁驿是仙霞古道繁盛时期的一个重要缩影。唐代始设驿，延至明清，为古代中原入闽第一驿。明清时在此设枫岭营守备衙门，驻千总、把总，外委有马、步、战守兵共四百二十六名以及烟墩火药局，教场坪等军事设施。千百年来战事不断，南宋抗金名将韩世忠追击叛军于渔梁，擒获兵变首领庙傅、刘正彦。与此同时，众多文人学者经此驿站也不惜笔墨，留下大量佳作美文。爱国诗人陆游赴仙霞宿渔梁，作《宿渔梁无鼓起行有感》诗二首；清代琉球国使者程顺则留下《夜宿渔梁》诗文；蔡襄、刘克庄、黄公度、朱熹、林则徐等名流皆留足迹，广置诗篇。明代地理学家徐霞客入闽，三度投宿于渔梁。清代诗人袁枚有诗《渔梁道上作绝句》：“山腰逼仄小车停，竹作长篱树作屏。远望自家行李过，画来都是好丹青。”

明代王世懋《闽部疏》载“凡福之丝绸，漳之纱绢，泉之蓝，福延之铁，福漳之橘，福兴之荔枝，泉漳之糖，顺昌之纸，无日不走分水关及浦城小关，下吴越如流水。”小关的关墙与驿亭遗址仍在，四周红豆杉、香樟等古树林立，似乎仍在骄傲地述说着那段曾经见证的繁华历史。浦城城关大西门勘头街后侧的“江山街”，长 600 米，就是数百年来一支数以万计的俗称“江山担”的挑夫队伍的大本营。他们头戴竹笠，脚穿草鞋，肩挑着浙皖的丝绸、瓷器、茶叶和福建的土特产等货品频繁地往来于仙霞古道上。建于南宋绍兴七年（1137）的朴树桥是浦城县境内仅见有明确造桥纪年石刻的桥梁，桥头北侧引桥的桥面卵石上清晰可见独轮车车辙印痕。

Take Yuliang Post and Xiaoguan in Pucheng as examples. Yuliang Post is an important epitome of the prosperous period of Xianxia Ancient Road. It was founded in the Tang Dynasty and was the first post station in the ancient Central Plains to enter Fujian. During the Ming and Qing Dynasties, Fengling camp was set up here to guard the yamen (the government office in fedual China), with 426 cavalry men, infantry and garrison, as well as military facilities such as Gunpowder Bureau and military training fields. For thousands of years, wars have continued. At the same time, many literary scholars did not hesitate to write when passing through this post station, leaving behind a large number of excellent works and beautiful articles. In the Ming Dynasty, Wang Shimao's "All Fujian's silk, Zhangzhou's tough silk, Quanzhou's blueberry, Fuyan's iron, Fuzhang's oranges, Fuxing's lychee, Quanzhang's sugar, Shunchang's paper all pass through Fenshui Pass and Pucheng Pass every day." The walls of the pass and the ruins of the post house are still there, surrounded by ancient trees such as Taxus chinensis and Cinnamomum camphora, which seems to be proudly recounting the prosperous history it once witnessed.

左上图：浦城夕阳岭古道上的夕阳寺 朱晨辉 摄

左下图：浦城临江镇的夕阳岭古道 吴军 摄

右上图：江山街曾是古道挑夫的大本营，这口水井原是附近挑夫的生活水源 吴军 摄

右下图：浦城的三山会馆，曾是昔日浦城最重要的商业区，是福州旅浦同乡所建。也是浦城与浙赣、福州等地商贸频繁往来的重要例证 吴军 摄

The upper left picture: Sunset Temple on the Ancient Road of Sunset Ridge in Pucheng. Photographed by Zhu Chenhui

The lower left picture: Sunset Ridge Ancient Road in Linjiang Town, Pucheng. Photographed by Wu Jun

The upper right picture: Jiangshan Street used to be the base camp of ancient road porters. This well was originally the living water source of nearby porters. Photographed by Wu Jun

The lower right picture: Sanshan Guild Hall in Pucheng was once the most important commercial area in Pucheng and was built by Fuzhou travelers in Puchengu. It is also an important example of the frequent trade exchanges between Pucheng and Zhejiang, Jiangxi, Fuzhou and other places. Photographed by Wu Jun

浦城县水北镇观前村是仙霞古道和南浦溪，闽浙两省重要的水陆联运交通命脉

Guanqian Village, Shuibei Town, Pucheng County, is an important land and water transportation lifeline between Xianxia Ancient Road, Nanpu River and Fujian and Zhejiang provinces.

漳浦盘陀岭

漳浦在唐代设有专供往来官员住宿和传递文书的漳浦驿。宋时，改漳浦驿为仙云驿，为便利行人，在驿道上设12个铺作为驿的分站，以庵立铺或逢铺立庵，以僧兼管铺事。元朝设临漳（漳浦）、云霄、甘棠3驿。明朝发展到十里一铺，设卒以递公文，又于各驿设公馆，招待过往官员。当时在驿内各常设担夫50名、专递公文驿夫4名。清代全县分设24铺，各设铺司1名，铺夫4名。

盘陀岭位于梁山山脉，梁山最高近1000米，有九十九峰之说。盘陀岭自古为闽粤的主要通道，汉在此建蒲葵关。唐代曾建有驿楼，李德裕流放至此，留有《登盘陀岭驿楼》诗篇。明代遗物有4根方形石柱，刻有“天启六年（1626）仲冬，长泰陈天柱僧良叔募建”“三霄邑交界至此止”等。

盘陀岭界碑位于白云寺对面，为《云霄漳浦界碑》。碑高1.74米，宽0.90米，厚0.25米，花岗岩刻制，下配底座。碑上端抹角，边沿凸出6厘米，额浮雕双龙戏珠图案，碑面上端镌“大清”，字径10厘米。碑文内容为：“遵奉提督军门杨、游、穆，抚督镇宪批断：浦云两营照县志以盘陀岭顶分水为界。南属云霄营辖，北属漳浦营管辖。公同勒石，永为遵守。康熙五十二年（1713）九月十九日立。”字径6厘米。

PANTUO RIDGE IN ZHANGPU

In the Tang Dynasty, Zhangpu set up Zhangpu Posthouse for officials to get accommodation and transfer documents. In the Song Dynasty, Zhangpu Posthouse was changed to Xianyun Posthouse. In order to facilitate pedestrians, 12 shops were set up on the post road as sub-stations of the Posthouse, with temples setting up shops or setting up temples in every shop, and monks concurrently managing the shops. Pantuo Ridge is located in the Liangshan Mountains, with a maximum of nearly 1,000 meters in LiangshanMountain. Pantuo Ridge has been the main passage between Fujian and Guangdong since ancient times, where the Han Dynasty built Pugui Pass.

漳浦盘陀岭界碑为云霄、漳浦两县界碑　楼建龙 摄

The boundary monument of Pantuo Ridge in Zhangpu is thatof Yunxiao and Zhangpu counties. Photographed by Lou Jianlong

The upper picture: Wushan Mountain in Yunxiao used to be an important hub and transportation route for the prefectural party Committee organs in southern Fujian to connect with the outside world. Photographed by Li Jintai

The lower left picture: Pantuo Ridge has been the main passage between Fujian and Guangdong since ancient times, and has built post buildings. Photographed by Lou Jianlong

The lower right picture: Pantuo Ridge at the junction of Yunxiao and Zhangpu West County has been a key pass since ancient times. Pukui Pass was set up here in the Han Dynasty and Zhangpu Posthouse was set up here in the Tang Dynasty. The mountains here are high and dangerous. Only Yangchang Stone Trail can pass through, which is the bottleneck of traffic between Fujian and Guangdong. Businessmen and travellers regarded it as a dangerous road. Photographed by Ruan Renyi

上　图：云霄的乌山曾是中共闽南地委机关连接外界的重要枢纽和交通要道　李晋泰 摄

左下图：盘陀岭自古为闽粤的主要通道，曾建有驿楼　楼建龙 摄

右下图：云霄和漳浦两县交界处的盘陀岭，自古就是关隘重地，汉代在此设蒲葵关，唐代在此设漳浦驿，这里山高岭险，仅有羊肠石径可通行，是闽粤交通之瓶颈，商旅皆视为险途　阮任艺 摄

集美深青驿

宋代，同安至泉州、漳州有驿道相通。元、明、清三朝，以同安为起点，有道路可通南安、安溪、长泰、集美、刘五店等地，另有五通至江头古道、漳泉古道、小盈岭古道、东田古道等。

南宋绍兴二十一年至二十五年，理学家朱熹授任同安主簿，辟泉漳古驿道，同安县境内共设驿站两处，即大同驿和鱼孚驿，上接泉州南安县的康店驿，下接漳州通源驿。古驿道设有小盈、店头、沈井、洪塘、县前、乌泥、新塘、苎溪、安民、鱼孚、深青、仙店等 12 铺，全长 69 里。宋时在深青溪架设木桥，为深青桥和驿道之初建雏形。

元代，大同驿更名为同安驿，鱼孚驿移建于深青村，名深青驿，上接泉州清源站，下接漳州江东驿。据嘉庆《同安县志》记载："深青驿，在县西 60 里，宋名鱼孚，在安民铺之侧，元移今所。明洪武十四年，知县方子张重建。景泰元年，上书薛琏令主簿蔡璘重建，上至大轮驿 60 里，下至漳州府龙溪县江东驿 60 里。原系驿丞专理。国朝乾隆二十年裁汰，归县管理。现在额设赡夫 60 名，抄单、走递、防夫等 6 名，兜夫 15 名。"

深青驿初设茂林庵，明洪武十四年（1381）及景泰元年（1450）两次扩建驿楼、驿馆、驿兵楼、马房等，逐渐成为一个设施、人员完备的驿站。明弘治年间，贞岱苏氏大量迁入深青村，人口迅速增长，他们又顺道建起驿口街，从店铺祠堂发展到有当铺、药店、客栈、饭馆、打铁铺、肉铺、食品杂货铺等，驿口街两侧还延续建巷如石狮巷、驿口巷、驿蛇巷等。明隆庆年间，深青驿成为颇有规模的小集镇。

SHENQING POSTHOUSE IN JIMEI

In the Song Dynasty, there were post roads from Tong'an to Quanzhou and Zhangzhou. In the Yuan, Ming and Qing Dynasties, starting from Tong'an, there were roads leading to Nan'an, Anxi, Changtai, Jimei, Liuwudian and other places, and there were also the AncientRoad from Wutong to Jiangtou, Zhangquan Ancient Road, Xiaoyingling Ancient Road and Dongtian Ancient Road,etc.

At the beginning, Maolin Temple was set up in Shenqing Posthouse. In 1381 and 1450, the post building, posthouse, post soldier building, stable, etc. were expanded twice. And it gradually becamea post station with complete facilities and personnel. During the reign of Qin Long in the Ming Dynasty, ShenqingPosthouse became a large-scale small market town.

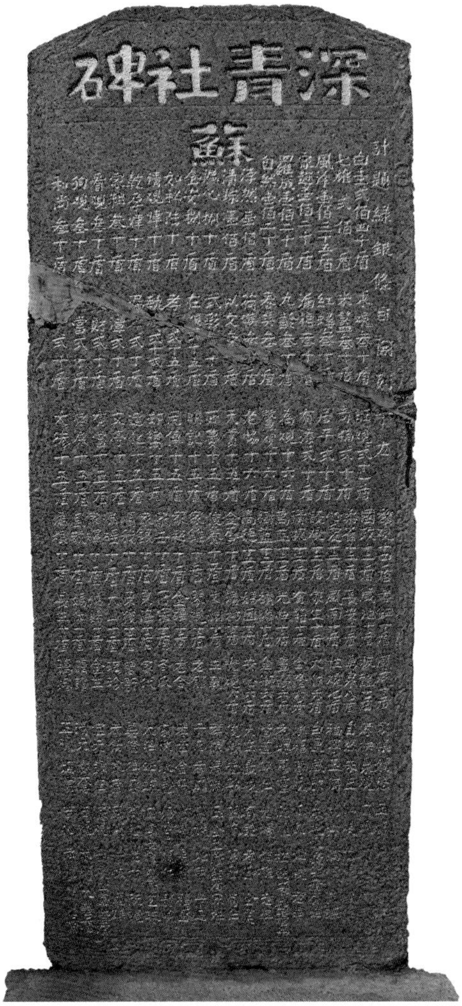

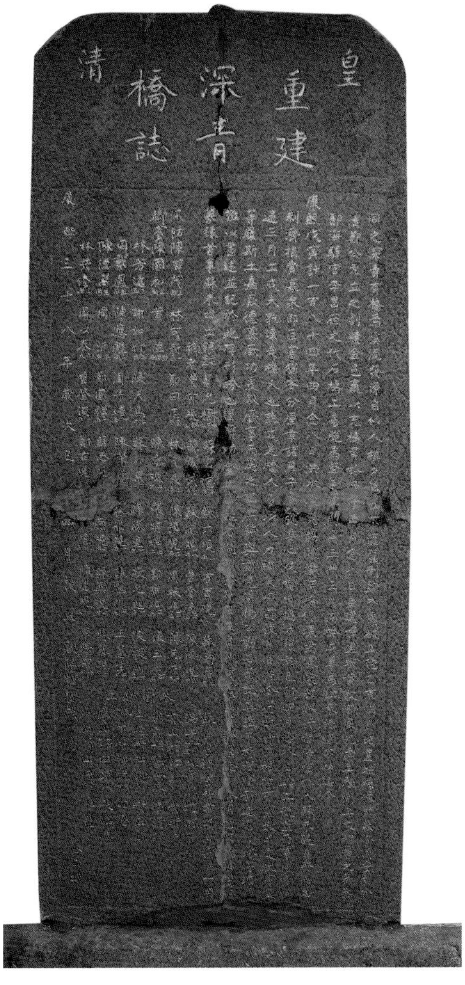

左　图：深青驿遗址位于厦门集美区灌口镇深青村，是古代同安连接漳州、泉州两地的古驿站之一。图为遗址上留存的五通石碑　楼建龙 摄

右上图：深青驿古道上的古庙供行旅之人祭拜　楼建龙 摄

右下图：清代重建深青桥所立石碑　楼建龙 摄

The left picture: The site of Shenqing Post is located in Shenqing Village, Guankou Town, Jimei District, Xiamen. It is one of the ancient post stations connecting Zhangzhou and Quanzhou in ancient Tong'an. The picture shows the Wutong Stone Tablet left on the site. Photographed by Lou Jianlong

The upper right picture: The ancient temple on the ancient road of Shenqingyi is for travelers to worship. Photographed by Lou Jianlong

The lower right picture: The stone tablet standing on Shenqing Bridge rebuilted in the Qing Dynasty. Photographed by Lou Jianlong

上　图：厦门同安深青驿桥始建于南宋，初为木板桥，后改为石桥　崔建楠 摄

下　图：深青桥，其桥墩为船型，船尖逆水而立，大大减少了水流对桥墩的冲击力　阮任艺 摄

The upper picture: Shenqing Post Bridge in Tong'an of Xiamen was built in the Southern Song Dynasty. It was originally a wooden bridge and later changed to a stone bridge. Photographed by Cui Jiannan

The lower picture: The pier of Shenqing Bridge is ship-shaped, and the tip of the ship stands against the water, which greatly reduces the impact force of water flow on the pier. Photographed by Ruan Renyi

The upper picture: The post building of Shenqing Post, which was built in the Yuan Dynasty, straddles the ancient post road at the entrance of Shenqing Village. The four characters "驿楼古地 (Ancient Land of Posthouse)" on the gate house are one of the few ancient post sites in China at present. Photographed by Ruan Renyi

The lower left picture: Colored Sculpture of Maolin Temple in Shenqing Post. Photographed by Ruan Renyi

The lower right picture: Maolin Temple in Shenqing Posthouse honors Patriarch Qingshui and the True King of Qing Yuan. Photographed by Cui Jiannan

上　图：始建于元代的深青驿驿楼横跨于深青村口的古驿道上，门楼上书“驿楼古地”四字 是目前国内存留不多的古代邮驿遗址之一 阮任艺 摄

左下图：深青驿茂林庵的彩塑 阮任艺 摄

右下图：深青驿茂林庵供奉的是清水祖师和清元真君 崔建楠 摄

周宁麻岭巡检

MALING AGENCY OF PATROL INSPECTION IN ZHOUNING

麻岭是周宁通往政和的古道必经之地，山高岭峻。麻岭巡检司离宁德一百八十里，与寿宁泗桥交界。明洪武二年（1369）改设赤岩巡检司，嘉靖三十五年（1556）筑周墩城，建东洋行县，由宁德县主薄驻征赋税。

巡检司遗址位于浦源镇麻岭巅岔口东南面坡下200米处。据清乾隆《宁德县志》记载，麻岭巡检司“元时设，明因之”；明宣德年间（1426~1435），有塘兵十。建筑坐北朝南，呈品字形依山而建，下两间宽13.3米 ×9.4米，靠东墙南北向各设石梁门一个，均为宽1.73米，高2.2米，门洞深1.56米。上一间面积约10米 ×9米。遗址东西两面和中间的山墙高5米，其余墙体高约1.5米，基座厚0.8~1米，毛石砌体。

麻岭卷石亭建在海拔1333米的大麻岭古道间。据《周宁县交通志》记载，清雍正八年（1730）七月，由上洋村民张贡十（张玉政）独资建造。涵洞为亭，石拱净跨3.55米，高2.8米，宽4.2米，拱壁及两侧用青条石砌筑。

Maling is the only place for the ancient road from Zhouning to Zhenghe, with highand steep mountains. Maling Agency of Patrol Inspection is 180 miles away from Ningde and borders Siqiao of Shouning.

Juanshi Pavilion in Maling is built between the Damaling ancient Road at an altitude of 1333 meters. According to "Traffic Records of Zhouning County", in July 1730, it was built solely by Zhang Gongshi (Zhang Yuzheng), a villager from Shangyang.

左上图：麻岭山高险峻，古道依山而建 楼建龙 摄

左下图：麻岭巡检司遗址 楼建龙 摄

右上图：巡检司大门 楼建龙 摄

右下图：麻岭古道上的卷石亭由当地热心村民所建 楼建龙 摄

The upper left picture: Maling Mountain is high and steep, and the ancient road is built on the mountain. Photographed by Lou Jianlong

The lower left picture: Site of Patrol Inspection Department on Maling Mountain. Photographed by Lou Jianlong

The upper right picture: Gate of Patrol Inspection Department. Photographed by Lou Jianlong

The lower right picture: Juanting pavilion on the ancient Maling Road was built by local enthusiastic villagers. Photographed by Lou Jianlong

路亭接引，送别赋游

"长亭外，古道边，芳草碧连天！"李叔同先生于1914年创作的《送别》里的场景已经家喻户晓。实际上，古道沿线"五里一亭，十里一铺"的设置，虽然只是对应于出行人员沿路憩息的需要，却是与古道相伴相息的必需配置以及"人文关怀"的典型例证。长路漫漫，清风相引之间，不时出现的寂寂孤立的路亭，是奔赴于崎岖古道之上旅人的暂憩场所，也成为文人墨客挥发情思的重要溯源。

路亭大多位于古道所经的荒郊野渡，或是山腰岭巅，但也有一类位于城镇之外三五里之地，成为人们送别或赋游之处，因而留下大量的纪事或抒情咏怀词句。屏南的大观亭位于南门外，在城南三里，咸丰年间(1851~1861)由龙源村陆姓改建。亭木构，单檐歇山顶，四扇十六柱，方形，外侧有椅靠，供路人休息之用。副贡张钦孟有诗："画栋绕时烟，亭高势参天。眼看千嶂表，人倚五云边。扑地鱼鳞合，环山雉堞连。伊谁来放鹤？小住话神仙"。廪生周珠联诗："嵯峨岭表俯层峦，便算南来一大观。坐爱松间风谡谡，披襟小憩夏生寒"。

矗立于福建古道上的路亭，不同地区的外观、构造以及建造材料等却各不相同。相比较而言，闽东地区的路亭最为正规，多采取清水木结构、庙亭合一的形式，一般是将路亭与观音庙合二为一，也有合祀大王、土地的。闽西北的路亭形式较为多样，有土木结构的，也有砖木结构，以及一类独特的石构券顶形式。闽西的路亭以青砖匡斗砖墙木构梁架为主，内墙居中常有神龛或纪事石刻。闽中南区的路亭较为简单，一般为三面土墙围护、山墙搁檩。闽东南区的路亭多为与庵庙相近的独立式石亭，亭子形式多样，也有做成上下两层，底部为过道、顶层供奉各路神明，也有与宫庙合为一体的。

THE ROAD PAVILION BECOMES A PLACE FOR RECEPTION AND WRITING POEMS WHEN BIDDING FAREWELL

The setting of "every five-mileshas one pavilion and every ten-miles has one shop" along the ancient road is only corresponding to the needs of travelers to rest along the road, but it is also a typical example of "humanistic care". With a long way to go, the road pavilion appeared from time to time are a temporary resting place for travelers on the rugged ancient roads in Fujian, and have also become an important source for scholars to volatilize their thoughts.

Most of the road pavilions are located in the wild suburbs or hillsides where the ancient road passes, but there are also some places located 3 to 5 miles away from the town, which have become places for people to bid farewell or travel, thus leaving behind a large number of chronicles or lyrical poems.

The pavilions standing on the ancient roads in Fujian have different appearance, structure and building materials in different regions. The road pavilions in eastern Fujian are the most formal, mostly in the form of clear water wood structure and the combination of temples and pavilions. Generally, the road pavilions and Guanyin Temple are combined into one. There are various forms of road pavilions in Northwest Fujian, including civil structure, brick-wood structure, and a unique form of stone structure coupon roof. The road pavilions in western Fujian are mainly made of wooden frame with black brick wall, usually with shrines or chronicle stone carvings in the middle of the inner wall. The road pavilions in the central and southern districts of Fujian are relatively simple and are generally enclosed by three earth walls. Most of them are independent stone pavilions similar to temples, which take various forms and are also made into upper and lower floors, and the bottom is a corridor and the top is dedicated to various gods.

上　图：福温古道上前岐镇挑矾古道道亭　赖小兵 摄
下　图：松溪铁岭黄坑村黄坑关，关隘修建的长凳可供路人休息　严硕 摄

The upper picture: Alum Picking Ancient Road Pavilion of Qiangqi Town on Fuwen Ancient Road. Photographed by Lai Xiaobing

The lower picture: In Huangkeng Pass, Huangkeng Village, Tieling, Songxi, benches built at the pass can be used for passers-by to rest. Photographed by Yan Shuo

木结构路亭

闽侯溪岭亭

又名喝岭亭，位于廷坪乡池坑村上房自然村三岔路口。明间后部设神龛，主祀玄天上帝。亭始建于明代，清同治、光绪重修。木构方形亭式建筑，歇山顶，抬梁穿斗混合式木构架，面阔一间并两廊，宽5.25米；进深四步梁前后穿枋用六柱，深7.25米。金柱高3.15米，柱头有卷杀，置圆形大斗和十字斗栱以承上层梁架。前后额枋上各施一斗三升重栱平身科2朵。屋顶覆青瓦，举折平缓，清水脊。原有翘角已失落，卯口尚存。建筑风格简朴粗犷，尚存明代建筑风格。供桌上有清光绪二十七年（1901）和同治十一年（1872）的青石香炉各一件。

WOODEN PAVILION

Xiling Pavilion in Minhou

Also known as Heling Pavilion, it is located at the intersection of Shangfang Village in Chikeng Village, Tingping Township. A shrine was set up at the back of the Ming Dynasty to worship the Xuantian God. The pavilion was built in the Ming Dynasty and was rebuilt in the regin of Tongzhi and Guangxu in the Qing Dynasty.

始建于明代的溪岭亭，别致的木构方形亭式建筑，可供行脚的路人歇息，祭拜 楼建龙 摄

Xiling Pavilion, built in the Ming Dynasty, is a unique wooden square pavilion for passers-by to rest and worship. Photographed by Lou Jianlong

上　图：闽侯溪岭亭始建于明代，清代重修　楼建龙 摄
左下图：溪岭亭内混合式木构架抬梁　楼建龙 摄
右下图：溪岭亭还供有香火，供人祭拜祈福　楼建龙 摄

The upper picture: Xiling Pavilion in Minhou was built in the Ming Dynasty and rebuilt in the Qing Dynasty. Photographed by Lou Jianlong

The lower left picture: Lifting beams with mixed wooden frame in Xiling Pavilion. Photographed by Lou Jianlong

The lower right picture: Xiling Pavilion also has incense for people to worship and pray for blessings. Photographed by Lou Jianlong

涵洞式石拱亭

政和分都亭

位于澄源乡北斗村北约2000米的葫芦岗两山垭口、由北斗村通往外屯的古道上。亭建于清光绪三十二年（1906），为石拱涵洞式，东西两侧有墙，残长15米，亭南北进深6.96米。南北两面开拱门，为长方形条石砌造，门两侧上方各开一个方形气窗。亭内东西宽5.3米，内高4.3、总高约6米。拱门高2.45米，宽1.72米。

政和分都亭记事碑 吴军 摄

Chronicle tablet of Fendu Pavilion in Zhenghe. Photographed by Wu Jun

CULVERT-TYPE STONE ARCH PAVILION

Fendu Pavilion in Zhenghe

Located at the two mountain passes of Hulugang, 2,000 meters north of Beidou Village in Chengyuan Township, and the ancient road from Beidou Village to Waitun. The pavilion was built in 1906 and is of the stone arch culvert-type with walls on the east and west sides.

左　图：政和分都亭隘口，是闽北通往闽东、浙南的必经之地，是重要的茶盐古道　吴军 摄

右　图：分都亭上留存的石碑，记录着古隘口曾经的繁荣　楼建龙 摄

The left picture: The pass of Fendu Pavilion in Zhenghe is the only way from northern Fujian to eastern Fujian and southern Zhejiang, and is an important ancient tea and salt road. Photographed by Wu Jun

The right picture: The stone tablets preserved on Fendu Pavilion record the prosperity of the ancient pass. Photographed by Lou Jianlong

泰宁万古亭

位于大龙乡陈坑村村头自然村白石崖对面山顶，本地人称之为“亭岭洞”，周边山脉地势险要，泰宁大布、龙安通往明溪的古驿道由北往南经由此处。岭上的万古亭北侧为泰宁地界，南侧为明溪地界。亭始建于清康熙二十四年（1685），东西宽 4.5 米，南北进深 4.8 米，高 2.5 米。通体用本地产花岗岩石砌筑，亭顶为拱形，拱券纵联法砌筑，于南边大门内侧左右各镶嵌青石碑，碑文均为正楷，东边书“万古亭”，碑宽 0.5 米，高 1.2 米，厚 0.10 米；西边写“永远碑”，正面碑文均为捐赠人姓名及捐赠银两数额，背面有刻字，但字迹模糊；碑宽 0.5、高 1.2、厚 0.10 米。南门额前自西向东有“经……万”七字。

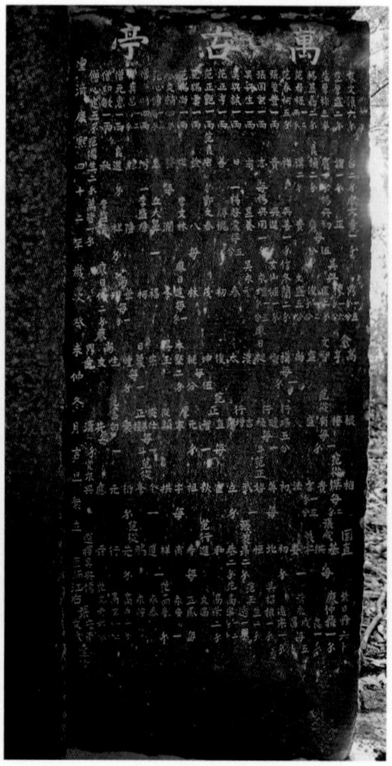

左　图：泰宁万古亭重建石碑
楼建龙 摄

中　图：泰宁万古亭捐赠重修所立石碑
楼建龙 摄

右　图：泰宁万古亭是古道上泰宁与明溪的分界亭，建于清代，由民间捐资兴建　楼建龙 摄

The left picture: The rebuilt stone tablet of Wangu Pavilion in Taining. Photographed by Lou Jianlong

The middle picture: Monuments erected by donation and reconstruction of Wangu Pavilion in Taining. Photographed by Lou Jianlong

The right picture: Wangu Pavilion in Taining is the boundary pavilion between Taining and Mingxi on the ancient road, which was built in the Qing Dynasty and was donated by the people. Photographed by Lou Jianlong

Taining Wangu Pavilion

Built in 1685, Taining Wangu Pavilion is located on the top of the mountain opposite Baishi cliff, Cuntou Nature Village, Chenkeng Village, Dalong Township. The local people call it "Tingling Cave". The surrounding mountains are of dangerous terrain. The ancient post road leading to Mingxi from Dabu and Long'an in Taining passes through here from north to south.

匡斗砖墙路亭

宁化水油塘树德亭

位于济村乡龙头村水油塘自然村，为古时宁化龙头通往江西福村必经之路。亭始建于民国六年，平面呈长方形，砖木结构。通面阔 4.8 米，通进深 6.17 米。面阔 1 间，架梁直接安于墙体上，硬山顶。西南面、东北面各开圆形对称透窗，内墙上嵌有“龙头村水油塘鼎建树德亭善助”碑一块。

位于宁化济村乡龙头村水油塘自然村的树德亭是宁化通往江西的必经之路 楼建龙 摄

Shude Pavilion, located in Shuiyoutang Nature Village, Longtou Village, JicunTownship, Ninghua, is the only way from Ninghua to Jiangxi Province. Photographed by Lou Jianlong

Kuangdou Brick-wall Pavilion

Shude Pavilion of Shuiyoutang in Ninghua

Located in Shuiyoutang Nature Village, Longtou Village, Jicun Township, it was the only way from Longtou in Ninghuato Fucun Village in Jiangxi Province in ancient times. The pavilion was built in the 6th year of the Republic of China. Its plane is rectangular,with brick and wood structure.

左上图：树德亭局部一角
楼建龙 摄
右上图：树德亭的砖石结构，虽经百年，依旧无损
楼建龙 摄
下 图：树德亭内的捐赠名单
楼建龙 摄

The upper left picture: A partial corner of Shude Pavilion. Photographed by Lou Jianlong

The upper right picture: The masonry structure of Shude Pavilion is still intact after 100 years. Photographed by Lou Jianlong

The lower picture: The donation list in Shude Pavilion. Photographed by Lou Jianlong

将乐泽坊毓秀亭

又名狐狸顶亭，位于安仁乡泽坊村头狐狸岭顶。亭坐北向南，总面积36.3平方米，平面呈长方形。亭面阔一间，进深4柱，为抬梁减柱造，硬山顶。砖木结构，亭柱共12根。南北两侧各辟券顶门。亭的东墙中央开圆形窗，西墙中央设壁龛。亭的南北为古道，北走狐狸岭、泽坊村至安仁乡，南通安仁的蜈蚣鼻大南坑、元洋坑至邵武。

左上图：将乐泽坊毓秀亭又名狐狸顶亭，位于安仁乡泽坊村头狐狸岭顶 楼建龙 摄

左下图：毓秀亭内可供路人歇脚、休憩 楼建龙 摄

右 图：毓秀亭的南北为古道，北走狐狸岭、泽坊村至安仁乡，南通安仁的蜈蚣鼻大南坑、元洋坑至邵武 楼建龙 摄

The upper left picture: Yuxiu Pavilion in Zefang of Jiangle, also known as Fox Top Pavilion, is located at the top of Fox Ridge at the head of Zefang Village in Anren Township. Photographed by Lou Jianlong

The lower left picture: Yuxiu Pavilion can be used by passers-by to rest and have a rest. Photographed by Lou Jianlong

The right picture: The north and south of Yuxiu Pavilion are ancient roads, with Fox Ridge and Zefang Village leading to Anren Township in the north, Centipede Nose Danankeng and Yuanyang Keng leading to Shaowu in Anren, Nanton in the south. Photographed by Lou Jianlong

Yuxiu Pavilion in Zefang of Jiangle

Also known as Fox Top Pavilion, it is located at the top of Fox Ridge at the head of Zefang Village in Anren Township. The north and south of the pavilion are ancient roads, with Fox Ridge and Zefang Village to Anren Township in the north, centipede nose Da Nan Keng and Yuanyang Keng to Shaowu in Anren, Nantong.

清流田口路亭

当地俗称茶亭，位于田源乡田口村东北面约 50 米的田畴中，坐东朝西，通面阔 4 米，通进深 7 米。建于清光绪年间，砖木结构。面阔三间，抬梁结构，进深六柱，硬山顶，两边开圆拱门。边墙一侧正中设圆窗，另一侧设神龛。墙为三合土筑成，外墙是沙灰土，亭内墙壁写有 20 世纪 60 年代的标语。

左　图：田口路亭内的壁龛　楼建龙 摄
右　图：清流的田源乡田口路亭是供过往路人歇脚、休息的茶亭　楼建龙 摄

The left picture: Niches in Tiankou Road Pavilion. Photographed by Lou Jianlong

The right picture: The clean Tiankou Road Pavilion in Tianyuan Township is a tea pavilion for passers-by to rest. Photographed by Lou Jianlong

Tiankou Road Pavilion in Qingliu County

The local common name is Tea Pavilion, which is located in the farmland, about 50 meters northeast of Tiankou Village in Tianyuan Township, which was built in Guangxu of Qing Dynasty with a brick-wood structure. A round window is set up in the middle of one side of the side wall and a shrine is set up on the other side. The walls of the pavilion have slogans from the 1960s.

岩上节孝坊

节孝坊位于建宁县里心镇岩上村，周边的历史构筑物还有水井、水尾庙及其附属“广积库”、石碑三通、石拱桥、红豆杉等。穿节孝坊亭而过的是由建宁通往江西广昌的重要驿道。坊亭由左、右二座石牌坊并中间加筑路亭组成，平面呈长方形，二面各宽4.32米，长5.17米。牌坊整体石砌，全部用辉绿岩条石叠砌而成，总高约6.38米（地面至牌坊脊饰顶部），坐西朝东。石牌坊均为四柱三间五楼式，总宽4.32米，其中明间宽2.16（柱中至柱中，下同），二次间宽0.91米。明间辟为门洞，高3.13米；二次间用块石封堵，墙角刻出须弥座圭角装饰等。门上额枋正面，阴刻立坊主题，即“旌表儒童张卫澜之妻谢氏”。额枋之上，是阳刻的“节孝”匾，匾二侧浮刻加官碑，再二侧是纪事碑，阴刻张大宾及其子孙女婿、建坊石匠、为建坊出过力的11名官员百姓名和建坊时间等。匾额之上，居中立高起的“奉旨恩荣”碑，碑之二侧的次楼下方，是浮刻的孝行人物图像。二处石碑坊间用条石加筑边墙，围出完整的室内休息空间，供过往行人歇脚之用。过亭地面用条石整齐铺砌，梁架采用五架抬梁形式；屋面覆二面瓦坡顶，脊高约5.32米。

Archway-type Pavilion

Arch of Chastity and Filial Piety in Yanshang

Arch of Chastity and Filial Piety is located at Shuiwei village. The surrounding historical structures include the water well, Shuiwei Temple and its affiliated "Guangji Reservoir", three stone tablets, stone arch bridge, Taxus chinensis, etc. Passing through Arch of Chastity and Filial Piety is an important post road from Jianning to Guangchang in Jiangxi Province.

建宁通往江西广昌的重要交通驿道穿节孝坊而过　楼建龙 摄

The important traffic post road from Jianning to Guangchang in Jiangxi passes through Jiexiao Arch. Photographed by Lou Jianlong

上 图：岩上节孝坊的砖雕依然保存完好 楼建龙 摄

下 图：节孝坊附近水尾石碑 楼建龙 摄

The upper picture: The brick carvings of Jiexiao Arch in Yanshang are still well preserved. Photographed by Lou Jianlong

The lower picture: Shuiwei Stone tablet near Jiexiao Arch. Photographed by Lou Jianlong

石构路亭

龙海木棉亭

位于龙海市九湖镇木棉村国道324线旁。现存碑刻共六通，为明代抗倭名将俞大猷所立，后人又在碑前建一亭名“木棉亭”。距木棉亭不远的木棉庵，乃宋代郑虎臣诛杀贾似道处，贾似道系宋末权奸。德佑元年（1275）元军南下，贾以右丞相领兵救鄂州（今湖北武昌），一战大败，全军覆灭。贾似道畏罪潜逃，后被贬循州安置。郑虎臣系会稽县尉，奉命监押贾似道，途经木棉庵，遂将贾似道处死。后人为颂扬郑虎臣的正义之举，遂于此筑亭立碑纪念。

左　图：木棉亭前，后人为颂扬郑虎臣的正义之举，筑亭立碑纪念　楼建龙 摄

右　图：龙海市九湖镇木棉村国道 324 线旁，现存碑刻共六通，为明代抗倭名将俞大猷所立　楼建龙 摄

The left picture: In front of Mumian Pavilion, people celebrated Zheng Huchen's just act and built a pavilion with a monument to commemorate it. Photographed by Lou Jianlong

The right picture: Beside the 324 National Highway in Mumian Village, Jiuhu Town, Longhai City, there are six existing inscriptions, which were set up by Yu Dayou, a famous anti-Japanese soldier in the Ming Dynasty. Photographed by Lou Jianlong

Stone-structure Pavilion

Mumian Pavilion in Longhai

Located beside 324 National Highway in Mumian Village, Jiuhu Town, Longhai City. There are six existing steles, which were erected by Yu Dayou, a famous anti-Japanese soldier in the Ming Dynasty. Later generations built a pavilion named "Mumian Pavilion" in front of the stone tablet.

左　图：清光绪年间重修所立石碑　楼建龙 摄

右　图：清乾隆年间乡里捐赠重修所立石碑　楼建龙 摄

The left picture: The stone tablet rebuilt in the Guangxu period of the Qing Dynasty. Photographed by Lou Jianlong

The right picture: During the reign of Emperor Qianlong of the Qing Dynasty, local people donated to rebuild the stone tablet erected. Photographed by Lou Jianlong

惠安百崎接官亭

位于百崎回族乡白奇渡口，面对后渚江。为百崎回民的始祖郭仲远于明洪武年间（1368~1398）捐资建造，旨在让过江候客小憩，盛夏时兼备凉茶，以供路人解渴。亭为石构凉亭，四角攒尖式，坐北朝南，正面长 7 米，前后宽 6.7 米，通高 5 米，亭中 4 根金柱围成一小“口”形，其外 12 根檐柱围成一大“口”形，16 个础位平面恰好构成一个“回”字形。亭盖由 20 根石梁及 16 根方形石柱支撑；盖顶四披，各披都由石板拼成等腰三角形，四条隆起的亭脊汇向葫芦形顶刹。

Baiqi Jieguan Pavilion in Huian County

Located at Baiqi Ferry, Baiqi Hui Nationality Township, facing Houzhu River. Guo Zhongyuan, the ancestor of Baiqi Hui people, donated money to build it from 1368 to 1398, so as to let people across the river wait for a rest and to provide herbal tea in summer for passers-by to quench their thirst. The pavilion is a stone pavilion with sharp corners and faces south.

惠安百崎接官亭 楼建龙 摄
Jieguan Pavilion in Baiqi of Huian. Photographed by Lou Jianlong

木石成桥，凌空渡水

桥路相连，桥梁用以凌空渡水，本身就属于古道的有机组成。以立县于清雍正十三年（1735）的屏南为例，建县之初，县治（今双溪镇）内外的路桥体系已经基本完备。其官道上通闽北四府、浙江，远及京城，南往古田并达省垣，西去南平及江西腹地，东出宁德、福安港口。各向道路上，“关、隘、桥、梁因地制宜，连类及之”。在县治四周，建南安桥、劝农桥、源里桥、百花桥，桥距城二里，临溪而建，故又统称二里桥；四面山岭之上，驿道之间各建路亭，以供休憩，亭距城五里，统称五里亭；并于水尾山上，创建瑞光塔，以为“发轫龙门，题名雁塔”之愿。相互连接对应的驿道、桥、亭、塔等建制完整，堪称古代县域之内道路亭桥匹配成网的典型实例。

福建古代各类桥梁数量众多，但因为需要与所经过古道周边的山形与水势相适应，所以各区的桥梁风格并不相同。概括而言，闽东北区古道所经，多有“V”字形的高山深谷，岭道需上下往复，所以发展出独具特色、凌空跨越山涧的贯木拱廊桥，以及山涧底部、可有效抵御山洪的石梁桥、柱梁桥、石拱桥、石碇步等。闽西北古道翻越高山而下，经历之处多溪谷宽广，所以沿途桥梁需长距离飞渡，故以多孔木伸臂梁廊桥、单孔木拱廊桥为主，长虹卧波，桥屋内外多有彩画装饰，外形“翼翼楚楚”，与村落风水理念相符，因此发展出丰富的“走桥”习俗。闽西客家地区地势封闭，但河流相对并不宽广，桥梁形式以石拱或木伸臂廊屋为主，但对风水理念更为重视，所以在桥梁两侧多建宫庙，形成用桥梁关锁村落风水的丰富的水尾宫庙建筑群。闽中南区山高水急，溪流纵横密布，所以大多是横跨溪涧的单跨石伸臂梁桥或单孔石拱桥，数量多，但体量一般较小；同时，在桥边多植有高大的乔木，作为树神，与树下桥旁的土地神龛一起，护佑行走之人的安全。与之相比，闽东南古道需要跨越的多属大江大河，桥梁只能采取长距离的多孔石梁墩桥形式，虽然耗资巨大，但所起到作用也是无与伦比，以其高技术含量，为福建赢得“闽中桥梁甲天下”的美誉。

上　图：始建于明代的寿宁大宝桥是从坑底乡前往杨梅洲的必经之路　赖小兵 摄

下　图：连城永隆桥是闽西尚存的古屋桥中最古老的一座　崔建楠 摄

The upper picture: Dabao Bridge in Shouning, which was built in the Ming Dynasty, is the only way from Kengdi Township to Yangmei Island. Photographed by Lai Xiaobing

The lower picture: Yonglong Bridge in Liancheng is the oldest one of the existing ancient house bridges in western Fujian. Photographed by Cui Jiannan

政和花桥乡的走桥习俗是南北方多种民俗文化融合在福建地区的传承，“走桥”即“走百病”，意在祈福消灾　赖小兵 摄

The custom of walking the bridge in Huaqiao Township, Zhenghe is the inheritance of the integration of various folk cultures in the south and the north in Fujian. "Walking the bridge" means "walking all kinds of diseases" and is intended to pray for blessings and eliminate disasters. Photographed by Lai Xiaobing

THE BRIDGE IS MADE OF WOOD AND STONE, CROSSING THE WATER AND THE SKY

The bridge and road are connected, and the bridge itself is part of the ancient road. There are a large number of bridges in ancient Fujian, but the styles of bridges in different districts are not the same because they need to adapt to the mountain shape and water potential around the ancient road. Most of the ancient roads in the northern part of eastern Fujian pass through high mountains and deep valleys in the shape of "V". Therefore, a unique wooden arcade bridge has been developed that volleys across mountain streams. The ancient road in northwest Fujian climbed over high mountains and went down, experiencing many broad valleys. Therefore, it was mainly composed of porous wooden cantilever beam covered bridges and single-hole wooden arcade covered bridges. The inside and outside of the bridge houses were decorated with colorful paintings, which was consistent with the fengshui concept of the village. Therefore, a rich custom of "walking on the bridge" was developed. The Hakka area in western Fujian is closed in terrain, but the rivers are relatively not wide. The bridge is mainly in the form of stone arches or wooden cantilever corridor houses, but more attention is paid to the fengshui concept. Therefore, more temples are built on both sides of the bridge. The mountains in the southern district of central Fujian are high and the streams are densely distributed, so most of them are single-span stone cantilever beam bridges or single-hole stone arch bridges spanning the streams, with a large number but a small size. At the same time, tall trees are planted at the edge of the bridge as tree gods to protect the safety of the walking people together with the land shrine beside the bridge under the tree. In contrast, most of the ancient roads in southeast Fujian need to cross large rivers. Bridges can only take the form of long-distance porous stone beam pier bridges. Although the cost is huge, the role played is incomparable. With its high-tech content, Fujian has won the reputation of "the best bridge in the world in central Fujian".

千乘桥

原名“祥峰桥”，位于棠口村，南北向横跨于棠口溪，创建于宋理宗年间。明末清初毁于火，至清康熙五十四年（1715）倡募重建，雍正七年（1729）落成。嘉庆十四年（1809）“两河伯争长，荡然无存”，以小舟渡之。嘉庆二十五年（1820）生员周大权等募建，因结构牢固、承载力强，故改称“千乘桥”。桥的周边还有祥峰寺、文昌阁（八角亭）、夫人宫、三圣夫人宫、林公庙、“节孝”石碑坊、齐天大圣庙、土地庙等附属文物古建筑，共同组成了丰富的水尾人文景观。

桥一墩二孔，桥身沿南北方向展开，左右 24 间，宽 4.9 米，总长 62.70 米。两岸桥台高约 10.14 米，北端桥台接有 37 级、南端桥台接有 20 级的台阶，通往地面；内侧做金刚墙，上起拱桥。中部桥墩用条石纵横叠砌，平面呈船形，长 9.73 米、宽 3.78 米，来水方向做成尖形，首部上昂，墩尖雕成鸡喙的形状；桥墩剖面为“凸”字形，顶面平，做为桥屋当心间的地面，在内收的二肩处分立左右两侧拱架的立柱。二孔桥身内部均用大木相贯，由第一受力系统的左右九组、每组三根长拱，与第二受力系统的左右八组、每组五根短拱共同组成稳定的受力组合体系；桥身内部使用斜撑，并在中、下方横木（大牛头、下牛头）与立柱间分设二组剪刀撑以加强桥身的前后稳定；拱架二外侧的立柱（将军柱）均向上伸出，兼做桥屋的侧面立柱，使桥面与桥下木构架联结成为稳定的一个整体。拱桥矢高 5.72 米，离水高度 9.70 米，南、北二个拱架的单拱跨度分别为 28.74 米和 26.48 米。

Qiancheng Bridge

Formerly known as "Xiangfeng Bridge", it is located in Tangkou Village and spans Tangkou Creek in the north-south direction, which was built in the Song Dynasty. In the 25th year of Jiaqing's reign (1820), students Zhou Daquan and others raised funds to build it. Due to its firm structure and strong bearing capacity, it was renamed "Qiancheng Bridge".

上　图：始建于宋代的千乘桥横跨棠口溪
赖小兵 摄
左下图：千乘桥周边的大圣庙、土地庙等附属文物古建筑，共同组成了丰富的周边人文景观　赖小兵 摄
右下图：千乘桥周边的文昌阁（八角亭）
赖小兵 摄

The upper picture: Qiancheng Bridge, which was built in the Song Dynasty, spans Tangkou Creek. Photographed by Lai Xiaobing

The lower left picture: The ancient cultural relics and buildings around Qiancheng Bridge, such as the Temple of Great Sage and the temple of the God of Earth, together form a rich surrounding cultural landscape. Photographed by Lai Xiaobing

The lower right picture: Wenchang pavilion (Bajiao Pavilion) around Qiancheng bridge. Photographed by Lai Xiaobing

万安桥

初名龙江公济桥，俗名长桥、彩虹桥，始建于宋代。正中桥墩背面嵌有一块石碑，碑文云："弟子江稹舍钱一拾三贯又谷三十四石，结石墩一造，为考妣二亲承此良因，又为合家男女及自身各乞保平安。元祐五年（1090）庚午九月谨题。"由此可以证明，万安桥所在的长桥溪至迟在北宋时就有造桥之举了。

1932 年再度复建，桥身向西北岸延伸为 38 开间 156 柱，桥西北端建有重檐桥亭。传说在此次重建中有一工匠从拱架上跌落河中而安然无恙，故更名为万安桥。桥身沿西北－东南方向展开，左右 37 间，五墩六孔，总长 98.20 米，宽 4.7 米，是我国现存最长的贯木拱廊桥。万安桥与深处深山峡谷中、数量上占绝大多数的单孔贯木拱廊桥有着较大的差别，它以多墩多跨、上木下石的结构形式，将我国造桥传统中木拱、石墩二大技术完美结合，从而解决了贯木拱廊桥单跨长度有限、不能在较宽河床上应用的制约，成为我国古代多跨多拱贯木拱廊桥的杰出代表。

左　图：每年端午节，屏南万安桥有“走桥”的古老风俗　张峥嵘 摄

中　图：万安桥是周边百姓休闲聚会的场所　赖小兵 摄

右　图：万安桥是我国现存最长的贯木拱廊桥　张峥嵘 摄

The left picture: Every year during the Dragon Boat Festival, Wan'an Bridge in Pingnan has an ancient custom of "walking the bridge". Photographed by Zhang Zhengrong

The middle picture: Wan'an Bridge is a place for the surrounding people to relax and meet. Photographed by Lai Xiaobing

The right picture: Wan'an bridge is the longest existing through wood arch bridge in China. Photographed by Zhang Zhengrong

Wan'an Bridge

The first name was Longjiang Gongji Bridge, commonly known as Changqiao and Rainbow Bridge, which was built in the Song Dynasty. It was rebuilt again in 1932. The bridge body extends to the northwest bank with 38 bays and 156 columns. A double-eaved bridge pavilion is built at the northwest end of the bridge. Legend has it that during the reconstruction, a craftsman fell from the arch and fell into the river unharmed, so he changed his name to Wan'an Bridge.

霞浦竹江汐路桥

位于沙江镇竹江村与小马村间东吾洋海域，系连接陆地与竹江岛的海上古石路。民国版《霞浦县志》卷之五《水利志》载：“竹江汐路桥。清嘉庆时，廪贡郑志鳌（字启昂）因竹江孤岛无路可行，悯涉川之劳，掘泥埕丈余许，磉石平叠而上至泥面，甃以石，插竹江上，直达小马堡，计蜿蜒七里余，遇有港处石板较广，石柱较高，下可通小舟、竹筏。港凡七，桥之数如之。至今水落时，往来络绎不绝，人称坦途焉。”

古石路为西北—东南走向，长 3056.65 米，其间有七座古石桥。因路和桥建在滩涂上，涨潮淹没，退潮（汐）方可通行，故称汐路桥。汐路桥兼具路和桥功能，由清朝竹江乡伸郑启昂耗巨资于嘉庆十六年（1811）建造。其建造过程十分艰难，全靠人工铺设。路基底用松木打桩，桩上铺垫杂木草皮，然后铺上条石，条石横竖叠三层，再铺设路面。七座古石桥，最宽 1.8 米，桥最高 2.9 米，最长 30 米；其中有四座桥，桥孔上下二层，引桥边有诸多小孔，具有排潮防潮和抗大潮能力。

左　图：霞浦沙江镇竹江村的竹江汐路桥，因建在滩涂上，其造桥过程十分艰难　吴军　摄

右　图：因路和桥建在滩涂上，涨潮淹没，退潮（汐）方可通行，故称汐路桥　吴军　摄

The left picture: Xilu Bridge of Zhujiang, located in Zhujiang Village, Shajiang Town, Xiapu, was very difficult to build because it is built on the beach. Photographed by Wu Jun

The right picture: Because roads and bridges are built on tidal flats, they are flooded by high tide and can only pass through when the tide ebbs (tide), so they are called Xilu Bridge. Photographed by Wu Jun

Xilu Bridge in Zhujiang of Xiapu

Located in the Dongwuyang sea area between Zhujiang Village and Xiaoma Village in Shajiang Town, it is an ancient stone road connecting land and Zhujiang Island. The ancient stone road runs from northwest to southeast with seven ancient stone bridges. Because roads and bridges are built on tidal flats, people can pass through only when the tide ebbs while they are submerged when the tide is low, so it is called Xilu Bridge.

会清桥

紧临贡川镇，横跨胡贡溪，始建于明末，竣工于清初，时值明、清易代之际，故名会清桥。另一说，是因为桥建于胡贡溪与沙溪交汇之处，溪水一浊一清而名。该桥为石拱廊屋桥，长 40.8 米，宽 8.2 米。其下部为石墩石拱，.2 墩 3 孔，中孔净跨 13.2 米，左右孔各 11.7 米。其上建有木屋，桥面铺石、立柱、盖房，构成一条长廊式走道。

安仁桥

位于青水畲族乡三房自然村北面溢洋溪上。由林氏先祖于唐显庆元年（656）建造，后毁，清嘉庆八年（1803）重建。桥身呈西北—东南走向，为木伸臂梁廊桥。桥身总长 28.1 米，宽 6.2 米，建筑面积 181.3 平方米。桥屋为歇山顶，面阔九间，进深四柱，前后七架梁，四面檐檩下设挡雨板。在迎水面的开间设有神龛，供奉“观音菩萨”，桥中心顶部设藻井。桥两侧设金刚墙，用岩石条砌而成，宽 14 米；跨河长度 18 米，底层用 8 根直径 60 厘米粗大梁水杉架构、第二层横用 28 根直径 40 厘米小梁架铺，第三层用宽 40 厘米宽 5 公分厚的杉木板铺面。桥屋顶中立葫芦刹，飞檐翘角，瓦上檐下雕刻彩绘镶嵌各种历史人物故事和民间吉祥物等。

桥西北面 5 米处建有“崇清宫”，宫坐西北朝东南，面阔 7.8 米，进深 7.9 米。供奉赵大元帅、张公法主、南朝大帝、马氏真仙、五谷神农等佛像。

会清桥位于永安市贡川镇集风村，建于明天启六年（1626 年），因桥建于胡贡溪与沙溪交汇处，而二溪一浊一清，泾渭分明，故取名会清桥 周跃东 摄

Huiqing Bridge is located in Jifeng Village, Gongchuan Town, Yong'an City, whichwas built in 1626, the sixth year of the Tianqi regin of the Ming Dynasty. It was named Huiqing Bridge because it was built at the junction of Hugong Creek and Shaxi, and the two streams were muddy and clear, which were quite distinct from each other. Photographed by Zhou Yuedong

YONG'AN COVERED BRIDGE

Huiqing Bridge

Close to Gongchuan Town and across Hugong Creek, it was built in the late Ming Dynasty and completed in the early Qing Dynasty. It was named Huiqing Bridge while the Ming Dynasty changed into the Qing Dynasty.

Anren Bridge

It is located on Yiyang Creek to the north of Sanfang Nature Village in She Nationality Township of Qingshui. There is a shrine in the bay facing the water to worship "Guanyin Bodhisattva". The roof of the bridge are carved and painted and inlaid with stories of various historical figures and folk mascots on the tiles and under the eaves.

漳州江东桥

古称“虎渡桥”，又名“通济桥”，是一座多孔石伸臂梁桥，位于龙文区与角美交界处，横跨九龙江北溪下游。两岸峻山夹峙，江宽流急，地势险要，古称“三省通衢”。相传初建桥时，桥墩屡建不稳，偶有猛虎负子过江，遂依虎道勘得水中礁石，乃就石垒墩，桥墩遂固，故名虎渡桥。而《漳州府志》则说此处“为郡之寅方，因名虎渡”。

南宋绍熙年间（1190~1194），郡守越逊伯在这里以联艘建造浮桥，开此处造桥历史的先声。嘉定七年（1214），郡守庄夏始于此垒石为墩建木桥。宋嘉熙元年（1237）木桥被火烧毁。漳州郡守李韶倡议改建石桥，并捐私钱 50 万，再拨政府库钱万缗，又发动和尚廷睿师徒四处募款以济。由郡人陈正义董其事，历时三年又一个月，花钱 30 万缗。造成的石桥“其长三千尺，址高百尺，酾水一十五道，梁跨于址者五十有八，长八十尺，广博皆六尺有奇。东西结亭以憩往来者。”

江东桥的石梁每条长 22 至 23 米、宽 1.15 至 1.5 米、厚 1.3 至 1.6 米，重量近 200 吨。这是桥梁建筑中的伟大创举，中外建桥史上的奇迹。我国桥梁专家茅以升在《中国石拱桥》一文中说：“福建漳州的江东桥，修建于八百年前，有的石梁一块就有二百来吨重，究竟是怎样安装上去的，至今还不完全知道。”英国剑桥大学博士李约瑟在《中国科学技术史》一书中也说：“江东桥是一个有趣的历史性问题。”在罗哲文主编的《中国古代建筑》书中，第一章就提及：“虎渡桥重达二百吨的石梁，工匠们如何把它们架上波涛汹涌的急流之上，至今仍然令人为之惊叹。”

JIANGDONG BRIDGE IN ZHANGZHOU

It is a multi-hole stone cantilever beam bridge, located at the junction of Longwen District and Jiaomei, spanning the lower reaches of the North Stream of Jiulong River. Each stone beamof Jiangdong Bridge is 22 to 23 meters long, 1.15 to 1.5 meters wide, 1.3 to 1.6 meters thick and weighs nearly 200 tons. This is a great pioneering work in bridge construction and a miracle in the history of bridge construction at home and abroad.

上　图：漳州江东古桥横跨于九龙江北溪下游　李晋泰 摄
左下图：漳州江东古桥宋代石梁墩有的重达 200 吨，堪称桥梁建筑中的奇迹　阮任艺 摄
右下图：古桥的石梁仍稳架于桥墩之上，如今已成为 324 国道的要塞　阮任艺 摄

The upper picture: Jiangdong Ancient Bridge of Zhangzhou spans the lower reaches of the North Streamof the Jiulong River. Photographed by Li Jintai

The lower left picture: Some of the piers of Jiangdong Ancient Bridge of Zhangzhou in the Song Dynasty weighed 200 tons, which can be called a miracle in the bridge construction. Photographed by Ruan Renyi

The lower right picture: The stone beam of the ancient bridge is still stable on the pier, and now it has become the fortress of 324 National Highway. Photographed by Ruan Renyi

泉州跨海长桥

SEA-CROSSING LONG BRIDGE IN QUANZHOU

洛阳桥

位于洛江区桥南村与惠安县洛阳镇洛阳街交界的洛阳江入海口，距市区10公里。这里原为古泉州湾洛阳港，未建桥时，往来皆赖舟船渡江。由于水面宽阔，水流湍急，常因风浪暴起而舟覆人溺。宋庆历年间（1041~1048），郡人李宠甃石为墩，架木板为浮桥，供行人过往。皇祐五年（1053），泉郡王实、卢锡、许忠、义波、宗善等十五人兴筑万安渡石桥。嘉祐元年（1056）二月至四年十二月，由蔡襄督造竣工。

洛阳桥系花岗石砌筑，现长731米，宽4.5米。桥墩45座，两侧作护栏，有500根栏杆石柱，其中28根为狮身栏柱，所用石桥板最大的长11米，宽0.98米，厚0.8米；每条桥板重达数吨至十余吨。

洛阳桥建于“水阔五里，深不可址”的江海交汇处，是中国历史上第一座跨海梁式大石桥。首先应用垒石、匝石、叠石，形成一条横跨江底的矮石堤，作为建桥立墩的基址，并开创了现代称为“筏形基础”的新型桥基，为后世建造跨海石桥提供了宝贵经验。

Luoyang Bridge

Located at the mouth of Luoyang River at the junction of Qiaonan Village, Luojiang District and Luoyang Street, Luoyang Town, Hui'an County. Luoyang Bridge is the first large sea-crossing stone beam bridge in Chinese history. First of all, a low stone dike spanning the bottom of the river was formed by using stacking stones, turning stones and stacking stones as the base site for building bridge piers, and a new type of bridge foundation called "raft foundation" was created in modern times, which provided valuable experience for later generations to build sea-crossing stone bridges.

左上图：洛阳桥是中国历史上第一座跨海梁式大石桥，昔日，不仅是连接福州和泉州的驿道，还是整个惠安县最重要的交通要道 陈海平 摄

左下图：洛阳桥原名“万安桥”，为北宋泉州太守蔡襄主持所建，桥头的《万安桥记》石碑记载着建桥历史 蒋一曦 摄

右 图：洛阳桥上精美的佛像，月光菩萨塔，这是全桥罕见的纪年文物，准确无误地记载了这座千年大石桥的建造年代 赖小兵 摄

The upper left picture: Luoyang Bridge is the first greatstone bridge across the sea in Chinese history. In the past, it was not only a post road connecting Fuzhou and Quanzhou, but also the most important traffic artery in Hui'an County. Photographed by Chen Haiping

The lower left picture: Luoyang Bridge, formerly known as "Wan'an Bridge", was built under the auspices of Cai Xiang, Governor of Quanzhou in the Northern Song Dynasty. The stone tablet "Notes of Wan'an Bridge" at the bridge head records the history of bridge construction. Photographed by Jiang Yixi

The right picture: The exquisite Buddha statue and Moonlight Bodhisattva Pagoda on Luoyang Bridge are rare chronological relics of the whole bridge, which accurately record the construction date of this millennium stone bridge. Photographed by Lai Xiaobing

The upper pictrue: The stone stele group on Anping Bridge. Photographed by Lai Xiaobing

The lower left pictrue: The stone stele group records the history of bridge construction. Photographed by Lai Xiaobing

The lower right pictrue: The stone statue at the head of Anping Bridge. Photographed by Lai Xiaobing

安平桥

位于晋江安海与南安水头之间的海湾上，是我国著名的古长桥，素有“天下无桥长此桥”的美誉。

安平桥于宋绍兴八年（1138）由安海黄护、黄逸父子和僧智渊倡建，后由郡守赵令衿督造，于绍兴二十二年（1152）十一月竣工。安平桥为东西走向，自东而西依此排列有：瑞光塔、超然亭、澄渟院、望高楼、憩亭、两侧水中石塔、水心亭（中亭）、新兴宫、两侧水中石塔、憩亭、隘门、海潮庵等。

安平桥筑墩时，按港道深浅、水流缓急分别筑建长方形、船形、半船形三种形式的桥墩。长方形墩筑于上下游都不深峻的水域，船形墩筑于水流湍急、水域较宽的港道，利于分流排水，半船形墩筑于一面较深的水域，便于迎水分流。

安平桥墩基采用一层木排的“睡木沉基法”，以达到桥墩能整体均衡沉降的目的。有的还在睡木两端打入支架的桩木，有的还在墩底海泥中渗入石砾、粗沙，这是睡木沉基结合沙基的筑基法，较“筏型基础”省工、省料，是建桥技术的又一创新。

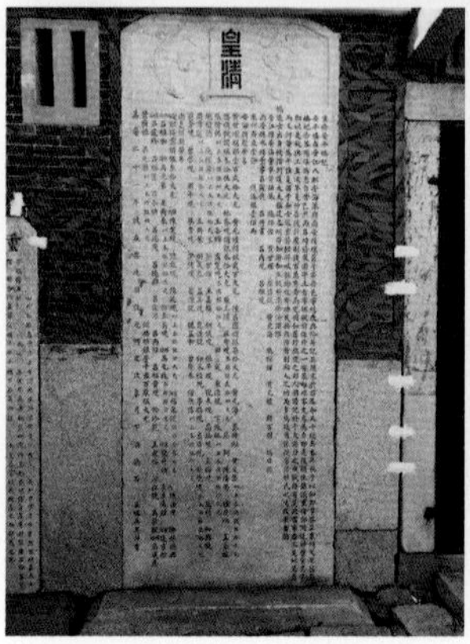

上　图：安平桥水心亭碑林　赖小兵 摄

左下图：水心亭碑林记载着修桥的历史　赖小兵 摄

右下图：安平桥亭的护桥将军石雕像　赖小兵 摄

Anping Bridge

Located in the bay between Anhai in Jinjiangand Shuitou in Nanan, it is a famous ancient long bridge in our country and has the reputation of "no bridge in the world is longer than this bridge". The pier foundation of Anping Bridge adopts the "sleeping wood sinking foundation method" of a layer of wooden rafts. Some still drive the pile wood into the support at both ends of the sleeping wood, and some still infiltrate gravel and coarse sand into the sea mud at the bottom of the pier, which is another innovation in bridge construction technology.

安平桥是中国现存古代最长的石桥，也是中国现存最长的海港大石桥 林燕春 摄

Anping Bridge is the longest existing stone bridge in ancient China, and it is also the longest existing harbor great stone bridgein China. Photographed by Lin Yanchun

莆田宁海桥

宁海桥

自唐代起，就开辟有自福州通往广南(广东)的驿道。宋代，随着兴化平原的开发，改变以往依山作势、遇水绕道的交通状况，闭塞的山区也因兴化县的设立而得以开发。自此，福(州)兴(化)泉(州)驿道、莆(田)仙(游)驿道、仙(游)惠(安)驿道、莆(田)新(县)驿道、莆田城东驿道等初具规模，并开始种植路边树。

涵江至黄石属城东驿道的一部分，长9公里，沿途多为平地，石板铺设。途经上梧、梧郊、镇前、宁海桥、林墩、华堤、井后等村。明郑岳《山斋集》卷11《修宁海桥记》云：宁海“为上下诸郡要津”。宁海桥位于木兰溪下游的入海口，古为宁海渡，故名宁海桥。宁海桥为连接莆田南、北两大洋平原的重要交通要道，每年端午节，拂晓站在桥上观日出，旭日初升，极似一面大圆镜，放射出万道金光；桥下波光粼粼，犹如金龙逐波，十分壮观，故有“宁海初日”之雅称，为“莆田二十四景”之一。

桥初建于元代元统二年(1334年)，由僧人越浦发起募捐建造。桥址原定在今址上有几百米处，该处水面较窄，但水流湍急，发生多起施工事故，未能建成。之后越浦前往泉州参观洛阳桥后，选现址另建。后经六圮六建，到清雍正十年(1732)第七次修建，历时15年才建成功。为伸臂式石梁桥，14墩，分水15门，通长225.7米，宽5.8米，桥面用75块长10~13米，宽、厚各约1米的巨大石梁架设而成；墩为两头尖的船形，上砌三层悬臂，以减少石梁跨度。宁海桥的架桥历史信息丰富，条石上都刻有捐施者的姓名和捐资数额，桥面两旁设有栏杆，望柱上雕刻姿态各异的石狮；同时，桥的两端各设有两尊明代雕造的高约3米、戴盔披甲执长剑的护桥将军石像。

宁海桥又名东济桥，位于木兰溪的入海处，古为宁海渡，因这里溪海汇集，潮大流急，泥沙滚滚，建桥工程十分艰巨。从元代元统二年（1334年）至清康熙十九年（1680年）的三百多年间，六建六圮。桥头两端竖有明代“护桥将军”石像各2尊 崔建楠 摄

Ninghai bridge, also known as Dongji bridge, is located at the entrance to the sea of Mulan Creek, which was Ninghai Ferry in ancient times. Because of the confluence of rivers and seas, the tide is high and the current is rapid, with rolling sediment, so the construction of Ninghai bridge was very arduous. During the 300-odd years from the 2nd year of Yuantong reign in the Yuan Dynasty (1334) to the 19th year of Kangxi reign in the Qing Dynasty (1680), six bridges were built six times. At both ends of the bridge, there are two stone statues of "bridge protecting general" in the Ming Dynasty. Photographed by Cui Jiannan

Ninghai Bridge in Putian

Ninghai Bridge was first built in 1334 of the Yuan Dynasty, which was raised and built by the monk Yuepu. The erection history of Ninghai Bridge is rich in information. The names and amounts of donations are engraved on each rectangularstone. Railings are set on both sides of the bridge deck, and stone lions with different postures are carved on the pillars; At both ends of the bridge are stone statues of two bridge protection generals carved in the Ming Dynasty, about 3 meters high, wearing helmets, armour and keeping a long sword.

上　图：古宁海桥上捐建者的石刻
　　　崔建楠 摄
左下图：古宁海桥还“藏”在现代大桥的下面 崔建楠 摄
右下图：宁海桥头石狮 阮任艺 摄

The upper picture: Stone Carvings of donors on the Ancient Ninghai Bridge. Photographed by Cui Jiannan

The lower left picture: The ancient Ninghai Bridge is still "hidden" under the modern bridge. Photographed by Cui Jiannan

The lower right picture: The stone lion at the head of Ninghai bridge. Photographed by Ruan Renyi

福清龙江桥

位于福清海口镇海口村西龙江之上。北宋政和三年（1113），太平寺僧惠国、守思倡议，后乡人林迁、林霸、陈侈和僧人妙觉等继续募缘集资建造，于北宋宣和六年（1124）竣工，耗钱500万缗（每缗1000文）。初名螺江桥，南宋绍兴王十年（1160），少卿林栗根据“江南沙合接龙首”的古语，更名为“龙江桥”。

龙江桥是座多跨伸臂梁式石桥，桥墩、梁、桥板、栏杆等均用石材。桥身东西走向，长476米，宽约4.6米，现存三十九墩，四十孔，舟型墩，墩长9.2米，高6米，宽3.6米。桥梁用9.5米，宽0.67~0.75米的条石铺成，首尾互相扣合搭接。桥头立一对八角七层楼阁式实心石塔，高5.05米，须弥座，葫芦刹顶，塔壁每面浮雕佛像一尊。

LONGJIANG BRIDGE IN FUQING

Located on the west Longjiang River in Haikou Village, Haikou Town, Fuqing, Longjiang Bridge is a multi-span cantilever beam stone bridge. The piers, beams, bridge slabs and railings are all made of stone. At the bridge head stands a pair of solid stone pagodas with an ctagonal and seven-storey loft style, and with a relief Buddha on each side of the pagoda wall.

左上图：龙江古桥桥墩采用种蛎固础的做法，桥基吃水以下长满牡蛎　赖小兵 摄

右上图：海口镇宋代龙江古桥　卢胜富 摄

下　图：龙江古桥头的石塔浮雕　赖小兵 摄

The upper left picture: The pier of Longjiang Ancient Bridge adopts the method of planting oysters to fix the foundation. Oysters grow below the draft of the bridge foundation. Photographed by Lai Xiaobing

The upper right picture: Longjiang Ancient Bridge of the Song Dynasty in Haikou Town. Photographed by Lu Shengfu

The lower picture: The relief sculpture of Stone Pagoda at the head of Longjiang Ancient Bridge. Photographed by Lai Xiaobing

第四章

Chapter IV

山水福建 闽道人文

福建

FUJIAN WITH MOUNTAINS AND RIVERS, HUMAN CULTURE OF FUJIAN ROADS

In ancient times, it was a pleasure to donate for repairing roads, and the government and the people took it as a righteous act.Fujian is rich in mountains and rivers, during which ancient roads walk. Building roadsthrough mountains and bridging upon streams, road opening and water control have become two major difficulties that must be faced directly in the construction of ancient roads in Fujian.

The difficulty of building roads is well known to all. But once it is completed, it can be recorded in history. There are countless records in history books about the good deeds of building roads and bridges. In addition to historical records, more folk acts of righteousness were recorded and passed down in the form of stone carvings. These carvings are still scattered on the roadsides, silently telling these memorable history. Stone carvings can be roughly divided into two types, one is the stone tablet and the other is the inscription. These stone carvings have been relatively completely preserved by the repairers of past dynasties and passed on from generation to generation.

古代，捐修道路以济行人，是好义急公之事，也被上自官方、下自民间认为是“深可嘉尚”之举。福建“八山一水一分田”，古道行走其间，逢山开路，遇水搭桥，开道与治水，成为古道修造中必须直面的两大难事。

梁克家在《三山志》卷五之《地理类·驿铺》中，“北取温州路”条目中，记述了当年修路铺桥一事：“嘉祐三年，知怀安县樊纪，僦工致治，乃奠高为夷，正曲为直，凹回者培，陷者续，迄今利之。主簿王知微记。又治路，自北门入岩溪，抵青山，又培土筑趋府道，积德、承平、移风三乡地庳泞，悉砌石以便民。至溪涧或江浦之阻，梁石以渡者五十一，木为桥十有六，皆利民之著者。”

修路之难，人尽皆知，但一路之成，青史留载，善名永成。纵观史书，修路筑桥的善举不胜枚举。清乾隆版《屏南县志》记载有知县沈钟为监生叶雄声平粜修路而请加奖励之事：“惟甘棠至古田北界嵩洲岭一带，计长三千余丈，尚未开平，依然鸟道，往来行旅，未免艰难。生夙钦德化，愿襄盛举……愿将膳余租谷三百余石，平价发粜，以济民食；并愿将发粜之价捐修道路，以便行旅。”同样，正德嘉靖间，柘荣因仙岭与外界交通不便，行人须翻山越岭绕道而行，劳顿不堪，有名宗远者，历时3年，耗费大量钱财，建成从仙岭经榴坪，过福安沙坑至雷公亭的一条长达17.5公里的石路，并在中途的福安县上白石沙井渡口处，设置渡船一只，置买渡田，雇人划船，免费让行人过渡。此外，宗远还建造通济桥、利济桥、局前桥、日桥、月桥、暗桥等6座桥梁，以及井前亭、种德亭、留芳亭、长冈亭等4座凉亭。行人有口皆碑，福宁知州题匾“德义兼隆”予以表彰，并上报朝廷，钦赐冠带荣身。

除了史书记录外，更多的民间义举，会以刻石以书的方式传诵下来。这些刻石如今仍然散布于路旁道头，默默地述说着这些值得纪念的往事。刻石大致可以分为两类，一为石碑，二为题刻。这些刻石被历代修缮者相对完整地保存下来，成为当地旌善扬名的重要方法，而代代传咏。

修路旌善，碑铭纪事

相对于摩崖题刻，修路石碑一般体量较小，因为可以在异地镌刻后搬至指定地点树立，所以碑面字数可以较多，字的尺寸较小，但撰写及刻工多为名家，艺术价值较高。修路石碑的内容以捐资碑、纪事碑为主，立于古道路旁，或大树下，或溪渡边，或庵亭前，或与摩崖题刻相近而立，形成行旅途中又一处驻足休憩、观赏品读的所在。

柘荣溪口造桥碑

柘荣地处闽浙边界，境内山高岭陡，人们外出只能步行、乘轿；货运全靠肩挑、背驮。据立于溪口村永安桥头的咸丰二年《资寿、庆安、同安三桥碑记》载："溪口隶霞邑而地近鼎邑，鼎故海物所聚，往来贸易者路由于此"。溪口村自古跨溪建有多座桥梁，形成环村而立的桥群。现存之桥群由二条石碇步、二座石梁柱桥及一座石拱桥组成，其中石碇步与梁柱桥均位于溪口村东面之凤里溪上，石拱桥即永安桥则跨村南面之玉山溪（又称石山溪）而建。

永安桥为单孔半圆石拱桥，拱券砌法为纵联式。此类石桥在闽浙山区常用于跨度较大的溪流之上，但因建造难度较大，所以保存下来的数量亦不甚多。据唐寰澄先生所著之《中国大百科全书·桥梁卷》所录，我国古代石拱桥以半圆拱居多，其中又以单孔拱桥的拱跨较大，多在10~20米之间，而永安桥之

上　图：柘荣溪口村石梁柱桥和石碇步桥　赖小兵 摄

下　图：溪口永安桥虽为常见的单孔半圆石拱桥，但因建桥的跨度较大，因而难度也大　楼建龙 摄

The upper picture: The stone beam column bridge and heavy stone bridge in Xikou Village of Zherong. Photographed by Lai Xiaobing

The lower picture: Although Yong'an Bridge in Xikou is a common single-hole semi-circular stone arch bridge, it was difficult to build it due to its large span. Photographed by Lou Jianlong

上　图：溪口永安桥——闽东最大的单孔石拱桥，古代从柘荣往福温古道的必经之路　赖小兵 摄

下　图：永安桥栏杆中部东侧石栏板刻“永安桥”三字　楼建龙 摄

The upper picture: Yong’an Bridge in Xikou, the largest single-hole stone arch bridge in eastern Fujian, is the only way from Zherong to Fuwen ancient road in ancient times. Photographed by Lai Xiaobing

The lower picture: "Yong'an Bridge" is inscribed on the stone fence slab on the east side of the middle of the railing of Yong'an Bridge. Photographed by Lou Jianlong

柘荣溪口造桥碑 楼建龙 摄
Bridge-building Monument in Xikou of Zherong. Photographed by Lou Jianlong

拱跨达 23.76 米。在永安桥北面宽坪立有八通石碑，详细记录了清朝咸丰、同治、光绪年间村民们集资修桥的义举。其中北侧五通石碑，一通为长安桥记（光绪七年），四通为永安桥捐资碑（同治二年）；东北角立碑三通，即资寿、庆安、同安三桥碑记（咸丰二年）。

据《资寿、庆安、同安三桥碑记》所记，“（溪口）旧左右二溪纵横交阻，自开辟以来，仅列石为步以渡，遇山水发时，行人不可涉足，缺憾不平久矣。咸丰元年辛亥月，庠贡生宜园吴君倡议并建三桥，命仲子从于林君、袁君等同为董事，且于附近募捐，共成义举，盖不独有其功也。越明年壬子十二月，三桥告成，继以修路，总费银一千柒拾两有奇，微吴君之力殆不及此。既竣事，咸谓桥安而寿，所以安人寿，爰名其右溪大桥曰资寿，名其左溪上桥曰庆安，下桥曰同安。属郡学生陶甄记其略为此并列捐资历者姓名勒之贞珉，以垂永远云。”

由碑文而知，石碇步是溪口村历史上最早建筑、同时也是最主要的渡水设施。溪口村历史上共建有五条碇步，四条建于左溪即凤里溪上，最长的一条位于右溪即玉山溪溪尾，建于清咸丰三年（1853），原有 99 墩，后增建至 101 墩、103 墩。碑文之中村南面玉山溪上的资寿桥现已无存，村东面凤里溪上游的庆安桥早期亦毁于水，之后于光绪七年（1881）重建，改称长安桥；溪下游的同安桥则一直保存至今，即今天位于凤里溪水尾处的石梁柱桥。

桥北立永安桥、庆安桥、资寿桥、同安桥等碑志八通　赖小兵 摄

In the north of the bridge, there are eight inscriptions such as Yong'an Bridge, Qing'an Bridge, Zishou Bridge and Tong'an Bridge. Photographed by Lai Xiaobing

BUILDING ROADS FOR COMMENDING GOODNESS, INSCRIPTIONS FOR CHRONICLES

Compared with inscriptionsengraved on a cliff, road-building stone tablets are generally smaller in size, because they can be transported and moved, so the number of words on the stone tablet's surface is larger and the size of words is smaller, but most of the writers and engravers are famous and have high artistic value. The content of the road-building stone tablet is mainly a donation stele and a chronicle stele, which stands on the roadside of the ancient road, or under a big tree, or at the edge of a stream, or in front of a temple pavilion, or close to the cliff inscription, forming a place to stop and rest and watch and read during the journey.

XIKOU BRIDGE-BUILDING MONUMENT IN ZHERONG

Zherong is located at the border between Fujian and Zhejiang, with high mountains and steep ridges. People could only walk and take sedan chairs when going out;The freight is all carried by one's shoulders and backs. The ancient road was formed in Sui and Tang Dynasties and took shape in Song and Yuan Dynasties. Xikou Village has built many bridges across the stream since ancient times, forming a group of bridges around the village. The existing bridge group consists of two stone anchorage bridges, two stone beam-column bridges and one stone arch bridge. The stone arch bridge, namely Yong'an Bridge, is built across Yushan Creek (also known as Shishan Creek) to the south of the village.

霞浦观音亭修路碑

霞浦境内古道路亭，多是土木结构，有双向或三向通路的屋亭或四面通行的凉亭，以及木架加盖茅草的草亭。现保存尚完整的有半岭观音亭、罗公亭、云海亭、长寿亭、渔洋岭亭等，半岭观音亭寨由观音亭寺、观音亭寨及古驿道三部分共同组成，庙因路兴，寨由庙名。

半岭古驿道至迟在北宋年间已经形成，自古就是闽浙（福温）通道所经之地。驿道保存极其完整，最宽处约 3 米，用卵石及块石整齐铺砌成台阶，蜿蜒上下于崇山坡地之间。半岭古驿道于观音亭寨之间沿山势由西南而东北再折向北，下行横穿寨堡而过，寨内长度约 88.7 米（南、北两门间水平距离）。驿道下行三里许坑壑下有溪，原有大小四座石拱桥，并有多通修桥修路石碑，后桥毁碑存，所存之 14 通石碑现集中移立于观音亭寺之前坪保存。碑文所记之募捐人等遍及浙闽粤各地，其中包括为数不少的闽西烟叶商人等。

观音亭寺，原名观音院，位于寨堡西南部，依山面向古驿道而建。寺始建于明洪武二年（1369），由门楼、前殿、后殿及前殿两侧附属建筑组成，总宽 29.5 米，进深 21.4 米；外部砖墙围护，占地面积 426.8 平方米。后殿于清康熙五年（1666）、乾隆辛亥年（1791）、光绪己卯年（1879）多次重修，抬梁式木构架保留清后期建筑风格。

左　图：现位于观音亭寺前坪的石碑 楼建龙 摄
右　图：霞浦观音亭前的僧人 吴军 摄

The left picture: The stone tablet located at Guanyin Pavilion in Siqianping Village now. Photographed by Lou Jianlong

The right picture: Monks in front of Guanyin Pavilion in Xiapu . Photographed by Wu Jun

观音亭寺之前方，是兀立高起的山壁，原来是观音亭寨的敌楼所在。从敌楼往东再弧折向北，沿山崖砌石壁，即现存基本完好的观音亭寨的寨墙。寨墙大致为南北走向的弧圈形，其西面利用高峻的山崖，南、北有门，东面则用块石砌筑寨墙。寨堡南北长约 86 米，东西宽约 63 米；墙体残高约 5 米，三面外墙现存总长约 131.84 米。

观音亭寨的北门保存较好。寨门跨古驿道而建，块石叠砌，顶部叠涩出肩，上承长条形板石。寨门宽约 1.76 米，深约 2.75 米，净高 2.86 米。寨门门额镌“观音亭寨”四字，并有“同治元年（1862）孟春月”“知福宁府事……题”的上、下款识。

Xiapu Guanyin Pavilion Village

Guanyin Pavilion Village in Banlingconsists of three parts: Guanyin Pavilion Temple, Guanyin Pavilion Village and Banling Ancient Post Road. The temple is famous for its roads and the village is named after the temple.

Banling Ancient Post Road was formed in the Northern Song Dynasty at the latest and has been the place where Fujian and Zhejiang (Wenzhou) passages pass since ancient times. The post road is well preserved and about 3 meters wide. There are streams down the road, and used to be four stone arch bridges of different sizes, and many stone tablets for repairing bridges and roads. Later, the bridge was destroyed and the stone tablets were stored. The 14 stone tablets stored are now concentrated in front of Guanyin Pavilion Temple for preservation. The fund-raisers recorded in the inscription are all over Zhejiang, Fujian and Guangdong, including many tobacco merchants in southwest Fujian.

左　图：半岭古驿道上的观音亭寨　楼建龙 摄
右　图：霞浦观音亭寺　楼建龙 摄

The left picture: Guanyin Pavilion Village on Banling Ancient Post Road. Photographed by Lou Jianlong

The right picture: Guanyin Pavilion Temple in Xiapu. Photographed by Lou Jianlong

漳浦陈仓岭修路碑

闽南特别是漳州的地理形势与闽东相似，但山海之间尚有相对开阔且平坦的滨海平原，成为连接闽粤之间的重要南北大通道。漳州南有漳江，北有九龙江，其支流深入博平岭山脉腹地，穿壑过涧，滩险濑急。但溪流下游缓潭漫流，水碧沙平，多可行舟。

漳浦陈仓岭修路碑位于马坪镇马墟村，是当时漳州马坪通往龙海白水的要道所经。古道共有660级台阶，每层台阶长约有0.9米，宽约0.4米，青石质地。古道弯弯曲曲，呈“之”字形，延绵近千米。古道边立有三座漳浦与龙海的交界碑，清雍正十一年（1733）立。碑刻并列同向，坐西向东，均为黄岗岩质，其中两座碑首均题有“陈仓岭”三字。三座中最高的碑刻高1.35米、宽0.54米，碑正面阴刻：“陈仓岭，漳浦海澄县交界碑，光绪元年（1875）贰月建，漳浦县樊海澄县华等仝立”；中间的碑刻高0.94米、宽0.35米，碑正面阴刻：“陈仓岭，漳浦海澄县合立界碑”；另一块无题首碑刻，高0.98米、宽0.35米，碑之正面，阴刻：“陈仓岭碑记，漳浦口海澄蔡雍正五年（1727）”。古道附近尚有“仓岭亭碑记”两座石碑，均带碑座，一座碑身高1.61米、宽0.65米，碑座长0.89米、高0.30米，另一座碑身高1.47米、宽0.68米，碑座长0.90米、高0.30米，均刻有碑文。

ROAD-BUILDING MONUMENT IN CHENCANGLING OF ZHANGPU

The geographical situation of Zhangzhou is similar to that of eastern Fujian. There is a relatively open and flat coastal plain between mountains and seas, which has become an important north-south channel connecting Fujian and Guangdong. Zhangzhou has Zhangjiang River in the south and Jiulong River in the north, which are mostly navigable.

The road-building Monument in Chencangling of Zhangpu is located in Maxu Village, Maping Town, which was the main route from Maping Town in Zhangzhou to Baishui in Longhai at that time. The ancient road has 660 steps, which is winding and in the form of "Zhi", stretching for nearly 1,000 meters.

上　图：俯瞰陈仓岭　楼建龙 摄

左下图：漳州马坪通往龙海白水古道附近刻有“仓岭亭碑记”的石碑（一）　楼建龙 摄

右下图：漳州马坪通往龙海白水古道附近刻有“仓岭亭碑记”的石碑（二）　楼建龙 摄

The upper picture: Overlooking Chencang Ridge. Photographed by Lou Jianlong

The lower left picture: The stone tablet carved with "Cangling Pavilion Inscription" near the ancient road from Maping to Longhai in Zhangzhou (1). Photographed by Lou Jianlong

The lower right picture: The stone tablet carved with "Cangling Pavilion Inscription" near the ancient road from Maping to Longhai in Zhangzhou (2). Photographed by Lou Jianlong

仓山修路碑

仓山龙江石步造路碑，花岗岩刻制，抹角首高长 1.8 米，宽 0.46 米，厚 0.19 米。碑文直刻 6 行，全文抄录如下：“吾乡田园一带土路左达官路，右通塔仔。原亦要途，每逢阴雨即见泥泺，行人往来实觉艰难，□与□目击神伤，愿个勉力指资铺成石路□高一尺，计长百余丈，兼修半道浦水道，疏通源流。本族踊跃助工，邻里皆悦，照仍旧址并无侵碍，因而绘图呈请闽邑，主张诣勘立碑等，因蒙二位在案，兹经改铺完竣，勒石以誌。道光癸未岁（1823）□□□里人林厚□、林厚全立。”此碑是石步历史的实物见证。

仓山龙江石步造路碑 楼建龙 摄

Shibu Road-building Monument in Longjiang of Cangshan. Photographed by Lou Jianlong

CANGSHAN ROAD-BUILDING MONUMENT

The road-building Monument in Shibu Village, Longjiang, Cangshan District, Fuzho, carved with granite and 6 lines of inscriptions, which recorded the historical development process of roads in Shibu Village from difficult to flat.

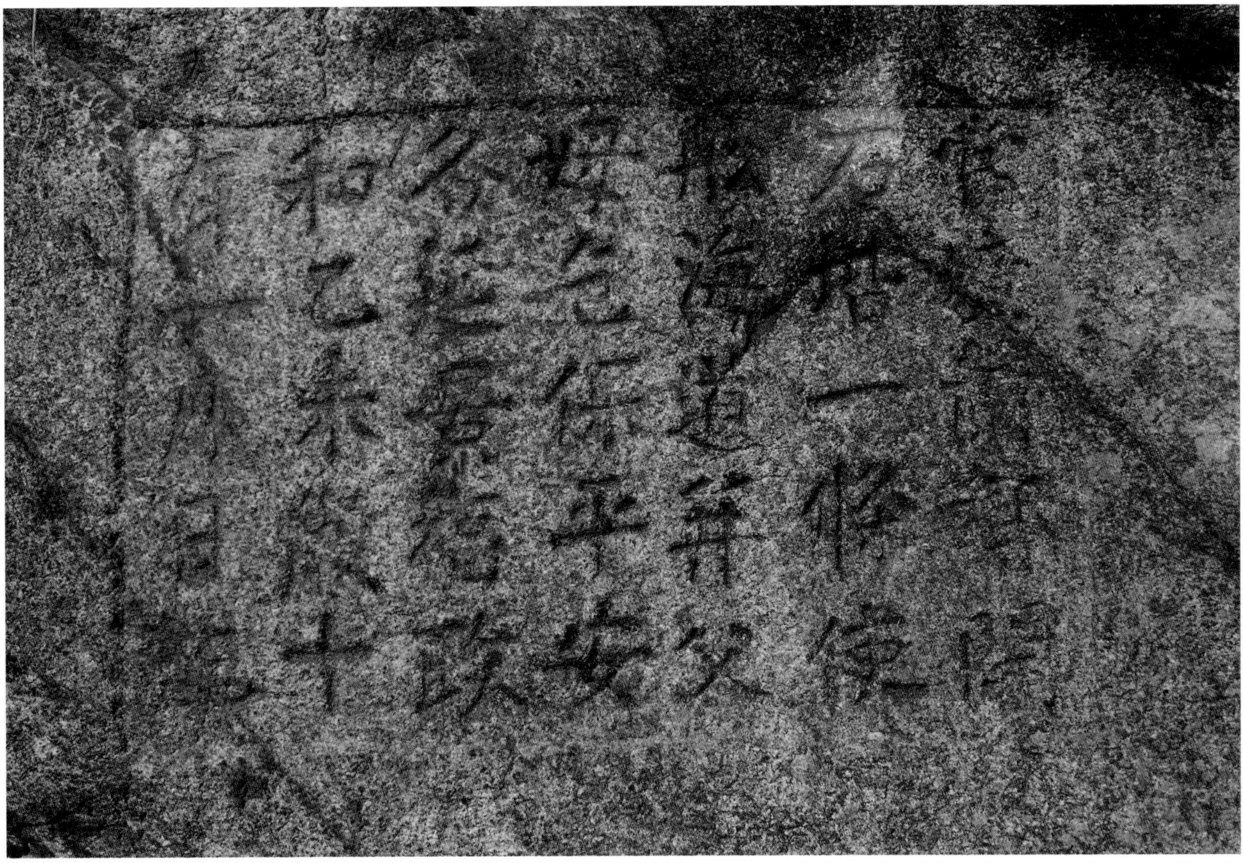

福州牛山石蹬道修路碑

Road-building tablet in the rocky mountain path of Niushan, Fujian

题刻垂彰，共襄盛绩

修路题刻作为歌咏功德的主要形式，因为要依托于大石或巨岩，所以主要分布在山间与水边。石刻的形式较为多样，可以是一块简单的路石，也可以是镌刻许多文字的题记，或是大幅的摩崖等等，大小不一，与周边环境以及后期树立的石碑等对映成趣。

泰宁题刻

芦庵滩摩崖石刻

位于泰宁县开善乡池潭村，清代摩崖石刻。石刻坐北朝南。全文楷书“化险为夷”等 19 行共 161 字，篇幅宽 4 米，高 2.5 米，分布面积 10 平方米。金溪河口险滩，礁石嶙峋，船只多被冲沉。楚南刘钧于光绪二十三年（1897）开凿芦庵滩，以利船只畅通，题刻“化险为夷”于石壁。

金溪河水在石刻前，自西向东流，石刻在北侧岸边。两岸山峰险峻，植被茂盛。河滩名为芦庵滩，地势险要。

左　图：泰宁开善乡池潭村古道　楼建龙 摄
右　图：泰宁芦庵滩摩崖石刻　楼建龙 摄

The left picture: The Ancient Road in Chitan Village, Kaishan Township, Taining. Photographed by Lou Jianlong

The right picture: Cliff stone carvings in Lu'an Beach, Taining. Photographed by Lou Jianlong

INSCRIPTIONS AREENGRAVEDFOR INHERITANCE AND RECOGNITION, TO MAKE GREAT ACHIEVEMENTS TOGETHER

Road-building inscriptions generally rely on large rocks, so they are mainly distributed in mountains and water's edges, whichis the main form for singing merits. Stone carvings come in various forms and sizes.

TAINING INSCRIPTION

Cliff Stone Carving in Lu'an Beach

Located in Chitan Village, Kaishan Township, Taining County, it is a cliff stone inscription in Qing Dynasty, which faces south with the back to the north. The estuary of Jinxi River is densely covered with dangerous beaches, and ships are mostly washed down. Lu'an Beach has a dangerous terrain. In order to facilitate the passage of ships, Liu Jun in South Chudug Lu'an Beach in 1897 and inscribed " 化险为夷 (change danger into safety)" on the stone wall.

猿岭山石刻

位于上青乡永兴村半岭自然村猿岭山腰石壁上，半岭村与邵武相邻，有古驿道与邵武和平相通。

石刻始刻于北宋大观四年（1110），坐东朝西，刻于青石之上，高 2.7 米，宽 1.8 米，分布面积 5 平方米。石刻内容为《安仁邓晚记》，阴刻楷体竖列，全文为“于崇宁甲申年修改猿岭大路，东去白土，西来护民寺前；次修本县白石岭，上来崇化市，下去白屋前；并改换大杉岭路，修下透龙门，上来入西坊及造桥，兼画宝盖岩。先邓父法堂灰壁，砌砖换阶，开岩前路至官道，甃换，母亲善缘，并夫妻在天庆观题，长□□二名於丁丑年……时大观四年庚寅岁二月初九日，邓晚置立，外甥黄旌书刻”，共计 120 余字，阐述了修建猿岭山大路的经过。

Stone Carving of Yuanling Mountain

Located on the stone wall of Yuanling in Banling Nature Village, Yongxing Village, Shangqing Township, Taining, Banling Village is adjacent to Shaowu, and there is an ancient Banling Road that communicates peacefully with Shaowu. The stone carving was first carved in 1110 and the content is Deng Wan's Records in Anrenwith more than 120 words in total, which mainly expounds the process of building the mountain road of Yuanling.

左　图：泰宁上青乡永兴村半岭自然村猿岭山腰石壁上的猿岭山石刻　楼建龙 摄

右　图：半岭村古驿道，通往邵武和平　楼建龙 摄

The left picture: Stone carvings of Yuanling Mountain on the rock wall of Yuanling Mountain hillside in Banling Nature Village, Yongxing Village, Shangqing Township, Taining. Photographed by Lou Jianlong

The right picture: The ancient post road in Banling Village leads to Heping in Shaowu. Photographed by Lou Jianlong

闽侯拔仕官路碑

BASHI OFFICIAL-ROAD MONUMENT IN MINHOU

位于荆溪镇关西村。拔仕官路为宋代驿道，也是晋京官路。这条利用不规整的石块铺设的古驿道，断断续续约有 3 公里，路面宽处有 2 米多。路旁的三段摩崖石刻均与古驿道紧密相关。

其一，“拔仕”榜书。楷体，字径 0.5 米，刻在村东的悬崖上，宽 0.8 米，高 1.3 米。落款“合沙陈公益书，宝庆乙酉（1225）秋立”楷书铭文，字径 0.1 米。拔仕村，原属侯官县，宋太平兴国六年（981）至明万历八年（1580）划归怀安县，为古时关源里三十六墩之一。

其二，沙溪修路记碑。位于“拔仕”榜书北侧的岩壁上，岩高 2.4 米，宽 2.3 米。上阴刻：“福州怀安县修沙溪路记，怀安县令樊纪，到官之次年，尝沿事沙溪口，由拔仕岭过新蓝至鸡菜岭。距县百里而遥，路险而石恶，行人苦之。其石有嘴于旁而啄衣者，牙于中而啮足者，蹲于前而梗步者。因购工力，率皆琢去，易艰涩为平易。虽引杖索涂者，亦无颠踣之虞。夫历年且深，陵谷尚有变更者，况道路乎。苟缺者能补，陷者能平，断者能接，敢望于继政君子。时嘉祐三年（1058）八月二十四日记。文林郎守县尉叶武，将仕郎守主簿王知微，都经划主幽居僧垂拱，监役僧戒达、传昭，住外汤院释庆聪书。”楷书铭文 14 行，字径 0.11 米。

其三，募修官路碑。高 1.6、宽 1.4 米，上阴刻楷书计 10 行：“都劝首林慈，发心起首铺境内官路，每丈管钱一贯四百文，并募缘舍钱姓名于右……宣和元年（1119）岁次己亥劝首林简立碑”等，字径 0.1 米。“官路”二字出现于北宋时期的石刻之中，十分罕见。

Located in Guanxi Village, Jingxi Town. Bashi Official Road is a post road in the Song Dynasty and also an official road leading to the capital. This ancient post road is about 3 kilometers intermittently and has a road width of more than 2 meters. The three sections of cliff carvings along the road are closely related to the ancient post road.

“拔仕”榜书一方　楼建龙 摄

One side of the "Ba Shi"list. Photographed by Lou Jianlong

The upper picture: Bashi Official Road in Minhou is a post road in the Song Dynasty. Stone carvings along the road record the history of the post road. Photographed by Lou Jianlong

The lower left picture: Donation list for repairing the official road. Photographed by Lou Jianlong

The lower right picture: Road-building monument in Shaxi. Photographed by Lou Jianlong

上　图：闽侯拔仕官路为宋代驿道，路旁的石刻记载着驿道的历史　楼建龙 摄

左下图：修官路捐赠名单　楼建龙 摄

右下图：沙溪修路记碑　楼建龙 摄

长乐登文道题刻

左　图：登文道码头修建于明万历年间，是闽江口岸商旅行人水上交通的要冲之一，是重要的船舶停靠点和对外通航的口岸　楼建龙 摄

右　图：长乐登文道题刻　楼建龙 摄

The left picture: Dengwendao Wharf was built in the Wanli period of the Ming Dynasty, which is one of the key points for commercial and pedestrian water transportation at Minjiang Port. It is also an important docking point for ships and a port for foreign navigation. Photographed by Lou Jianlong

The right picture: Inscription of Dengwendao in Changle. Photographed by Lou Jianlong

登文道在长乐潭头的文石村，修建于明万历二十年（1592）。这里是江海交接的关口，也是水上进出省会的门户。原来登文道长约 200 米，现在退潮时，还可以走出几十米。道头是双条石铺面，每条巨石长约 3 米，宽半米多，厚近半米。一些条石上刻有文字，有的还清晰可辨，如“龙门高家舍道一门”“枫林姜助造”等。

摩崖题刻二方分布于登文道道观崖壁上。分别为：一、“登文道”摩崖题刻，文中载“社友、耆英”，款识“万历己丑（1589）”。二、登文道摩崖题刻，幅高 1.2 米，额横刻楷书“皇明，登文道”，文楷书竖刻“余辈募缘造道，奔劳四载，今已成功。间有愚顽，不思工程浩大，在此系船。诚恐致坏，刻石谕知，尔等各宜体悉，违者呈究不徇。缘首何文叶、陈琼道、刘仕康、陈文芳、陈子道、僧传兴。万历壬辰（1592）春林杰书”。另有花岗石碑三通，分别是：一、重修登文道碑，清乾隆二十年（1755）立。碑高 2.85 米，宽 0.48 米，楷体，字径 0.06 米。二、接修登文道碑，清光绪十一年（1885）立。碑高 2.3 米，宽 0.65 米，楷体，字径 0.06 米。三、接修登文道碑，清光绪十三年（1887）立。碑高 2.35 米，宽 0.68 米，楷体，字径 0.06 米。

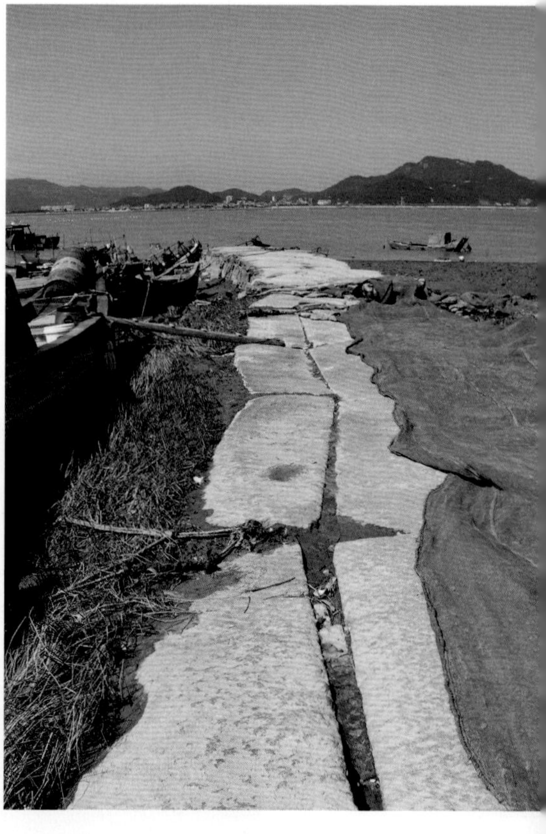

Dengwen Road Inscription in Changle

Dengwen Road was built in Wenshi Village, Tantou Town, Changle, in the 20th year of Emperor Wanli in the Ming Dynasty (1592). This is the gateway between rivers and seas, and it is also the gateway to and from the provincial capital by water. Cliff inscriptions are distributed on the cliff of Dengwen Road Taoist Temple.

甲高岭石刻

甲高岭古道起始于山墩村白岩山，终止于云龙乡际上村凤凰山。路宽约 1.2 米，全程用大小不一的石块铺设，保存大致完好，古道二旁古松参天。石刻位于古道一旁的巨石上。石面宽 3.4 米，高 1.9 米，字体为楷书阴刻、由右至左横书。字径分别为“甲”字高 0.50 米、宽 0.42 米，“高”字高 0.55 米、宽 0.40 米，“岭”字高 0.60 米、宽 0.44 米；落款为“淳祐壬子（1252）仲春口”数小字。该题刻相传为南宋状元郑性之所书。

左　图：甲高岭古道　吴军 摄

右　图：相传，南宋状元郑性之当年是从这里走出闽清进京赶考的。他在淳祐年间告老还乡，并在此铺路建亭，挥毫题写“甲高岭”三大字于石壁上　楼建龙 摄

The left picture: Jiagaoling Ancient Road. Photographed by Wu Jun

The right picture: According to legend, Zheng Xingzhi, the number one scholar in the Southern Song Dynasty, went out of Minqing and went to the capital for examination. He returned to his hometown during Chunyou's reign, paving roads and building pavilions here, and inscribing "Jiagaoling" on the rock wall. Photographed by Lou Jianlong

Minqing Ancient Road Chronological Stone Carvings

Jiagaoling Stone Carving

Jiagaoling Ancient Road starts at Baiyan Mountain in Shandun Village and ends at Fenghuang Mountain in Jishang Village of Yunlong Township. The stone carvings are located on boulders beside the ancient road. The inscription is said to have been written by Zheng Xingzhi, the number one scholar in the Southern Song Dynasty.

万松岭石刻

位于梅溪镇樟洋村东面万松岭古道旁。在一宽 1.5 米、高 2.8 米的大石上镌刻“万松岭”三大字，为纵式三行排列，“万松岭”三字为楷书阴刻，位居中行，字高 0.82 米，宽 0.60 米，左右刻旁款 “清溪郑、性之书”，字经 0.20 米见方。在该石刻右侧有民国石刻“听涛”，落款“徐尧昭书”。

郑性之（1172~1255），原名自诚，嘉定元年（1208）状元，曾任知枢密院事，最高军事长官兼参知政事（相当于副丞相），是宋朝名臣，《宋史》有传。宋梁克家《三山志》说：“郑自诚状元，字信之，后改名性之，闽清人”。

左　图：“听涛”题刻位于“万松岭”题刻旁，为民国时期（1934~1936）闽清县县长徐尧炤（湖南浏阳人）所书 楼建龙 摄

右　图：宋代时，万松岭是樟洋村连接外界的交通要道。相传，郑性之在闽清县城“梅溪书院”读书时，常往返于此。后郑性之中得科举状元回乡，经万松岭，写下了“万松岭”三大字刻于石上 吴军 摄

The left picture: The inscription of "Tingtao" is located next to the inscription of "Wansongling". It was written by Xu Yaozhao (a native of Liuyang, Hunan), the magistrate of Minqing county during the Republic of China (1934-1936). Photographed by Lou Jianlong

The right picture: In the Song Dynasty, Wansongling was the main traffic route connecting Zhangyang Village with the outside world. According to legend, Zheng Xingzhi often traveled here when he was studying in the "Meixi Academy" in Minqing County. After Zheng Xing, the number one scholar in the imperial examination returned to his hometown. After passing through Wansongling, he wrote the three characters "Wansongling" and engraved it on the stone. Photographed by Wu Jun

Wansongling Stone Carving

Located beside Wansongling Ancient Road to the east of Zhangyang Village in Meixi Town. In the Song Dynasty, Wansongling was the main traffic route connecting Zhangyang Village with the outside world. According to legend, Zheng Xingzhi returned to his hometown as the number one scholar in the imperial examination. After passing through Wansongling, he wrote the three characters " 万松岭 (Wansongling)" and engraved them on the stone.

石郑岭驿道

位于闽清县梅溪镇石郑村东面岭头山峦。驿道为台阶形式，由西山脚向东山顶延伸呈蜿蜒状，全长约 300 米。路面以大小不一的卵石作不规则铺就，面宽 1 至 1.25 米不等，保存较好。这条驿道，古时是邻近马洋、石郑通往闽清乃至外界唯一的道路；据记载，南宋状元郑性之青少年时期曾经居住在石郑村。

Shizhengling Post Road

Located in the mountains of Lingtou Villageto the east of Shizheng Village in Meixi Town. The post road is well preserved. In ancient times, it was the only road to Minqing and even the outside world near Mayang and Shizheng. According to records, Zheng Xingzhi, the number one scholar in the Southern Song Dynasty, once lived in Shizheng Village as a teenager.

左　图：闽清石郑岭古驿道上的寺庙　楼建龙 摄
中　图：闽清石郑岭古驿道　楼建龙 摄
右　图：闽清石郑岭古驿道上的寺庙香火旺盛　楼建龙 摄

The left picture: The temple on the ancient post road of Shizhengling in Minqing is full of incense. Photographed by Lou Jianlong

The middle picture: The ancient post road of Shizhengling in Minqing. Photographed by Lou Jianlong

The right picture: The temple on the ancient post road of Shizhengling in Minqing. Photographed by Lou Jianlong

福清一都古道石刻

福清于南宋景定五年（1264）在境内设渔溪驿、太平驿。元朝改驿为铺，全县设5铺，为石塍铺、太平铺、假面铺（即金印铺）、渔溪铺和蒜岭铺。明、清增设至15铺，分两条路线：一条是从福州通向闽南的南驿道，北自闽县的大田驿入县境，经常思铺、磨石铺、太平铺、高车铺、宏路铺、金印铺、玻璃铺、渔溪铺、苏溪铺、蒜岭铺，南出莆田县的莆阳驿，为南北之通衢；另一条连接福清东、南沿海与县治，从县前铺向西接宏路铺，向南经南门铺、锦屏铺，折向东至海口铺，向南至三山铺、万安卫。

此外，福清另有多条通往四邻的县际古道。其中之一，是从东张经一都进入永泰，也可从一都转抵莆田大洋。

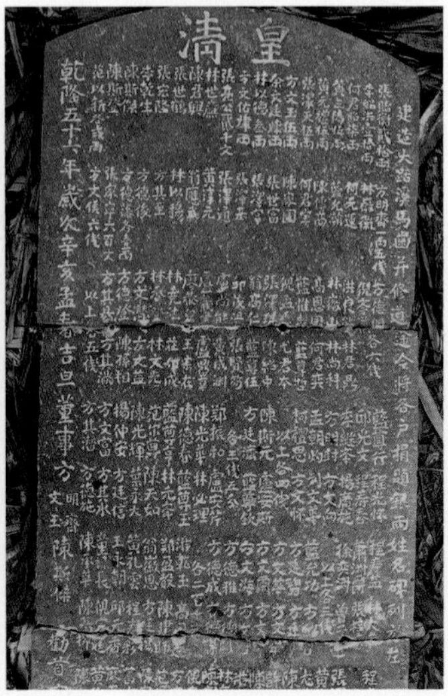

左　图：福清一都古道山壁上的石刻　楼建龙 摄

中　图：福清一都古道上的石碑　楼建龙 摄

右　图：作为永泰、福清、福州、莆田四地往来的交通要道，一都镇至今还保留着两条古驿道。一条是永福驿道，曾是永泰通往福州、福清唯一的官方驿道；另一条是莆福古道，又称“十八踏”，是莆田学子进京赶考的重要通道　楼建龙 摄

The left picture: Stone inscriptions on the mountain wall of Yidu Ancient Road in Fuqing. Photographed by Lou Jianlong

The middle picture: The stone tablet on Yidu Ancient Road in Fuqing. Photographed by Lou Jianlong

The right picture: As the main traffic routes between Yongtai, Fuqing, Fuzhou and Putian, Yidu Town still retains two ancient post roads. One is Yongfu Post Road, which was once the only official post road from Yongtai to Fuzhou and Fuqing. The other is Pufu Ancient Road, also known as "Eighteen Steps", which is an important passage for Putian students to go to the capital for examination. Photographed by Lou Jianlong

Stone Carving of Yidu Ancient Road in Fuqing

Fuqing set up Yuxi Posthouse and Taiping Posthouse in 1264 during the Southern Song Dynasty. In the Yuan Dynasty, post stations were changed to shops, and 5 shops were set up throughout the county. As the main traffic route between Yongtai, Fuqing, Fuzhou and Putian, Yidu Town still retains two ancient post roads. One is Yongfu Post Road, which was once the only official post road from Yongtai to Fuzhou and Fuqing; The other is Pufu Ancient Road, also known as "Eighteen Steps", which was an important passage for Putian students to go to the capital to sit an examination.

诏安砌岭路石刻

诏安地处福建省东南端之闽粤交界处，地势由西北向东南倾斜，海湾深入内陆，梅岭港为泉州港和广州港的中继站，清嘉庆间有船行 10 多家，通航于国内各大港口及东南亚一带。

境内有南诏驿，为福建东南沿海大驿道上最南的一处驿站。除纵贯县境南北的官马大路外，另有道路通往铜山、悬钟、琉璃岭、龙过岗等处。

石泉山石刻位于桥东镇牙头村石泉井路边。文字刻在一块巨石断面上，坐东南向西北。字幅长约 5 米余，高 3 米。共有六碑，楷篆两种字体。从右至左分别为：明崇祯庚辰岁（1640）刻“皇明大都督郑捐砌岭路兵民戴德碑”，万历三十六年（1608）三月刻“皇明大都阃祝公去思碑”，万历三十九年（1611）八月刻“皇明大都阃埜公去思碑”，万历三十九（1611）十二月刻“皇明大总戎麟武杨公去思碑”，万历三十八年（1601）刻“皇明大总主春台杨公德政碑”和另一处只能辨出“大都督郑公谕和功德碑”等字。

左　图：诏安分水关碑　楼建龙 摄

右　图：诏安分水关长乐寺内乾隆年间留存的石碑　楼建龙 摄

The left picture:Fenshuiguan Monument in Zhao'an. Photographed by Lou Jianlong

The right picture: The stone tablet retained in Changle Temple of Fenshuiguan in Zhao'an during the Period of the Qianlong regin. Photographed by Lou Jianlong

Qiling Road Stone Carving in Zhao'an

Zhao'an is located at the southeast end of Fujian, at the junction of Fujian and Guangdong. There is Nanzhao Post Station in the territory, which is the southernmost post station on the major post road along the southeast coast of Fujian.

Shiquan Mountain Stone Carving is located on the roadside of Shiquan Well, Yatou Village, Qiaodong Town. The text is carved on the section of a huge stone in memory of Zheng Zhilong, Zheng Chenggong's father.

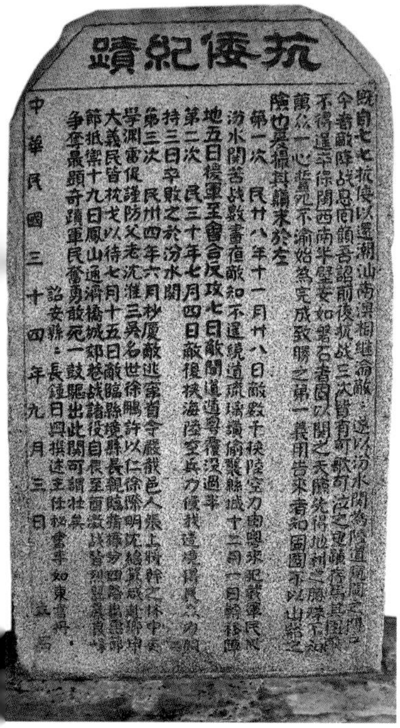

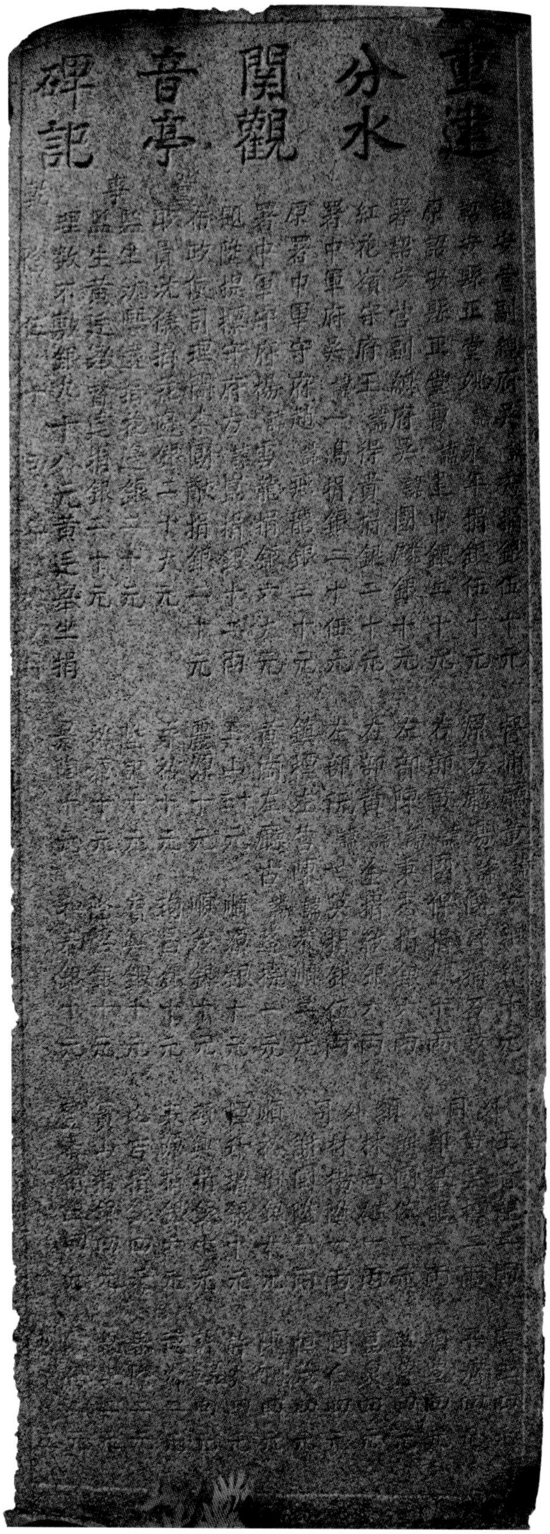

拍摄后记

选择浦城作为福建古驿道拍摄的第一站，是有多方考量的。一是浦城地处闽、浙、赣三省交界处，境内古道众多，可说的话题自然不少；二是闽浙、闽赣分界的仙霞岭雄踞于此，这条历史上入闽最便捷最早的驿道，贯穿着福建历史发展的始末。从地图上看，这一带山脉连绵，岭路崎岖，川流不息的闽江水系蜿蜒其间，由仙霞入闽至浦城，由观前泛舟，下建宁过延平可通津千里直抵福州。这条古代的“高速公路”水陆相连，正是诠释福建山水地貌的最典型的古驿道。

浦城境内的第一站便是仙霞古道。闻名遐迩的仙霞岭长达百里，横跨闽浙两省， 到达仙霞古道枫岭关的时候正是午后，立关南望，天空中，云破处，一缕阳光正好洒在关隘之上，隘口临闽浙边界，关门有 1 米多宽、3 米多高，看上去就像一个小小的桥洞。跨过这处关口，沿着下山的古道往南走，便是福建地界的浦城盘亭乡深坑村，相较于其他福建境内的古驿道，这段仙霞驿道要宽敞的许多，驿道中间形态不一的鹅卵石依旧保留着原有的风貌，两边的野茶与树木有序的生长着，透过隘口，四下无人，没有挑夫的身影，没有南来北往的客商，也没有匆匆赶考的学子，只有满地的枯叶和零星走过的采茶人。细细想来曾经的战场，繁华的商贸之路，诸多悲喜，都不过是岁月长河中的一段往事，唯有当年的驿道，仿佛在时光的清浅里，等待着今人的一场相遇。

福建北部全境皆山，远处峰岭连绵，虽然并不高耸，但随处可见悬崖峭壁，我猜想可能是由于地壳运动频繁，加之水系丰富，支流众多，经年累月的江河切割，才会形成这样地形地貌，正是这些大山，阻碍了福建与中原的联系。也正因为交通不发达，古代福建经济长期得不到发展，内陆地区尤为落后。让人惊叹的是在如此复杂和困难的地形中，坚毅的闽人前赴后继，竟然修建出了这样一条进出福建的驿道，那是需要怎样的勇气和想象力。从历史的进程来看，福建陆地文明与海洋文明的发展其实和福建山海相连的地形地貌有着极大的联系，进出中原的不便，迫使闽人开山修路，而另一方面向海而生，寻找出路可能是福建人的最好选择，或许正是每朝每代都不断拓展的驿道打通了福建陆地文明与海洋文明的任督二脉。

李白说“蜀道难，难于上青天”，遗憾的是诗仙没有机缘到达闽地，如果他不辞辛苦地进入，一定会感慨“闽道难，难于上青天”了。诗仙没有到过闽地，但闽地却从不缺少诗意，不计其数的文人墨客带着飞跃崇山峻岭的渴望，经由仙霞古道入闽，欧阳修、王安石、陆游、朱熹、杨万里等宋代文人广置诗篇。明代地理学家徐霞客踏歌而来，曾三次经仙霞古道入闽，留下了众多不朽的文字，再往后说，细数题刻在古道石壁上数以百计的历代诗文著作，则山阴道上，更是应接不暇。郁达夫在《仙霞记险》曾说：“要看山水的曲折，要试车路的崎岖，要将性命和命运去拼拼，想尝尝生死关头，千钧一发的冒险异味的人，仙霞古道不可不走。”我们无法理解历代文人骚客何以对远离中原的这条古道如此钟情，是对东南一隅神秘之地无限的吸引，还是蜗居山中的闽人征服自然的决心？也许两者皆有。

快马加鞭越过仙霞古道，古代中原入闽的第一道驿站渔梁驿就在眼前。从唐代到明清，这里就是商贾仕宦北上中原，学子考取功名的必经之所。“投宿渔梁溪绕屋，五更听雨拥篝炉”这是诗人陆游投宿渔梁驿有感而发写下的诗句。遥想初冬之时诗人南下，翻山越岭，无人相陪，百忧交集，夜半雨声绕渔梁，前路未卜，万般惆怅，这样的诗句是合乎他彼时的心境的。诗与远方总是相连，渔梁驿就是当年的“网红”打卡处，经由此地，除陆游外，还有蔡襄、黄公度、刘克庄、徐霞客、袁枚、林则徐等，也都曾来到渔梁并留下诗文。而从历史记载上可以看到两宋时期共有进士近30000名，而福建学子就有7000多名，堪称“科甲”大省，当时最便捷的通京之路，便是仙霞古道，渔梁驿则是赶考学子出省前的最佳歇脚之处，可以毫不夸张的说这条千年古道，是学子们的求学之道，也是孕育福建多元文化发展的历史之路。

在渔梁村的村口，一座飞檐流彩的亭子上，“渔梁驿”三个大字赫然醒目，亭子边上的渔梁小学干净整洁，崭新的跑道上，孩子们在疯跑，一群孩子围在我的镜头前，夸张地做着各种动作。在孩子们朗朗的书声中，静谧的渔梁驿，曾经的求学之路，那些消失的岁月，在我的图片里，蔓延开来。

仙霞古道，渔梁古驿，就这样慢慢铺开历史画卷，带我们走近古道背后的庞大体系。蜿蜒的古道书写着历史和回忆，它们是古时的军事之路，商旅之路，也是民族迁徙、文化融合之路。历史就这样慷慨地成就了八闽古道，而古道也慷慨地将文化馈赠给了今人。近年来，福建各地不断开发物质文化遗产和非物质文化遗产，古村落、古建筑的梳理都已形成体系，唯独对古驿道的梳理还处在初级和地方的开发阶段，本书则是首次对福建古驿道全貌进行完整的梳理。文字作者楼建龙先生，是福建省博物院考古研究所所长，三年的田野调查，不仅梳理了福建古驿道的形成、发展、变化的历史，更借由驿道的流变，勾连出驿道上的某些重要时间节点和历史事件与重要人物。从“黄尘腾万丈，驿马如流星”的古道再到关隘寨亭、送别赋游、碑铭纪事，作者以史为基，注重可读性，读来轻松从容，可谓化苦旅为坦途。

本书的另一精彩之处在于图片的呈现，图文对照极大丰富了时间、场景和细节的历史认知，这样的场景当然包括了地形地貌的航拍画面和局部的驿道、古渡、桥亭的真实记录，光影交错间既展示了驿道的历史发展进程，也体现了当下的福建古道在乡村振兴、精准扶贫与传统保护上的的活

化现状。为了给使读者提供更为丰富、详实的人文背景，又不影响正文阅读，编辑别出心裁的采用延伸阅读的方式，介绍与福建古驿道相关联的历史人物，从一个侧面展现出历代福建社会、经济、人文的变迁。本书的出版不仅弥补了福建古代交通驿道史的空白，更为重要的是从另一角度提供了研究福建历代经济、文化演变的历史档案；对于提升福建古道的文化内涵、现阶段的旅游开发具有积极的推进作用。

感谢本书的策划者原福建省委宣传部部长梁建勇先生，是他的提议让这个在福建传统文化中被人忽略但又极其重要的选题得以出版。感谢海峡出版发行集团领导对本书出版的关心与支持，原海峡出版发行集团董事长蒋达德先生看完本书初稿之后坚持要以中英文双语出版，为本书作为福建优秀传统文化代表 “走出去”定立格局；集团副总经理林彬女士多次参加出版选题讨论，对本书的内容、装帧都提出许多具体和独到意见，在此由衷的表示感激。

本书的拍摄工作历时两年，五条古驿道的拍摄工作由福建画报社摄影记者完成，大家翻山越岭，涉水跋涉数千公里，拍摄了上万张的图片，真切的体验了昔日“闽道难难于上青天”的艰辛之苦。其间，一些古道被活化，而更多的是杂草丛生，不复昔日景象，行走拍摄的艰难程度可想而知，原福建画报社社长、纪实摄影家崔建楠带领户外摄影师阮任艺，不辞辛苦参与此次闽粤古道、客家古道的拍摄工作，我社资深摄影吴军抱病坚持工作，都让我们心存敬意。沿途各地宣传部门也给予了极大的配合，他们陪同拍摄、帮我们寻找隐居山中的古道，在此一并感谢。福州手绘作者池志海在福建省博物馆考古研究所绘制的地图基础上，以古地图的绘画风格，再现了福建古驿道、关隘、桥亭的全貌，意在为今人提供一份详实的八闽古道行走线路，读者若有兴趣，可依图行走一番，来一场梦回唐宋明清的时光穿越之旅，闽道迢迢，乡愁仍在。

赖小兵

2020 年 9 月

POSTSCRIPT

There are many considerations in choosing Pucheng as the first stop for shooting Fujian's ancient post road. Firstly, Pucheng is located at the junction of Fujian, Zhejiang and Jiangxi provinces.With many ancient roads in the territory, there are naturally many topics to be discussed. Secondly, Xianxia Ridge, the boundary between Fujian and Zhejiang and also between Fujian and Jiangxi, dominates here. This is the most convenient and earliest post road to enter Fujian in history, which runs through the whole history of Fujian's development. Viewing it from the map, the mountains in this area are continuous, the ridge roads are rugged, and the endless Minjiang River system winds through it, entering Fujian to Pucheng via Xianxia. Boating from Guanqian via jianning to Yanping, we can reach Fuzhou straightly through thousands of miles of waterway. This ancient "expressway" is connected by land and water, which is the most typical ancient post road to interpret Fujian's landscape.

The first stop in Pucheng is Xianxia Ancient Road. The famous Xianxia Ridge is hundreds of miles long, spanning Fujian and Zhejiang. It was in the afternoon when we arrived at Fengling Pass on Xianxia Ancient Road. Standing at the pass and looking south, in the sky, where the clouds dispersed, a ray of sunlight was just over the pass. The pass faces the border between Fujian and Zhejiang. The pass gate is more than 1 meter wide and 3 meters high, which looks like a small bridge opening. Crossing this pass and going south along the ancient road down the mountain, it is Shenkeng Village, Panting Township, Pucheng, Fujian Province. Compared with other ancient post roads in Fujian, this section of Xianxia Post Road is much more spacious. The pebbles with different shapes in the middle of the post road still retain their original style. Wild tea and trees on both sides grow in an orderly way. Through the pass, there is no one around, no porter, no merchants being always on the move, no students rushing to take the examination, with only withered leaves all over the ground and tea pickers passing sporadically. Think carefully about the past battlefield, the prosperous commercial road, and many joys and sorrows, all of which are just a period of the past in the long river of time. Only the post road of that year, as if in the silence of time, is waiting for a meeting with modern people.

The whole territory of northern Fujian is full of mountains, with continuous peaks and ridges in the distance. Although they are not high, cliffs can be seen everywhere. I guess it is probably due to frequent crustal movement, abundant water systems, numerous tributaries and years of river cutting that such topography is formed. It is these mountains that hinder Fujian's connection with the Central Plains. It is also because of underdeveloped transportation that the economy of ancient Fujian has not developed for a long time, especially in inland areas. What is amazing is how courageous and imaginative it takes for the determined Fujian people to build such a post road to and from Fujian in such a complicated and rough terrain. Judging from the course of history, in fact, the development of Fujian's land civilization and marine civilization was closely related to the topography of

Fujian's mountains and seas connecting with each other. The inconvenience of entering and leaving the Central Plains forced Fujian people to cut mountains and build roads. On the other hand, they were born facing the sea, so finding a way out might be the best choice for Fujian people. Perhaps it was the post roads continuously expanded in every dynasty and every generation that opened up Fujian's land civilization and marine civilization.

Li Bai said that "The road to Sichuan is so steep, so it may be steeper than going to Heaven". Unfortunately, the poetic genius did not have a chance to reach Fujian. If he took the trouble to enter, he would certainly sigh with emotion that "The road to Fujian is so steep, so it may be steeper than going to Heaven". The poetic genius had never been to Fujian, but Fujian has never lacked poetry. Countless literati, eager to leap over the mountains, entered Fujian via the Xianxia Ancient Road. Literati in the Song Dynasty such as Ouyang Xiu, Wang Anshi, Lu You, Zhu Xi and Yang Wanli wrote a lot of poems. Xu Xiake, a geographer in the Ming Dynasty, accompanied by singing, entered Fujian three times through the Xianxia Ancient Road, leaving behind many immortal words. What's more, the hundreds of poems and essays of past dynasties inscribed on the cliff of the ancient road later were even more overwhelmed on the mountain road. Yu Dafu once said in "Adventure in Xianxia ": "It is necessary to look at the twists and turns of the mountains and rivers, to test the rugged road, to fight for one's life and fate, and to taste do or die. For those who want to taste the sense of adventure at the critical juncture, Xianxia Ancient Road is a must-go place." We cannot understand why scholars and poets of all ages are so fond of this ancient road far away from the Central Plains. Is it an infinite attraction to the mysterious place in the southeast corner, or is it the determination of Fujian people living in the mountains to conquer nature? Maybe both.

Fast across the Xianxia Ancient Road, Yuliang Posthouse, the first post station from the ancient Central Plains to Fujian, is just around the corner. From the Tang Dynasty to the Ming and Qing Dynasties, this is the only place which must be passed for businessmen and officials to go north to the Central Plains and for students to obtain fame. "The creek ran around the house when staying in Yuliang, I listened to the rain around the stove during the fifth watch of the night (from three o 'clock to five o 'clock in the morning)" was a poem written by poet Lu You when staying in Yuliang Posthouse. In the early winter, the poet went south and climbed mountains without anyone accompanied, full of all sorts of worries. The sound of rain circled Yuliang in the middle of the night. The road ahead was uncertain with all sorts of melancholy. Such a poem was in line with his state of mind at that time. Poetry is always connected with the distance. Yuliang Posthouse was the place where "Internet celebrities" must go in those days. Through this place, besides Lu You, Cai Xiang, Huang Gongdu, Liu Kezhuang, Xu Xiake, Yuan Mei, Lin Zexu and others also came to Yuliang and left behind poems. From historical records, we can see that there were nearly 30,000 Jinshi (a successful candidate in the highest imperial examinations) in the Song Dynasty. There are more than 7,000 students in Fujian, which can be called a province full of excellent scholars. At that time, the most convenient way to the capital city was Xianxia Ancient Road, while Yuliang Post Station was the best place to rest before the students left the province. It is not exaggerated to say that this ancient road with a long history for thousands of years was the way for students to study and the historical way to nurture Fujian's multicultural development.

On a pavilion with colorful cornices at the entrance of Yuliang Village, the three characters "Yu Liang Yi (Yuliang Posthouse)" stand out. Yuliang Primary School beside the pavilion is clean and tidy. On the brand-new runway, the children are running freely. A group of children gather around my camera and do various actions in an exaggerated way. In children's reading sound, the quiet Yuliang Posthouse, the past road to study and those disappeared years spread in my vision.

Xianxia Ancient Road and Yuliang Ancient Posthouse slowly spread out the historical picture scroll and take us closer to the huge system behind the ancient road. The winding ancient roads are written with history and memories. They are the ancient military road, the road of business travel, the road of ethnic migration and cultural integration. In this way, the history generously gives achievements to the ancient road of Fujian, and the ancient road also generously presents culture to modern people. In recent years, all parts of Fujian have continuously developed tangible and intangible cultural heritage. The sort-out of ancient villages and buildings has formed a system. Only the sort-out of ancient post roads is still in the primary and local development stages. This book is to completely sort out the whole picture of ancient post roads in Fujian for the first time. The author, Mr. Lou Jianlong, is the director of the Archaeological Research Institute of Fujian Provincial Museum. In his 3 years of field investigation, he has not only sorted out the history of the formation, development and change of Fujian's ancient post roads, but also connected some important time nodes, historical events and important figures on the post roads through the changes of the post roads. From the ancient road described as with "yellow dust rising high and posthouse horse like meteor" to the Pass Village Pavilion, the farewell tour and inscription chronicle, the author based on history, but paid more attention to readability and reading easily and calmly. It can be said that the bitter journey has turned into a smooth road.

Another highlight of this book is the presentation of pictures. The contrast between pictures and texts greatly enriches the historical cognition of time, scenes and details. Such scenes, of course, include aerial photographs of topography and landforms and real records of local post roads, ancient ferries and bridge pavilions. The light and shadow crisscross not only shows the historical development process of post roads, but also reflects the current activation status of Fujian ancient roads in rural revitalization, precise poverty alleviation and traditional protection. In order to provide readers with a richer and more detailed humanistic background without affecting the text reading, the editor introduced

the historical figures associated with Fujian's ancient post roads in an ingenious way by extending reading, showing the changes of Fujian's society, economy and humanity from one side. The publication of this book not only makes up for the gap in the history of Fujian's ancient traffic post roads, but also, more importantly, provides a historical file to study the economic and cultural evolution of Fujian's past dynasties from another angle. In order to enhance the cultural connotation of Fujian ancient road, the tourism development at this stage has a positive role in promoting.

Thanks to the planner of the book, Mr. Liang Jianyong, former director of the Propaganda Department of Fujian Provincial Party Committee. It was his proposal that enabled this neglected but extremely important topic in Fujian's traditional culture to be published. Thank the leaders of the Strait Publishing & Distribution Group for their concern and support for the publication of this book. After reading the first draft of this book, Mr. Jiang Dade, former chairman of the Strait Publishing & Distribution Group, insisted on publishing it in both Chinese and English, setting a pattern for the book to "go globle" as a representative of Fujian's excellent traditional culture. Ms. Lin Bin, deputy general manager of the Group, participated in many discussions on the topic selection of the publication and put forward many specific and unique opinions on the content and binding of the book. I would like to express my heartfelt gratitude here.

The shooting of this book took two years. The shooting of the five ancient post roads was completed by the photographers of Fujian Pictorial Office. Everyone climbed mountains and waded thousands of kilometers, and then took tens of thousands of pictures. They truly experienced the hardships of "the road to Fujian is so steep, so it may be steeper than going to Heaven" in the past. In the meantime, some ancient roads were activated, However, it is more overgrown with weeds, which is no longer the scene of the past. It is conceivable how difficult it is to walk and shoot. Mr. Cui Jiannan, former president of Fujian Pictorial Office and documentary photographer, led outdoor photographer Ruan Renyi to take pains to participate in the shooting of the ancient Fujian-Guangdong Road and the ancient Hakka Road. Wu Jun, a senior photographer of our agency, insisted on his work in illness, which made us respect him in our heart. Propaganda departments around the way also gave great cooperation. They accompanied us in the shooting and helped us find the ancient road in seclusion in the mountains. We are also grateful to them. Chi Zhihai, Fuzhou's hand-painted author, recreates the whole picture of Fujian's ancient post roads, passes and bridges in the painting style of ancient maps, aiming to provide today's people with a detailed walking route of the ancient roads in Fujian. If readers are interested, they can walk according to the map and have a dream of returning to the Tang, Song, Ming and Qing Dynasties. Fujian has a long way to go and the homesickness is still there.

Lai Xiaobing

September 2020

《福建古驿道》编委会

总 策 划：梁建勇

策　　划：蒋达德　林彬（女）

监　　制：黄伟岸

主　　编：赖小兵

撰　　文：楼建龙

摄　　影：赖小兵　吴　军　崔建楠　朱晨辉　阮任艺
楼建龙　那兴海　周跃东　陈秀容　陈龙林
袁松树　赵　勇　郭晓丹　严　硕　杨　欣
黄景业　郑惠平　刘建波　沈少华　李晋泰
张峥嵘　陈海平　蒋一曦　林燕春　卢胜富
何清和　邱汝泉　丁李青

设　　计：深圳市佳正航包装设计有限公司

封面设计：王　卉　郑必新

责任编辑：辛丽霞

编辑助理：吴承熹　阮静然

英文翻译：薇尔（北京）国际翻译有限公司

福建古驿道地图制作：福建省博物院考古研究所

福建古驿道手绘图：池志海

内页驿道绘图：林子茜

特别鸣谢：历史照片提供《影易时代》

EDITORIAL COMMITTEE OF FUJIAN ANCIENT POST ROAD

General Planner: Liang Jianyong

Planners: Jiang Dade, Lin Bin (Female)

Producer: Huang Wei'an

Editor-in-Chief: Lai Xiaobing

Author: Lou Jianlong

Photograph: Lai Xiaobing, Wu Jun, Cui Jiannan, Zhu Chenhui, Ruan Renyi, Lou Jianlong, Na Xinghai, Zhou Yuedong, Chen Xiurong, Chen Longlin, Yuan Songshu, Zhao Yong, Guo Xiaodan, Yan Shuo, Yang Xin, Huang Jingye, Zheng Huiping, Liu Jianbo, Shen Shaohua, Li Jingtai, Zhang Zhengrong, Chen Haiping, Jiang Yixi, Lin Yanchun, Lu Shengfu, He Qinghe, Qiu Ruquan, Ding Liqing

Design: Shenzhen Jiazhenghang Packaging Design Co., Ltd.

Cover Design: Wang Hui, Zheng Bixin

Editor-in-charge: Xin Lixia

Editorial Assistant: Wu Chengxi, Ruan Jingran

English Translator: Weier (Beijing) International Translation Co.,Ltd

Map Making of Ancient Post Roads in Fujian: Institute of Archaeology, Fujian Provincial Museum

Hand Drawing of Ancient Post Roads in Fujian: Chi Zhihai

Inside Page Post Road Drawing: Lin Zixi

Special Acknowledgement: Historical photos provided by Beijing Yingyi Shidai Cultural Development Co.,Ltd

图书在版编目（CIP）数据

福建古驿道 / 楼建龙著. -- 福州 : 海峡书局,
2020.11
ISBN 978-7-5567-0746-1
Ⅰ. ①福… Ⅱ. ①楼… Ⅲ. ①古道－文化遗址－研究
－福建 Ⅳ. ①K878.44
中国版本图书馆CIP数据核字(2020)第158961号

责任编辑：辛丽霞
编辑助理：吴承熹　阮静然

福建古驿道

出版发行：海峡书局
地　　址：福州市鼓楼区五一北路110号11层
邮　　编：350001
印　　刷：雅昌文化（集团）有限公司
开　　本：889毫米×1194毫米　1/16
印　　张：23
字　　数：287.5千字
版　　次：2020年11月第1版
印　　次：2020年11月第1次印刷
书　　号：ISBN 978-7-5567-0746-1
定　　价：236.00元